POLITICS, PRUDERY
& PERVERSIONS

POLITICS, PRUDERY & PERVERSIONS

THE CENSORING OF THE ENGLISH STAGE
1901–1968

NICHOLAS DE JONGH

METHUEN

Published by Methuen 2001

1 3 5 7 9 10 8 6 4 2

First published in hardback in 2000 by
Methuen Publishing Limited, 215 Vauxhall Bridge Road,
London SW1V 1EJ

Copyright © Nicholas de Jongh 2000

Nicholas de Jongh has asserted his rights under the
Copyright, Designs and Patents Act, 1988, to be identified
as the author of this work.

Methuen Publishing Limited Reg. No. 3543167

A CIP catalogue record for this book is available from the British Library.

ISBN 0 413 76150 9

Typeset by Deltatype Ltd, Birkenhead, Merseyside

Printed and bound in Great Britain by
Creative Print and Design (Wales), Ebbw Vale

To Thelma Holt and James Roose-Evans, who made a positive difference.

CONTENTS

Introduction   ix

1 Putting the Prime Minister on Stage   1

2 Putting Women Straight   35

3 Homosexual Relations   82

4 Playing Politics with the Stage   136

5 No Flushing, Please, We're British   165

6 The Importance of Being Saved   214

Epilogue: The Limits of Freedom   245

Index   255

ACKNOWLEDGEMENTS

This book could not have been written without the help, advice, information and interviews generously provided by those listed below. I am particularly grateful to Sir John Johnston, who went out of his way to provide information and help despite knowing how hostile I was to the system of theatre censorship. My thanks to Helen Montagu, Constance Cummings, Sir Peter Hall, Ned Sherrin, Michael Codron, Michael White, Lord Annan, Lord Jenkins of Hillhead, Thelma Holt, Lord Callaghan, Sir Alec Guinness, Frith Banbury, Geoffrey Dearmer, Ian Herbert, Sir John Johnston, Faith Brook, Jeremy Kingston, Michael Hallifax, Anthony Page, Eleanor Knight, Michael Earley, Sally Brown, John Peter, John Tydeman, William Gaskill, Ian Albery, Judy Monahan, Irving Wardle, Michael Wilcox, Peter Rankin, John Mortimer, Peter Wood, Tom Morris, Salley Vickers, Margot Weale, Kashif Merchant and Susan Black, who read the text for printing errors. My colleague on the *Sunday Times*, John Peter, read an early draft and made valuable suggestions.

Nicholas de Jongh was awarded the Theatre Book Prize 2000 for Politics, Prudery and Perversions *by the Society of Theatre Research. The Society encourages interest and research into theatre history and practice, past and present, through talks, publications, seminars and research grants. Membership is open to all. For further details write to the Society c/o The Theatre Museum, 1e Tavistock Street, London WC2E 7PA, or consult the website at www.str.org.uk.*

Note

Where a play's licensing is the subject of discussion, the reference is to the appropriate Lord Chamberlain's file.

INTRODUCTION

This book deals with a secret, or rather concealed system of censorship of the London stage from 1901, when the Edwardian age began, until 1968. It was only at this latter date that peculiar restrictions upon what could be said and depicted on public stages were lifted by an act of parliament. From 1737 the text of any play to be performed before a public audience in the United Kingdom had to be submitted to the Lord Chamberlain, one of the senior members of the royal household. The intention was that every word and action to be played out upon the public stage had to have the Chamberlain's sanction in advance of a play's performance.

I do not employ the dramatic adjectives 'secret' and 'concealed' loosely, for until 1991 the files of the Lord Chamberlain and his staff were withheld from the public domain. These files reveal what went on in the Chamberlain's shady closets. They provide, for the first time, surprising and often comic insights into the principles governing the practice of theatre censorship in the twentieth century and the views and values of the gentlemen who administered it.

The Stage Licensing Act of 1737 had entrusted the Lord Chamberlain with freshly defined duties of control over all plays due to be performed in Britain. The wording of the act was so vaguely framed that the Chamberlain could censor anything and could ban 'as often as he shall think fit'.[1] The processes by which the Chamberlain's Examiner of Plays worked were rarely disclosed and his reasons for censoring plays or cutting scenes, incidents or words were not publicly divulged. All the Chamberlain's or Examiner's communications with theatre producers who sought to present plays, or theatre managers responsible for selecting plays for particular theatres, were regarded as confidential. The Lord Chamberlain's judgement was final and he would not enter into discussion with playwrights. There was no court of appeal and no questions about his decisions could be tabled in the House of Commons or the Lords.

Compromises and concessions were, however, sometimes possible, if conducted quietly behind the scenes with the Chamberlain's staff. Victorian theatre managers, being generally concerned with profits, were careful not to antagonise the Lord Chamberlain's staff. So producers and playwrights were given practical incentives not to complain about censorship. One example is illustrative of the situation. Edward Garnett's 1907 play, *The Breaking Point*, concerns an unmarried woman who fears being impregnated by her married lover and kills herself. The Lord Chamberlain's Examiner, George Redford, wrote to the producer, Frederick Harrison, '*privately* [my italics] suggesting that the play should be withdrawn before it was submitted for a licence, in order to avoid friction and perhaps publicity.'[2] Garnett insisted that *The Breaking Point* be submitted for licensing and wrote to Redford angrily asking why the play had been banned. Redford refused to engage with this questioning. His letter of reply to Garnett was printed when the text of the play was later published, thereby emphasising that in England you were allowed to read what could not be said or depicted on stage. 'I trust you will absolve me from any discourtesy,' Redford said, 'if I point out that my official relations are only concerned with the Managers of theatres, I cannot suppose that [Harrison] has any doubt as to the reason.'[3] The ban upon the play was not lifted until 1952.

Some late-Victorian and Edwardian writers, critics and playwrights protested more frequently, systematically and vehemently about stage censorship than most of their twentieth-century counterparts. Theatre-going again became a fashionable and respectable recreation for the middle classes of the later nineteenth century. Some members of this new audience chafed against the Lord Chamberlain's restraints and craved plays that challenged conventional views) There were four parliamentary inquiries into stage censorship between 1853 and 1909, but these merely served to stiffen the powers of the Lord Chamberlain. Bernard Shaw eloquently ridiculed theatre censorship around the turn of the century. He protested regularly about the long ban upon his play *Mrs Warren's Profession* and was the goading leader of the troupe of famous writers who appeared before a 1909 parliamentary committee to plead for a relaxation of censorship. In contrast, from 1914–1956 West End theatre managers and a majority of producers, playwrights, actors and critics colluded in the practice of censorship and its confidential processes.

Lords Chamberlain, appointed by the monarch from the ranks of senior courtiers, naturally reflected the values and views of a conservative aristocracy. They were reactionaries, with little capacity for reflection. The men appointed by the Chamberlain to help run his department, the Comptrollers, were mostly upper-middle-class, retired senior officers from the armed services. In the twentieth century they tended to be intelligent and diplomatic, but were also often philistine, with little knowledge of serious drama and its traditions. These men appeared to have little awareness or appreciation of the modern movement in literature, drama, art and music. They relied on their gut feelings and they were full of guts; radical directors and producers tended to be treated with the cold shoulder of condescension. Anti-Semitic and anti-homosexual sentiments are also sometimes evident in the files, but these were not that unusual amongst that class in the earlier part of the century.

Occasionally there would be a Comptroller whom some avant-garde theatre producers and directors regarded as more sympathetic to the shock and challenge of the new theatre. Peter Wood, the director who had dealings with the Chamberlain's office over Joe Orton's *Loot* in 1965, recalled Lieutenant-Colonel Sir Eric Penn with affection. 'I knew him socially. He was very civilised, an absolute charmer, a little bit uncomfortable, I think, with having to do the job. If they had all been like him the Lord Chamberlain's office would have been a completely different place.'[4]

From 1909 until the late 1930s, whenever the Lord Chamberlain was uncertain whether to license a play, he sent the script to an advisory board for the benefit of its advice. These board members were invariably relics of the establishment. They included Asquith's Lord Chancellor, Lord Buckmaster, and superannuated theatre directors, producers and actors of conservative cast. Sir John Hare, Squire Bancroft and Johnston Forbes Robertson were among them. (One member, Sir Walter Raleigh, who was also an Oxford Professor of English Literature, wrote off Ibsen's *Ghosts* in 1914 saying, 'If it had been acted twenty years ago it would have been dead now.'[5] Bancroft and Hare revealed themselves to be stupid or ignorant, and sometimes both, when giving advice on plays. Hare suggested that there was a case for banning a production of Sophocles' *Oedipus Rex* in case it encouraged the writing of other plays with a similar theme. Bancroft dismissed Pirandello's *Six Characters in Search of an Author* as a work that ought to be sent back to Vienna, the place from which he believed it had come. These chauvinistic men often used their influence to suppress not to sustain.

The twentieth century Examiners, of whom there were usually two in office at one time, read the play-texts that had been submitted for a public performance licence. They provided résumés of each play, detailed any words, speeches or scenes that had to be censored and decided whether or not to recommend a licence. From 1937 until 1968, most important scripts found their way to Charles Heriot, Senior Examiner for the last ten years of his ignominious reign. He was a lecturer at Morley College, though he showed few signs of academic rigour. Conservative, anti-modernist, xenophobic, prim and puritanical, he often exceeded the bounds of his duty, being gratuitously abusive about plays and playwrights. His reports are infested with complaints about supposed indecency, bad language, insubordination and revolt against societal norms. Some plays that would become modern classics earned his sneering contempt; Genet and Tennessee Williams revolted him. Had his views and judgements seen the light of day while he still examined plays there would have been such an outcry that the whole censorship system might have been threatened.

Heriot's nominal superior, Geoffrey Dearmer, Examiner from 1936 to 1953 and Senior Examiner until 1958, seems to have been responsible for reporting on very few plays compared with his deputy. Dearmer, who had written poetry in the First World War trenches and became editor of BBC Radio's *Children's Hour*, proved to be far more independent-minded and impartial. He had been recommended to the Lord Chamberlain by the playwright and critic St John Ervine, was a friend of Bernard Shaw and a member of the Stage Society, that in the early years of the century presented occasional performances of avant-garde plays.

When I interviewed Dearmer he was one hundred years old and coherent. He seemed quite unaware of any objections to the Lord Chamberlain's practice of censorship. 'I only banned one play,' he said. 'It was about the second coming of Christ as a communist. Jesus was disguised as a member of the Party. It horrified people. I don't think I ever read a play about homosexuality. I remember one play with the line, "Where the monkey hides the nuts", which caused trouble. If squirrels could hide nuts why not monkeys? Cromer [the Lord Chamberlain] wrote, "It's not the name of the animal but the destiny of the nuts that causes problems."'[6]

This pompous remark was typical of Cromer. He approached drama with the firm smack of aristocratic prejudice. He gave a revealing indication of this approach in his memorandum on Strindberg's *Miss Julie*, which he chose to ban in 1925: 'There is the very questionable theme in these days of the relations between masters and servants which this play tends to undermine'.[7] In other words, plays that threatened the stability of class and rank had to be prohibited. In so saying he indicated his belief that the theatre was a forum of great social influence.

Such a stance now appears blinkered and obstinate, but the role of Lord Chamberlain must be viewed in its historical perspective. Armed with the evidence in the Lord Chamberlain's files, I have sought to describe and explain the principles governing the office, what was censored and why, and how the Lord Chamberlain dealt with the forces of opposition that eventually succeeded in deposing him. I trace the belief of successive Lords Chamberlain that the theatre could be a persuasive focus for social and political dissent to the sixteenth century. (The country was then destabilised by the upheavals of the Reformation and the government feared eruptions of social and religious unrest.) The population of London was small and the theatre, visited by all classes, was liable to be a potent form of influence and incitement; and there was no police force to control an excited mob. Stage censorship, in such circumstances, was sometimes justified as securing the stability of the realm.

The ideological foundations of twentieth-century theatre censorship were fortified by the nineteenth-century censors' principle that the theatre should reflect an idealised and conventionally moral view of society, and should avoid any serious questioning of orthodox values, any debating of contemporary political issues, or any form of social heterodoxy. Using material from the files, I have tried to suggest how the modern censors tried, with some success, (to preserve a Victorian notion of what the theatre should be.) Taking examples from the twentieth-century theatre's treatment of contemporary political issues and personalities, of marriage, sexual morality and female emancipation, I have sought to show how the Lords Chamberlain strove to ensure the stage was relatively detached from modern life; how they operated a political censorship sympathetic to Conservative and conservative belief; and how, until the 'Theatre Revolution' of the 1950s, censorship prevented the stage from becoming a forum for radical ideas or a pulpit from which to attack politicians.

The files, which are at the Public Record Office, cover most, if not all, of the plays submitted for licensing between 1901 and 1968. They contain Examiners' reports on playscripts, the internal memoranda of the Lords Chamberlain and their staff, and their external correspondence with theatre managers, directors and producers. A list of plays that the Lord Chamberlain ruled unsuitable for public performance during this period included some of the most remarkable plays of the twentieth century: Shaw's *Mrs Warren's Profession*, Ibsen's *Ghosts*, Pirandello's *Six Characters in Search of an Author*, Tolstoy's *Power of Darkness* and Granville Barker's *Waste*. The shock of the new agitated and appalled these censors. The angry young playwrights of the 1950s alarmed them. From their reports and inter-office memoranda of the 1960s it is not difficult to glean the impression of a group of like-minded men standing firm against the tide of what they perceived to be 'bearded lefties' undermining all that they held dear and valuable in Britain. And they fought to the very end in this endeavour.

In 1965 *Private Eye* mocked the Lord Chamberlain's approach to the theatre, floridly describing the incumbent 'in all his prudish glory, a heraldic figure in gold-embroidered regalia wielding the blue pencil with the face of the toothily beaming Lord Cobbold and the mind of a sex-mad hypocritical maiden aunt.' Sex-crazed maiden ladies, however, even those who do not practise the chastity they commend to others, do little harm. The Lords Chamberlain caused a great deal of damage. Their system of censorship suffocated the British stage in the twentieth century by limiting its freedoms; they refused to allow performances of important foreign plays that revolted against the stifling embrace of the status quo; they weakened the resolve of British writers and dramatists who did not even try to challenge their edicts for the first half of the century.

Relatively speaking, the twentieth-century English stage was subject to more censorship than in the reigns of Elizabeth I, James I and Charles I. Stultified and repressed, Britain's theatre became a reactionary, unintellectual outpost of Europe, scarcely involved with the modern theatre movement. In the light of this newly accessible evidence, we must ask how this came to be so, and how it came to an end.

Notes

1. Danbury Pickering (ed.), *The Statutes at Large* (Cambridge, 1765), XVII, p. 141.
2. Richard Findlater, *Banned* (London, 1967), p. 100.
3. Edward Garnett, *The Breaking Point* (London, 1907), pp. xxii–xxiii.
4. Peter Wood, interview with author, 4 September 1998.
5. Lord Chamberlain's file on *Ghosts*. I do not give the British Library numbering for his files on the play-scripts that I mention, but all files are easily accessed by the playwright's name.
6. Geoffrey Dearmer, interview with author, 4 January 1993.
7. Lord Chamberlain's file on *Miss Julie*.

PUTTING THE PRIME MINISTER ON STAGE

One summer morning in July 1967, at the weekly Cabinet meeting, Prime Minister Harold Wilson owned up to a strange fear of his. He was frightened of what damage the theatre might, in future, do to decent politicians. Mr Wilson was alarmed about the idea of liberating the stage and giving it licence to ridicule and impugn the reputations of public figures such as the Queen, the Prime Minister, foreign heads of state and politicians. For the Prime Minister and his Cabinet were that day considering how the British stage would work without the special form of censorship which had muzzled and controlled it since the Stage Licensing Act of 1737 and the Theatre Regulation Act of 1843.

Earlier that month, a joint select committee of the House of Commons and Lords had unanimously recommended that the Lord Chamberlain's control of the theatre be terminated and not be replaced by any other form of pre-censorship. Stage plays, the committee had said, should simply be subject to the laws of the land in the same way that novels and works of non-fiction were. The House of Commons had voted to accept the recommendation. On 25 July, Roy Jenkins, the Home Secretary, and an enthusiast for repeal of the Lord Chamberlain's censorial powers, had informed Lord Cobbold, the incumbent Lord Chamberlain, that the government accepted the report and that it would 'bring in new legislation'.[1]

All Cabinet ministers were believed to support the principle of reform; the Prime Minister, though, surprised his colleagues with his objections to complete repeal of the Chamberlain's power. 'The abolition of pre-censorship would leave the way open to the portrayal of living persons on stage,' he warned. The official cabinet papers for the July 1967 meeting, written in the neutered decorousness of civil service prose, disguise the nature of a conflict about freedom of expression that has never been made public. The recollections of Roy Jenkins and James Callaghan, at that time Chancellor of the Exchequer, help elucidate those distant discussions. Harold Wilson conceded that 'no exception could be taken to political satire as such' but wanted strict limits put upon the legislation to free the theatre. 'Harold Wilson was never keen on a bill [to end the Lord Chamberlain's theatre duties] and he was surprisingly supported by Richard Crossman [Leader of the House of Commons] who had a certain authoritarian disposition,' Roy Jenkins recalled. It was possible that Crossman was only being loyal to his leader, but Jenkins estimated that 'the entire cabinet [Crossman apart] was broadly in favour, but how passionately they all felt about it, I can't remember.'[2]

The Prime Minister told his colleagues he feared that without pre-censorship the British theatre could pose a threat to the 'public interest', that imposing hideaway to which politicians often resort when under embarrassing scrutiny. He imagined theatrical scenarios that portrayed 'public men for purposes of political or private advantage' to the nation's detriment. He contemplated a situation in which the sovereign or the president of some foreign country would be portrayed on stage, thereby causing offence in this country and abroad. It was pointed out to the Prime Minister that 'as attendance at theatre was optional, unlike TV, stage plays should . . . be left to the operation of the ordinary law and the good taste of the public.' One unnamed Cabinet member even reminded Wilson that 'it would be difficult to replace the Lord Chamberlain's censorship with a stricter requirement so that there would be no representation of living persons on the stage at all.'

It appears, therefore, that the Prime Minister was engaged in a last-ditch attempt to sabotage censorship reform. He said the traditional practice of the Lord Chamberlain, who shared his concern, was to prohibit all stage representation of the Queen 'and to give any other persons who might be portrayed [in a play] the opportunity to see the script and to make representations to him.' In Wilson's view the theatre was just too wild and dangerous an animal; a system of checks and restraints were required. For dramatists once more to be allowed to subject real-life people to scorn and ridicule would never do. There had to be 'safeguards against the theatre being used deliberately to discredit or create political hostility towards public figures.' This remark implies that he supported a special, politically motivated censorship that would not have disgraced a totalitarian state. It was an astonishing idea and one which would have commanded little support within his party or among backbench MPs.

When Wilson summed up the Cabinet debate, he conceded that there was 'general agreement with the joint select committee', but still insisted it was 'important that a solution be found to the problem of the portrayal of living persons on stage.'[3] Roy Jenkins was instructed, according to the minute, to go away and examine the options carefully, which meant he had the difficult task of devising a liberal theatre reform that would not conflict with Wilson's concern to protect public figures from being satirised in stage plays. The Prime Minister's non-conformist morality was at obvious odds with Jenkins' humane liberalism. Indeed it is surprising that Wilson chose Jenkins to be Home Secretary in 1965; he was a close friend of Wilson's rival and predecessor as Labour leader, Hugh Gaitskell. As a backbencher Jenkins had been a prime instigator of the Obscene Publications Act of 1959, which extended freedom of expression for writers of books. Yet Wilson's stance on theatre censorship was surprisng for such a pragmatic leader, for a politician who did not easily depart from the main stream of party policy. Why would the Prime Minister seek to outrage liberal opinion?

There is one tantalising piece of evidence that may partially explain Wilson's stance. It can be found in a cryptic sentence in the Lord Chamberlain's file on Edward Bond's *Early Morning* (1967), a fantasy in which Florence Nightingale not only was depicted in the throes of a lesbian relationship with Queen Victoria, but was also sexually caught up with both Gladstone and Disraeli. Worse was to follow for the play ends up in heaven, where Queen Victoria looks down in approval on people eating each other. The Lord Chamberlain, Lord Cobbold, was shocked. The play was banned. Two private performances were given and threats of further action came from the censor. The contretemps occurred while the bill to abolish stage censorship was making its way to the statute book, and on 28 March 1968, Cobbold minuted in the *Early Morning* file, 'I mentioned last night to the Queen, the present position about *Early Morning*. Her Majesty agreed that this should be put firmly in the Attorney [-General]'s lap. I also said I should be grateful if she would mention the censorship bill to the Prime Minister. I have sent over copies of his letter and my reply. The Queen will do so.'[4]

What was contained in this exchange of letters is unknown, but Wilson's relations with the Queen were said to be very cordial. It may be that the monarch, in one of her weekly audiences with the Prime Minister, expressed concern about the extent of the freedoms the theatre was to acquire. Wilson's address in Cabinet may have reflected royal concern as much as his own. Roy Jenkins is not convinced by this theory: 'I suppose [the Queen's] remark about the Attorney-General's lap could be taken as ambiguous,' he said. 'I do not know how much pressure was put on Wilson by the monarch. One never knows. But I doubt if the Queen spoke strongly for [repeal of the act].' In his memoirs, though, he refers to 'royal hesitations' when it came to the question of ending theatre censorship and later repeats, 'I think [the royal family] were a bit hesitant.' He recalls the Queen telling him about the royal family during the war when at Windsor: 'We were very dull here. Just a little family except for Lord Clarendon [the Lord Chamberlain], who sat in a tower censoring plays.'

In seeking to protect himself and public figures from stage plays' comic cuts and mocking satire, Wilson was following in the footsteps of Sir Robert Walpole, the Prime Minister who introduced new theatre censorship in 1737 to save his political skin. In the eighteenth century the London stage still enjoyed the potential to exert political influence and for years Walpole's political integrity had been impugned in stage satires. Henry

Fielding had implicitly charged Walpole with political and personal corruption in several of his plays, with Walpole's identity disguised though not concealed. Then, in 1737, with his administration weak, scandal-ridden and unpopular, Walpole was savaged in Fielding's *The Historical Register for the Year 1736*, a play rated as 'the most outspoken exposure of corruption in contemporary politics ever to be seen upon the political stage'. The character of Walpole appeared disguised as a corrupt fiddler 'who makes people dance to his tune by bribery'.[5] The *Daily Gazeteer* and some of Walpole's dwindling band of supporters urged the Prime Minister to introduce censorship and the Stage Licensing Act was his riposte.

There is, though, a far more plausible and amusing explanation of the decision to set himself against his Cabinet by arguing that only people who had died could be impersonated on stage. Only a few cabinet ministers probably knew that ever since April 1967 the Prime Minister and his wife had been brooding about the text of a play that had been sent to them by the Lord Chamberlain, and in which they featured as principal characters. The Wilsons had been asked by the Chamberlain to say what portions of the text they wished to be excised. No wonder. The play was a mocking farce, *Mrs Wilson's Diary*, based upon the fortnightly column of that name in *Private Eye*. Mr Wilson therefore had found himself in a position roughly similar to his eighteenth-century predecessor, Robert Walpole: he was embarrassed and enraged by stage plays attacking his probity. Both men itched to prevent playwrights from making fun of them or casting aspersions upon them. Walpole had been satirised though his identity was lightly disguised by the playwrights who mocked him.

George Brown, the Foreign Secretary, The Chancellor of the Exchequer, James Callaghan, Roy Jenkins, the Home Secretary and Colonel Wigg, the Prime Minister's Security Adviser, featured as minor characters in the play. All had been sent copies of *Mrs Wilson's Diary* by the Lord Chamberlain and given the chance to object to anything they thought offensive. None was sufficiently agitated to argue the case for banning plays in which living people appeared.

The authors of the *Private Eye* column, Richard Ingrams, then the magazine's editor and John Wells, a regular contributor, had hit upon the inspired idea of dramatising *Mrs Wilson's Diary*. By 1967 Wells and Ingrams had acquired reputations as notorious prickers of pretensions and their column made ample fun of Wilson's suburban lifestyle and values. But there were no serious attacks upon his politics.

The production was due to be staged by the radical company Theatre Workshop, run by Joan Littlewood at Stratford East. Miss Littlewood had already fallen foul of censors. A decade earlier her production of *You Weren't Always on Top* had run into significant trouble. During the run of the play an action not approved by the Lord Chamberlain had been interpolated. One of the actors had dared to imitate the voice of Sir Winston Churchill in a scene where a politician was shown opening a public lavatory. For this shocking example of lese-majesty the Director of Public Prosecutions, Sir Norman Skelhorn, had dragged Miss Littlewood and four other defendants to court where they were fined small sums after pleading the requisite level of poverty. *Mrs Wilson's Diary* may have irritated the Prime Minister, but it was semi-farcical with a marshmallow centre. It lacked any serious political edge, and could not be described as serious satire. It merely made fun of Wilson and his wife, depicting the pair as suburban folk, out of their depth in high society. The Prime Minister was portrayed as an aspirant Napoleon both a victim of Walter Mittyish delusions of invincibility and wild fears that his Cabinet colleagues were plotting against him. In the *Private Eye* column and the play the business of Wilson's government was refracted through the eyes of his wife Mary, who saw politics as an irritating intrusion into her domestic life.

Once the script had arrived at St James's Palace and been read by the Chief Examiner, Charles Heriot, lines of communication and consultation were opened with 10 Downing Street. The idea was that the politicians concerned should make recommendations to Cobbold about what should be removed from the script. 'This is a sniggering unfunny romp about the present

PM, his wife and other people in the public view with a touch of the paranoia to be found in the plays of Spike Milligan (plus the sudden violent obscenity),' Heriot scathingly reported in his 24 April judgement on the play-text, together with an astonishing recommendation that the script should be banned. It was, the Chief Examiner noted with a crapulous flourish typical of his examining style 'material well down to the level of that other paranoiac, Miss Littlewood.' But on the evidence of his report he could not find very much about which to complain at all, unless the mere mention of the First Lord of the Treasury on stage was to be forbidden. The Premier and his wife were merely represented as 'a dreadful suburban couple perpetually using the jargon of advertising.' Worse, apparently, was the role allotted to a parrot 'whose only utterances are obscene' but Heriot seemed far less concerned that the Foreign Secretary, George Brown, was 'of course depicted as a drunkard.'

The Chief Examiner, though, did catch the tone and the essential light-heartedness of the piece, even while admonishing the upstart authors for treating the Wilsons with haughty disdain. 'Wild swipes at undergraduate level are taken at various public figures. There is curiously no attempt at political satire,' he accurately observed. 'In an odd way it is a snobbish production – but the whole thing is beneath contempt. The thing is so cheap and gratuitously nasty and so completely worthless that it is not recommended for a licence.' But Heriot provided no example of what he termed 'gratuitous nastiness' and besides nastiness was not a legitimate reason for banning a play. The nature of the show's apolitical, enjoyable smutty innuendo is best conveyed by a brief scene, recalled by Peter Rankin, one of Miss Littlewood's assistants. In this extract Jenkins, or 'Smoothie-chops' as Wilson in the Ingrams-Wells's Diary used to call him (played here by Nigel Hawthorne), suavely condescends to the Premier's wife, who is characterised as a suburban lady swept up and bewildered by high politics.

ROY JENKINS: You must drop round and have a look at my Jason Pollocks.

MRS WILSON: And you must pop up and have a peep at my Holman Hunt.[6]

Days before Heriot had penned his diatribe against the play Cobbold had written a confidential memorandum for his senior staff, warning them of the attitude he intended to take when the play arrived. 'I have spoken privately to the PM about the Stratford theatre's reported intention to produce Mrs Wilson's diaries, [sic]' he wrote on 16 April 1967. 'I said our normal practice is to allow a good deal of teasing of public figures but that we should look very carefully at anything affecting private individuals (and should consider Mrs Wilson to some extent at least a private individual) and should not probably insist on an assurance that the individual did not object.'

Lord Cobbold was being severely economical with the truth. Public figures, when satirised in revues or depicted as characters in plays, had been protected by the edicts of successive twentieth-century Lords Chamberlain not only from the lash of criticism but even mere pinpricks. As recently as 1963, when Harold Macmillan was Prime Minister, *The Bedsitting Room*, a wild political fantasy by Spike Milligan and John Antrobus, suffered the most severe of political prunings. 'Omit the name of the Prime Minister; no representation of his voice is allowed,' the Lord Chamberlain's office warned. Political lines were tightly drawn all over the place: 'Omit references to the royal family, the Christmas Message and the Duke's shooting. Omit 'the Duke of Edinburgh is a wow with Greek dishes. No representation of Lord Home's [the Foreign Secretary] voice is allowed.'

A Labour prime minister, it seems from Cobbold's memorandum, could not expect such reverent protection from the Lord Chamberlain when up against the jeer and jovial smear of the new generation of satirists. Harold Wilson appears to have put on a brave face when talking to Cobbold about the play in April before it had even been submitted to the Lord Chamberlain and there had only been reports in the national press about its forthcoming production. 'Mr Wilson agreed that unless there was anything unduly offensive about Mrs Wilson and or the private individuals it would probably be wise not to refuse a licence,' the Lord Chamberlain noted.

What a wily old manipulator Cobbold proved to be on this

occasion. He had made it seem as if it would be bad form if Wilson were to complain about irreverent allusions to himself in a stage play. By 27 April Johnston had also read the play, commenting that he was not surprised that Heriot had recommended that the script be refused a licence. But the Assistant Comptroller may well have been diplomatic, appearing to support the testy Chief Examiner while in fact opposing a ban. 'In view of your conversation with the PM I suppose it might be allowed with cuts,' he wrote to Cobbold. 'All the principal characters are made to look very silly, but apart from George Brown's addiction to drink (which I suppose everyone knows) there is nothing particularly nasty or invidious.' These last words were a repudiation of Heriot's view.

Cobbold sensibly did not want to make a public issue out of *Mrs Wilson's Diary* by refusing to license the script. Perhaps he realised that public figures, in the age of television satire, could no longer hope to be treated with the respect that royalty still enjoyed. 'I feel pretty sure it would be a mistake to advertise it by refusing it a licence.' He instructed Johnston to discuss the idea of licensing the script with A. N. M. Halls, the PM's private secretary, and to let him know about the cuts that the Lord Chamberlain proposed to make.

The offending text was duly sent to 10 Downing Street at the end of April. On 1 May Halls told Johnston that he believed the Prime Minister would ask Mrs Wilson to read the play. But neither the premier nor his wife appear to have been keen to do just that. A week later Halls telephoned Johnston to say he had 'not made progress with the Wilsons.' The couple had 'discussed' the play but neither had read it and Mrs Wilson was 'not too keen' about the task. But the Prime Minister was 'still hoping to persuade her to.' George Brown, to whom Wilson had also spoken, was similarly reluctant to read the script 'because as he says he has had just about enough of this sort of thing.' Poor George Brown. His mishaps and undiplomatic pratfalls, inspired by too much alcohol, were indeed the stuff of mocking newspaper comment.

There seems to have been a feeling that Miss Littlewood would pose an embarrassing challenge to the government if the play were banned by the Lord Chamberlain. It was believed that Stratford East was prepared to adopt the Royal Court's risky practice of turning itself into a members-only theatre for the duration of the play's run, thereby exploiting a legally doubtful idea that unlicensed plays could be performed for members of a theatre society which they had applied to join at least 48 hours earlier. For Halls is reported as saying that he hoped Wilson would persuade Brown to read the play and condone its performance, because 'whatever George Brown says, the play will be put on under the auspices of a club.' It is not known to what Mr Wilson and his wife actually objected, because the Lord Chamberlain's file on *Mrs Wilson's Diary* has presumably been weeded of any communications from 10 Downing Street. There was, however, obviously close and sympathetic co-operation between the Lord Chamberlain's office and Wilson's.

By 18 May Halls noted that the script with Cobbold's proposed deletions had been seen by Mrs Wilson, the Foreign Secretary, the Chancellor of the Exchequer and Mrs Callaghan and Colonel Wigg. The 'Wilson copy' of the script was also delivered to St James's Palace that evening. The idea that Cabinet ministers should have the opportunity to pore over comic references to themselves in a forthcoming stage farce and be allowed to recommend deletions from the text seems bizarre today. Yet ministers were so allowed and availed themselves of the opportunity, a situation unprecedented in the twentieth century. That the Cabinet ministers were permitted surveillance of the script, and allowed to make recommendations about references to themselves, was a symptom of the fact that theate censorship was government-inspired.

A Cabinet paper from the period reveals how easy it was for those Cabinet ministers to propose vetoes to references to themselves in *Mrs Wilson's Diary*. There are two illuminating sentences in the paper, saying 'The Foreign Secretary has now read *Mrs Wilson's Diary*. The additional passages he wishes to see deleted are marked in red in the margin.' Mrs Callaghan had also asked that a couple of references to herself be removed. One of them reads in outrageous full: 'I shall never forget that time Audrey Callaghan was taken short by the tea-place.'[7]

Five days later a two-and-a-half-page list of disallowances was sent to Gerry Raffles, the manager of Theatre Royal Stratford East. The fact that the Audrey Callaghan reference is among the disallowances suggests the Cabinet ministers' recommendations had been included. But anyone scanning the Lord Chamberlain's letter to discover evidence of the deletion of political references will be disappointed. The situation was simply, sadly comical. Prudery was the governing concern. The script had been subjected to a thorough cleansing to ensure that politicians emerged purer than in real life. The greatest problem related to a naked statue of the President of the United States which was intended to stand proudly on stage. Nudity, even in the form of an innocent statue, was out of the question. 'The statue of President Johnson must not be naked,' it was insisted in the letter to Raffles. After Stratford East's manager submitted a pleading letter to Cobbold on 8 August about several of the disallowances, Cobbold insisted 'The statue must be decently attired.' The use of the word 'decently' raised nice questions as to how this could be achieved. Was Cobbold perhaps dreaming of a situation in which the President wore nothing but close-fitting underpants through which a massive presidential penis protruded?

Apart from this specification the Lord Chamberlain was only concerned with niggling points of decency. Farting could not be allowed. 'The delivery man must not have a tendency to break wind,' Cobbold's letter instructed. Expletives or expletive-strengthened insults such as 'buggaroff', 'bugger', and 'fuck the Pope' were excised. One of the subsequent compromises allowed was to interpolate the anti-Semitic 'The Pope's a Jew.' A charming verse-allusion to George Brown's randiness

'My charm kills all the ladies
Though lesser men may frown
The gentlemen all hide
And lock their ladies inside
I'm the debonair Mr Brown.'

had to go as did two or three allusions: 'the poof's delight', 'arse against the wall' and 'the great big cock.' There was also a note from Hill to Johnston saying 'I think remarks about the PM's sexual powers should be brought to the Lord Chamberlain's notice.' It is not clear, however, whether Cobbold was so informed.

On 15 August the Lord Chamberlain wrote a memorandum recording the fact that he had spoken to Sir Michael Palliser and told him that Stratford East had proposed some alterations where words and sentences had been disallowed. He, Cobbold, had allowed some, disallowed others. 'I thought it would be unwise and might add to publicity if I delayed by sending it [the revised script] round again.' Wilson then sent a message saying 'he was quite content' to leave everything to Cobbold's discretion. Wilson was at this stage presumably set upon ensuring that when the Lord Chamberlain's powers were repealed, there would be safeguards to ensure that no Prime Minister would in future have to put up with such mockery on stage.

A light-hearted mockery of contemporary British politicians was all the rage among the early 1960s generation of Oxbridge satirists and performers. It appears that the first time this century a Prime Minister was parodied upon a West End stage was in 1960. At the Fortune Theatre, Peter Cook wittily impersonated Harold Macmillan in one of the items in *Beyond the Fringe*, the revue that launched the careers of Alan Bennett, Jonathan Miller, Dudley Moore and Cook. The Lord Chamberlain, the Earl of Scarbrough, had made no objection to the sketch, perhaps because the scriptwriters concealed the fact that Macmillan was to be impersonated. After *Beyond the Fringe* had won rave reviews from theatre critics, the Lord Chamberlain did not ban the portrayal and even took the Queen to see the show. Not long after he had become Prime Minister in 1964, there were regular suggestions that Wilson did not approve of this revival of the tradition of poking fun at politicians and their politicking. The Saturday-night BBC TV show, *That Was the Week that Was*, and its successors had regularly featured less than flattering impersonations of Mr Wilson as a wily manipulator of the electorate's sympathies and a purveyor of a candour from which the crucial ingredient of sincerity had been removed. Ned Sherrin, a BBC producer often involved in such satirical shows recalled John Bird, who regularly did a lethal impersonation of Wilson on TV, coming back from a lunch at which Harold Wilson appeared. 'I remember John telling me that Wilson had been frightfully sucking up to him before the lunch and then had shown a very cold attitude to him after John had done an impersonation of the Prime Minister.' According to Sherrin, the BBC's Director-General, Hugh Greene had been 'wonderful. But some deal was done with Wilson to ensure that there was no reference to the way the Prime Minister was clinging to the coat-tail of Lyndon Johnson and supporting his bombing of Vietnam. When we dealt with this in a parody in the style of Longfellow's *Hiawatha* – quite a strong piece of writing – it was blocked because of some agreement with Wilson.'[8]

The Prime Minister's remarks at the July cabinet meeting substantiate these indications of his sensitivity to parody. Wilson reminded his colleagues that satirical portrayal of people in the public eye was no longer prohibited on television, although the Independent Television Authority, the watchdog for commercial television, ensured that lampooning of politicians could not degenerate into anything that was 'plainly motivated by political or personal malice.' Earlier that summer Lord Hill of Luton, the Chairman of the Independent Television Authority, and a former Conservative Cabinet minister, had been selected as the next Chairman of the BBC. Hill was reckoned to be just the man to restrain Hugh Greene, who had been accused of secularising the BBC and condoning sexual and moral laxity. It was confidently asserted that Hill's transfer had been dreamed up by Wilson himself to restrain Greene's liberalism and precipitate the Director-General's resignation. During the cabinet's discussion of theatre censorship, the Prime Minister even said that Hill had already assured him the BBC governors had sufficient power to deal with any satirical lese majesty. It looks, therefore, as if Wilson had already expressed his concern to the incoming BBC chairman about the mockery of politicians on television satire shows.

Although Home Office officials began work on a theatre censorship bill that autumn, there was a sudden, strange impasse. On 1 November 1967, *The Times* reported that the bill had been dropped because of difficulties in formulating it and the volume of Home Office legislation. Roy Jenkins has a startlingly different theory as to what had really happened. 'It was Crossman who blocked me. I got on quite well with him, but he was not a man of great loyalty and of a certain authoritarian disposition. He may though have been acting as agent for the Prime Minister on this occasion. Crossman recorded me at the time as getting "more imperious" about the bill.' It may also be that the Leader of the Commons regarded theatre censorship as a matter of little concern. Even though Crossman later became editor of the *New Statesman* he took no great pleasure in Jenkins' programme of liberal law reform – the easing of the laws relating to divorce, abortion, family planning and homosexuality. The abolition of theatre censorship, Crossman believed, was a further indication of the 1960s' surge to restrained liberalism and 'broke with traditional working-class moralism and with Fabian Puritanism'.[9] Crossman would later reveal that he disliked the 'unpleasant' Sexual Offences Act of 1967, which was the first stage in legalising certain homosexual acts. 'It may well be twenty years ahead of public opinion,' he wrote in his diaries.[10]

According to Sir John Johnston, Cobbold went to see Wilson on 29 November to discover what was happening to the censorship bill. The Prime Minister told the Lord Chamberlain that 'the general feeling of ministers was to let everything go free, but he himself wanted protection for the living and those recently dead.' Wilson was fighting a rearguard action against the Cabinet. Cobbold was Wilson's devoted ally in the theatre censorship battle and wrote to him after their meeting: 'There would be strong and widespread criticism of any new arrangements which failed to give adequate protection to those who cannot in practice take advantage of the ordinary laws of libel and slander.'[11] This was a reference presumably to the Queen.

The same day that Cobbold visited Wilson, James Callaghan succeeded Roy Jenkins at the Home Office. Perhaps Wilson believed that Jenkins' bluff successor, who was not known for liberal sympathies, would be prepared to abandon the stage censorship bill; he was wrong. George Strauss, who was a friend of Callaghan's and had chaired the Select Committee on Theatre Censorship, had a good chance of securing censorship reform through a private members' bill and Callaghan was sympathetic. 'Like most others at the time I thought that the role of the Lord Chamberlain was so farcical that censorship should be abolished,' Callaghan told me. 'I only came into the picture when I became Home Secretary. By that time Russell Strauss (as his friends called him) was actually drafting a private members' bill and had been given assistance of lawyers at the Home Office to ensure that it was in an acceptable shape.'[12]

Callaghan also hints that Wilson's opposition to the bill may have had something to do with the Queen. The new Home Secretary enjoyed a better relationship with Wilson than his predecessor and exploited the fact. 'One of my principal tasks was to reassure Harold Wilson that he would not be thought to be abandoning the Prime Minister's duty to the sovereign in these matters.' Callaghan's attitude in Cabinet was robust. 'The Home Secretary agreed with his predecessor's conclusion that the best course would be to make defamation in a play, as on TV, a ground for action for libel.' George Strauss had indicated that he was not prepared to include a provision to prohibit presentation of a living person on stage.[13] This time Wilson did not put up a fight. The alliance of Jenkins and Callaghan was more persuasive than that of Jenkins alone. Cobbold did go to see the Home Secretary on 14 December, in what was a very last-ditch attempt to keep the essence of theatre censorship by banning the representation of living people on stage. If the Lord Chamberlain had succeeded, stage censorship would have, in some ways, intensified. *Mrs Wilson's Diary* would never have reached the stage and the parody of Harold Macmillan, which even the Queen appeared to have enjoyed, would have been excised from *Beyond the Fringe*.

Callaghan told Cobbold that he would mention his concern

in Cabinet and did so in terms which left Wilson in no doubt that Cobbold's idea of limited censorship was impossible. Once this had been done, 'The only thing that was left to me was to smooth the sensitivities of Russell Strauss and Lord Cobbold [who] happened to be personal friends of mine, although not of each other.' Callaghan refused to let Cobbold know, in advance of the second reading of Strauss's bill, how the government would treat the Lord Chamberlain's concerns. Callaghan said, 'Although I had to smooth things over once or twice, you will see that my part was only that of a facilitator. The hard graft was done by others and especially by Russell Strauss who worked hard and lobbied hard for the bill over a long period and he rightly regarded its passage as a major achievement in his political life.' Strauss is undoubtedly the scarcely sung hero of the long campaign to free the theatre from the Lord Chamberlain's control.

In Callaghan's words, 'Basically [Cobbold's] attitude was that as he was to be guillotined, would I please get on with it. So I did.' Once the bill had become law and the Lord Chamberlain had failed in his attempts to neuter it, he became magnanimous in defeat, and maintained friendly relations with Jenkins. 'I made no progress with two Home Secretaries (Brooke, Conservative and Soskice, Labour). It was only with Roy Jenkins . . . who was interested in the subject and agreed with my views, that things got moving,' Cobbold noted. [14] The Lord Chamberlain, once he understood that the Labour administration was concerned about the practice of theatre censorship, expressed agreement that his office be divested of responsibility for licensing plays and censoring them. But in the House of Lords he unsuccessfully pressed the case that the stage should continue to be subject to wide and peculiar forms of censorship. He, like Wilson, wanted a ban upon the depiction on stage of living people and upon any references to such persons that were 'calculated to offend public feeling'. Jenkins looks back in gratitude to his successor's achievement in completing what he had initiated. 'It was one of the few measures Callaghan inherited from me and he presented it very sensibly and well.'

Mrs Wilson's Diary, in censored form, was finally staged at

Stratford East later that year and was regarded as no more politically slanted than a Ben Travers farce. 'A jolly romp with humour, good-natured and harmless, and in no way malicious,' the po-faced Sir John Johnston (then a Comptroller) approvingly recorded. Jerry Raffles had invited Johnston down to the first night. [15] Theatre tickets were offered to the Prime Minister but he declined the invitation. Pearl Binder, who was married to Elwyn Jones, then the Attorney-General and later Lord Chancellor, was the costume designer for Theatre Workshop's next show, and was invited to dinner at 10 Downing Street during the run. Peter Rankin at Stratford East asked her how *Mrs Wilson's Diary* compared with the real thing. 'She was cautious but said "You'd be surprised" in the sense of life at Number 10 being nuttier than the show.' [16] Art, or at least the Wells-Ingrams play, had done the decent thing and made the Wilsons less comic than they really were in their domestic life. The censoring process had had no real impact upon that.

The fear of theatre's potential to incite dissidence and threaten the security of the realm was not even new in Elizabeth I's reign. It can be traced back to classical Greece, as evidenced in Plato's *Republic*. Sir Robert Walpole, Harold Wilson and the Lords Chamberlain would have approved Plato's notion of what art should be and do – 'an adjunct of state policy, an instrument for the shaping of good citizens in accord with approved morality'. [17] That ideal, though, ran counter to the tendency of poetry and art to appeal to the unreasoning part of the mind. Poetry and drama, when representing 'sex and anger', had the effect of stimulating our lower self, with its less rational emotions. [18] Aristotle's *Poetics* provided a more subtle counterweight to this theory, with its notion of catharsis engendered by watching a tragic action. Ancient Rome betrayed a similar ambivalence towards theatre and actors were subject to withering prejudice by the time of the Empire. Performers came to be rated as no better than 'thieves, panderers, cut-throats and gladiators'. [19] They were forbidden to hold public office, 'The law bound them to their trade like serfs' and they became a 'hereditary and disgraced caste'. Castrated actors played feminine roles 'with much lascivious realism and the dramatic fare ran heavily to bawdry and sexual excitation.'[20]

Formal theatre censorship in England dates from 1543, soon after the Henrician Reformation had removed the English Church from papal control and its orthodoxies. This censorship was principally religious in its motivation, inspired by fears that the theatre might stimulate Catholic resistance to Protestantism and thereby pose threats to the stability of the state. That plays might encourage immorality was a secondary consideration. The framing of the 1543 act, with its aspirations to achieve 'the advancement of true religion', and 'the rebuking and reproaching of vices and the setting forth of virtues', suggests guiding aspirations to which twentieth-century theatre censors continued to adhere. Mystery plays and their seductive reiteration of Catholic doctrine, were reckoned particularly threatening. For those plays with 'homely diction which expressed the forms and dogmas of the old (Catholic) faith were far more attractive to a popular audience than the sophisticated and unfamiliar arguments of Protestant performers.'[21]

The Tudor notion that the performance of play could in some circumstances constitute a threat to the public peace was affirmed by a Royal Proclamation in 1549. Actors were not to perform 'any kynde of Interlude, Plaie or Dialogue or other matters as sette furthe in forme of plaie in any place publique or private.'[22] Ten years later Queen Elizabeth I, just months after her accession, codified a system of licensing plays, prohibiting those 'wherein either matters of religion or of the governaunce of the estate of the common weale shall be handled'.[23] Her reign was significant for the theatre: government, the Church of England, Privy Council, the Lord Mayor and the Common Council instituted new systems of control to restrict and regulate actors, plays and playhouses. These founts of authority never achieved unanimity about how stringent these new regulations should be, but they shared understandable anxieties about how large numbers congregating at theatres might lead to breakdowns of public order. There were scant means of controlling crowds.

London theatres in the sixteenth century were legitimately reckoned places liable to spread the plague. They were venues where the unemployed, the work-shy and petty criminals could congregate. Actors themselves were reckoned liable to be thieves or cheats. A repressive ordinance from the Common Council of London in 1574 warned of imprisonment and fines for the performance of plays containing 'anie unchastitie, sedicion nor such lyke unfytt and comelye matter'.[24] The brothels of Southwark lay in close proximity to the playhouses and prostitutes of either sex loitered in the environs, thereby offering a variety of pleasures, aesthetic and sexual, in one visit. In *The Anatomy of Abuses* (1583), Philip Stubbes, a moderate Puritan in terms of doctrine, but a fearsome harrier of the stage, asks rhetorically, 'Do they not induce whoredom and uncleanliness? Are they not rather plain devourers of maidenly virginity and chastity?'[25]

The population of London increased dramatically in the sixteenth century, from about 50,000 in Henry VIII's reign to between 160,000 and 180,000 by 1600.[26] But there was neither police force nor standing army to deal with any minor local insurrection, at a time when men without regular employment flocked to London. These unemployed men were reckoned to number an astonishing 30,000 in 1602. The principal playhouses were situated in Clerkenwell, Blackfriars and Southwark, areas beyond the control of city government and home to militant Protestants, anti-clericals and radical separatists.[27] And the theatres 'were close enough to the people who flocked to them to express this opposition to authority and good order.'[28] By the 1590s the capacity of London playhouses has been estimated at about 50,000 per week, with up to 3,000 people attending a single performance. Some of the audience belonged to what has been described as 'a large population living very near if not below the poverty line, little influenced by religious or political ideology but ready-made material for what began in the later seventeenth century to be called the mob.'[29]

In the last quarter of the sixteenth century the Lord Mayor and Common Council of London kept trying to rid the town of actors altogether, generally citing the theatre as a centre of sexual corruption and a forum for social dissidence. The Lord Mayor, Sir William Webb attributed the genesis of rioting in June 1592 to a mob that had gathered at a theatre on the pretext of seeing a play.[30] As the Council made clear in a letter to the Privy Council in July 1597, the City Fathers were concerned about 'the ill effects of plays on discipline and order, so difficult to maintain in the rapidly and chaotically growing city, with its mass of newcomers, uprooted people and unemployed.'[31] The letter referred specifically to 'divers apprentices and other servantes who have confessed unto us that the said Staige playes were the very places of theire Randevous appoynted' for meetings to hatch 'mutinus attemptes'.[32] The Elizabethan play and playhouse, therefore, were sometimes understandably perceived to pose threats to the stability of the state in ways which were unimaginable in the twentieth century. 'For the fatal weakness of this fragile regime was its lack of coercive power. The absence of either a professional army or a paid bureaucracy left it without the final arbiters of forceful compulsion.'[33]

The practice of censorship, as administered by the Elizabethan and Jacobean Masters of the Revels, was not, however, applied with consistent rigour. The Masters did not seek to prevent the production of all plays dealing with sensitive political issues. Elizabeth's court was an arena for competing factions and subtle forms of patronage. This circumstance permitted 'a wide range of comment on contemporary affairs so long as this was properly licensed, suitably veiled and not slanted with offensive particularity at a powerful constituency.'[34] Occasionally a play would be regarded as subversive and the response would be one of 'almost paranoid ferocity, threatening death, mutilation or prolonged imprisonment, so as to remind everyone of the limits of toleration.'[35] An extreme example is provided by that most defiant of writers Ben Jonson, who was gaoled for two months for his role as an actor in and co-author (with Thomas Nashe) of *The Isle of Dogs*.

When a performance of a play about Richard II, probably by Shakespeare and perhaps with the deposition scene included, was given on 7 February 1601, the night before the Earl of

Essex's botched attempt at a *coup d'état*, an investigation was launched in the belief that the two events were somehow connected. For in the late 1590s it was said that there were similarities between Elizabeth I and Richard II, particularly with regard to the power of their favourites. An inquiry by Lord Chief Justice Popham revealed that a dozen aristocrats had paid inducement money to the Chamberlain's men to play *Richard II* and that the performance was attended by large numbers of Essex's supporters. Neither actors nor conspirators were punished for the performance. Marlowe's *Edward II*, in which the monarch is deposed, was published in 1594, and there was no apparent complaint about the play's same-sex passion or the depiction of a fatal sodomising of the king. The Master of the Revels' role evolved during Elizabeth's reign into that of a usually benevolent scrutineer of plays performed in public. The Master usually offered protection both for playwrights and actors, and often gave reassurance to Justices of the Peace and the Common Council, who were peculiarly concerned about salacious material in plays. 'There is every indication that lewdness was the issue that disturbed [the Council] the most frequently, though it rarely seems to have been one the Masters of the Revels saw it as part of their remit to do anything about.'[36]

There were no major shifts in the forms, methods and degree of censorship during James I's reign. Censorship, its practice defined on the basis of deletions in play manuscripts and prosecutions of playwrights and theatre companies, concentrated upon 'personal satire on influential people, unfavourable presentation of friendly foreign powers or their sovereigns, comments on religious controversy ... representation of any ruling sovereign.'[37] Such guidelines served as the basis for censoring political and satirical aspects of plays until 1908. When it came to questions of decency the Master continued to maintain the detachment of his Elizabethan predecessors. 'Except for the specific bans on oaths and profane language introduced in 1606, the censor was scarcely concerned with questions of morality and good taste. At incest, adultery, rape, sexual invective and innuendo, or Rabelaisian sex-and-lavatory clowning he did not turn a hair.'[38] It was the politically motivated play, particularly when it implied criticism of the monarch, that sometimes brought down the punitive wrath of the sovereign. For a stage play might serve as a rallying point for opponents of government policy. Middleton's 1624 play *A Game at Chess* disguised its purposes under a thin veneer of allegory. The Spanish and English monarchs and the former Spanish Ambassador, disguised by representation as pieces of a chess set, disparaged not only the Catholic Church but also the plans to unite the two countries of Protestant England and Catholic Spain by marriage between James's son and a Spanish princess. The play was performed for nine evenings, before a complaint from the Spanish ambassador to the monarch. James made his rage felt after hearing of the delight the play aroused in its first audiences. Sir Edward Conway, the King's private secretary informed the Privy Council on 12 August that the Spanish Ambassador had complained to him about a 'very scandalous Comedie'. Five days later the Council ordered the play to be stopped. A warrant was issued for the arrest of Middleton, who had gone into hiding.[39]

Even in the politically fraught period of Charles I's rule, when he ruled without benefit of parliament, playwrights still managed to 'dramatise the conflicts and tensions at work in their society' and see their plays produced. There was 'a well-oiled machine of censorship that exerted strong constraints on the players' freedom of expression' but this machine 'could be circumvented with caution in the non-courtly theatre.'[40] The drama of the period was rich in 'absolute kings tyrannising over their realms, and subjects trapped between their loyalty to the crown and their need to speak out'; and the courtier plays of 1632–42 focused on 'anxieties and dissent existing within the court'.[41] Ambiguity, analogy and metaphor continued to serve as 'a creative and necessary instrument of theatrical operation.'[42] The closure of the theatres in 1642, thanks to a Puritan-dominated parliament, though not all Puritans were inherently hostile to theatre, marked a zenith of censorship and rising dread of the influence that the stage play might exert. The Restoration period, when women were at last allowed to act upon the stage, was remarkable for its liberality of expression. The most famous Restoration comedies, principally addressed to aristocratic audiences, were free to revel in a cynical amorality and to trade in sexual innuendo to such an extent that they became anathema to nineteenth and early twentieth-century audiences. Yet plays were still censored or banned altogether because of their religious and political allusions. Any anti-papal play might offend the sympathies of Charles II.

Reaction to the relative freedoms permitted the stage during Charles II's reign first came in the form of attacks upon the Restoration dramatists' disdain for conventional morality and their refusal to see the drama's duty as akin to that of the pulpit preacher. The Reverend Jeremy Collier's *Short View of the Immorality and Profaneness of the English Stage*, published in 1698, appealed to an inveterate distrust of the theatre, a distrust which was not simply Puritan or indeed puritanical. In his disapproving view the stage was set upon debauching the morally infirm, and contributing 'to the exaltation of vice and the mockery of virtue'. Glynne Wickham rated Collier's rallying cry as 'destined to infiltrate not only every non-conformist institution – Quakers, Baptists and later on the Methodists – but also academic life at every level and to cause the theatre to be regarded by half the population throughout the eighteenth and nineteenth centuries as at best frivolous and at worse subversive, and thus to be shunned if it could not be banned.'[43]

Collier's accusation was an index of the new morality ushered in by William III, the Dutch Protestant successor to James II. In a royal echo of Collier's outrage the monarch complained in 1698 that despite the orders of the Lord Chamberlain 'to prevent the profaneness and immorality of the Stage, several plays have lately been acted contrary to religion and good manners.'[44] But the office of the Master of the Revels – the Chamberlain's deputy still nominally responsible for the regulation of theatre – had lost its control over what was performed on the stage. The satires of Henry Fielding, who savaged the reputation of Prime Minister Robert Walpole and under cover of allegory accused him of political corruption, provided incentives to tighten control of the stage. Fielding had promised to use his talents to abuse 'while the liberty of the Press and Stage subsists'. [45] Walpole retaliated with the Stage Licensing Act of 1737, which restricted the number of theatres licensed in London to the few within the City of Westminster and its liberties and gave the Lord Chamberlain unlimited power to censor whatever he chose. Any new play which was to be produced 'for hire, gain or reward' had to be submitted for approval and licensing fourteen days before the first performance. Even plays that had already been produced could be banned if they were reckoned politically dangerous. *King Lear* was banned, for example, during the period of George III's madness. [46] Months after the passing of the act, two censors of plays were appointed to the Chamberlain's staff.

Lord Chesterfield presciently recognised the dangers of this arbitrary form of regulation and voiced his concern in the House of Lords that the stage did not require special forms of regulation. 'If poets and players are to be restrained, let them be restrained as other subjects are, by the known laws of their country,' he pleaded. 'A power lodged in the hands of one single man to judge and determine, without any limitation, without any control or appeal, is a sort of power unknown to our laws, inconsistent with our constitution. It is a higher, a more absolute power than we trust even to the King himself.' [47] The monarch was subsequently used on rare occasions by successive Lords Chamberlain as a court of last reference and authority, and at other times informally exerted influence on the way in which the Lord Chamberlain interpreted his censorial duties. Supplementary acts in 1752 and 1755 addressed the problems posed by theatres outside Westminster, giving magistrates powers to license them for limited periods. The fact that the act perpetuated the monopoly of two London theatres, Drury Lane and Covent Garden, to produce what was called 'legitimate' drama – plays without music – provided a loophole by which new playhouses in the city of Westminster could continue to operate. These new theatres, particularly in the early nineteenth century, submitted to the Lord Chamberlain a form of play described as a burletta – a very vague burlesque of Italian opera, with a few songs in each act. The musical interpolations, or indeed ballet, pantomime and spectacle, ensured that these productions could not be described as 'legitimate' plays, but 'with the music removed (in performance) ... there was little to distinguish burlettas from the regular drama.'[48] Over the River Thames legitimate plays enjoyed immunity from the Lord Chamberlain's licensing system.

In view of vociferous complaints about these anomalies, a House of Commons select committee was appointed in 1832 under the chairmanship of Bulwer Lytton, who was not only an MP but also a playwright, to consider the questions of theatre licensing and censorship. Lytton seems just the man to steer a committee towards the repeal or relaxation of theatrical censorship, for he was a radical Whig who was anxious to see the stage unshackled, and wrote three distinctly political plays which proclaimed his belief in republican democracy. His committee did not, however, dare go further than to make a recommendation, voted down in the House of Lords, that the Drury Lane and Covent Garden monopoly be terminated. The Theatre Regulation Act of 1843 fulfilled that recommendation. It also brought all theatres outside Westminster under the Lord Chamberlain's control, so that he was not only required to license playhouses but also to sanction the plays they performed. This act also reaffirmed the Lord Chamberlain's discretionary powers and extended their considerable range. The censor was allowed to prohibit a play's performance 'whenever he shall be of opinion that it is fitting for the Preservation of good Manners, Decorum or of the Public Peace.'[49] These terms of reference reveal the 'distinctly Victorian moral bias' that inspired the legislation.[50]

The nineteenth-century theatre, both before the 1843 act and after it, was remarkable for the scope and rigour of censorship of plays that challenged political, religious and sexual orthodoxy or were seen to threaten the established order. Governments in the first half of the century understandably believed the country to be prey to threats of social disorder, extension of the franchise and even republican revolution. The Examiners of Plays perceived 'a whole list of prohibited areas . . . the Irish problem, the Reform Bill, 'Chartism and the Royal Family.'[51] Anything 'inflammatory', in the vague words of George Colman, Examiner of Plays from 1824–36, was outlawed and censorship began to operate as an arm of firm government. In the 1830s, when there was agitation for the extension of suffrage, and when the Irish question loomed large and dangerous, plays which dealt with uprisings and political plots were banned. The Lord Chamberlain was also fearful of drama that represented thieving and murderous exploits in seductive and romantic terms. London's East End theatres often attempted to stage 'Newgate Dramas', as they were called, but the working classes who packed such playhouses were reckoned peculiarly susceptible to melodramas that did not conform to the theatre's moral responsibilities. 'It is highly desirable to elevate the tone of the drama,' a member of the Chamberlain's staff wrote in 1853 when the Examiner of Plays, William Donne, had banned a melodrama subtitled *The Neglected Child, the Vicious Youth and the Degraded Man*. 'It is specially necessary in the case of the saloons [minor theatres] who have a tendency to lower the morals and excite the passions of the classes who frequent these places of resort.'[52] The Lords Chamberlain, therefore, moulded a didactic theatre requiring 'the triumph of virtue over vice and a happy ending regardless of a probabilities of plot or character', drama that 'offered only an escape from life not an examination of it'.[53]

In the second half of the nineteenth century the importation of French plays, which light-heartedly dealt with adulterous liasons and uninhibited formication, concerned the Lord Chamberlain and his Examiner of Plays. In their view such plays would outrage audiences and posed a challenge to the notion that the stage should set a moral example. Thomas Southey had already approvingly noted in 1833 that English audiences had no interest in the plays of Dumas and Hugo with their 'adulteresses, prostitutes, seducers, bastards and foundlings'. Twenty years later the literary critic George Henry Lewes adhered to the same belief in the moral superiority of Anglo-Saxons when it came to play-watching. 'Paris may delight in such pictures, but London, thank God! has still enough instinctive repulsion against pruriency not to tolerate them,' he wrote in reference to Dumas's *La Dame aux camélias*. The Victorians would not wish to immerse themselves in 'a subject not only unfit to be brought before our sisters and our wives, but unfit to be brought before ourselves.'[54]

The prohibitive vigour of the Chamberlain ebbed and flowed according to social and political impulses and at certain times competing forces of liberation and repression were locked in struggle. Victoria's reign was remarkable for the strengthening of the Chamberlain's control over the theatre, and the banning or truncating of scripts that his Examiners of Plays reckoned were liable to incite political or social dissidence and question accepted morality. But there were three separate inquiries into stage censorship during this period, as well as sustained protests against the Chamberlain's restrictions. Bernard Shaw and the theatre critics J.T. Grein and William Archer, all champions of Henrik Ibsen, attempted to extend the boundaries of stage freedom. Similarly, the most consistent and sustained campaign against the censors' powers occurred in the Edwardian period when the Lord Chamberlain was at his most vigorously repressive.

The eagerness of the Victorians to regulate moral behaviour by repressive statutes was symptomatic of how they were both appalled and enthralled by the power of eros. The tension between proponents of orthodox morality and the more liberal free-thinkers became apparent in the nervous activities of the longest-serving Victorian Examiner of Plays, William Donne. He began to refer his decisions to the Lord Chamberlain for approval when doubtful French plays were submitted for licensing. Even the Lords Chamberlain did not always accurately reflect the beliefs and prejudices of the respectable middle classes, who returned to theatre-going in the second half of the century as it became a socially acceptable pursuit again. By the mid-1870s, 'white tie and tails were compulsory in the stalls' and the working-class audiences had been relegated to the gallery or the pit.[55] In April 1877, the Chamberlain licensed *The Pink Dominoes* (sic), an adapted importation from the French stage,

27

and caused uproar. In this new play a wife suspecting her husband of adultery set herself up as an *agent provocateur*. The *Daily Telegraph*, in both its review and correspondence columns, quivered with indignation at the idea that such things could be put on an English stage. 'On the score of decorum it is . . . right to protest in the strongest manner against the transfer to the English stage of a piece in which the coarsest suggestions are made the provocative of merriment,' it raged, while one of its readers suggested the Lord Chamberlain had failed in his supposed duty to ensure theatre-goers were not led into moral temptation.[56]

Objections to the stifling nature of theatre censorship, to a theatre of opulent escapism that did not care to deal with serious issues of life, developed in force and fluency from the 1880s. The minority movements of socialists, feminists, radicals and suffragists cohered to form a new kind of theatre audience for realist plays. Realistic drama, which constituted a vital sense of nineteenth-century theatre, did not view life through rose and diamond tinted spectacles. Matthew Arnold, William Archer, who was Ibsen's first English champion, and Bernard Shaw all argued for a new realistic English drama that criticised the hypocrisies and conventions of bourgeois life. Sydney Grundy, Arthur Pinero and H.A. Jones were late Victorian playwrights who resorted to some of the artificialities of Victorian drama, melodrama for example, but had Ibsenite tendencies. They aspired to write plays that faced up to the rigours of life and the grim facts of human relations. But even before the advent of Ibsen's plays in London there were attempts to escape the long arm of the Lord Chamberlain. The Shelley Society gave a private performance of Shelley's *The Cenci* in 1886 at Islington's Grand Theatre. The play had been banned by the Lord Chamberlain because it concerned a villainous father's incestuous passion for his daughter, but the society realised it could evade that edict by staging the play for a members-only audience – a supposed loophole in the censor's ambit. Plays that the Lord Chamberlain was likely to ban or had already prohibited were regularly presented in these special circumstances for the next eighty years until a magistrate closed the loophole. By then the Lord Chamberlain's control of the theatre was within two years of being terminated.

The Chamberlain often resented this defiance. When the manager of the Grand Theatre applied for a renewal of his licence the following year, he was 'warned against further complicity in such evasions of the law'.[57] It was Ibsen's *Ghosts*, however, given a single private performance by the Independent Theatre Society on 13 March 1891, at Soho's now defunct Royalty Theatre, that marked the opening of crucial hostilities. It was the most sensational of all nineteenth-century premières. The play pitched the Lord Chamberlain and radical critics and dramatists into the first skirmish of the long campaign to liberate the theatre from censorship. J.T. Grein, the theatre critic who founded the Independent Theatre Society, wrote a manifesto explaining that the aim of his society was to free the stage from the 'shackles of the censor' and to perform plays dealing with 'real human life'.[58]

The Examiner of Plays, E.F. Smyth Pigott was not impressed by such aspirations, or by Ibsen and his works. 'Do not come to me with Ibsen,' he told Grein in 1891. The Lord Chamberlain's Comptroller, Sir Ponsonby Fane, was much confused by the play and the playwright, recording in a memorandum that Ibsen was 'Danish', the play was called '*The Ghost*', and its producer was 'Mr Green'. Fane's assessment – that the play 'though harmless in language is suggestive of an unwholesome state of things' – was accurate in strictly technical terms. But Pigott's analysis of Ibsen was, as Shaw accused, an example of his 'vulgar, insular prejudice'. The outburst of abuse and outrage with which almost all the national newspaper reviewers greeted the play's première was inspired by its subtextual innuendoes and implications. In *Ghosts* Ibsen suggests that upper-middle-class married gentlemen could and sometimes did contract syphilis from their sexual activities with whores. He implies that such gentlemen could then transmit the malady to their wives who in turn would produce offspring doomed to die from the disease. The sanctity of respectable middle-class relations was being questioned. Mrs Alving, Ibsen's heroine, was just one of many Ibsen women eager to reject the uxorial duties imposed upon her by patriarchal society. But Victorian gentlemen would have recognised the ghost of Captain Alving, whose spirit looms through the play, as a truth-bringer too dangerous to be permitted an appearance on stage.

It was not a subject, some critics thought, that could even be discussed on stage in front of an audience that included ladies. 'Strange to say women were present in goodly numbers, women of education, women of refinement,' Clement Scott, the theatre critic of the *Daily Telegraph* complained in his first-night notice on 14 March. Scott, the Lord Chamberlain's file on *Ghosts* reveals, had been busy trying to persuade the censor to ban this private performance. The *Daily Telegraph* reminded its readers in a leading article on the same day that art was 'but the abbreviation of the Greek name for what is highest, most excellent and best', qualities of which the paper judged there was not a trace amidst the 'candid foulness' of Ibsen's plays.

On 16 March there was a meeting at the Home Office, attended by the Lord Chamberlain's senior official, to discuss what could be done to prevent such challenges to the censor. All West End theatre managers appear to have been subsequently advised, though in confidential terms, not to allow any performance of *Ghosts*. Bernard Shaw, who attempted to secure a members-only performance of *The Cenci* at the Haymarket Theatre the following year, wrote in a letter, 'It was said that [Pigott] was quite ready to wink at an invitation performance, but when Beerbohm Tree was on the point of lending us the Haymarket, an interview which he had with Pigott completely changed his tone . . . It was quite evident that he had been bound over by the censorship.'[59] This was the discreet method by which the Lord Chamberlain's staff worked.

That same year a select parliamentary committee of enquiry was overwhelmed with theatre managers arguing for the retention of censorship. Pigott tried to claim that his own efforts were 'the friendly and perfectly disinterested action of an advisor'. He merely cautioned theatre managers against allowing 'places of amusement' to become 'political arenas'. Yet his protestations of impartiality were belied by the comments he made to the committee about a specific playwright. 'I have studied Ibsen's plays pretty carefully,' he explained, and he had come to some dramatic and factually inaccurate conclusions. 'All the characters ... appear to me morally deranged. All the heroines are dissatisfied spinsters who look on marriage as a monopoly, or dissatisfied married women in a chronic state of rebellion not only against the conditions which nature has imposed on their sex, but against all the duties and obligations of mothers and wives; and as for the men they are all rascals or imbeciles.'[60] The select committee of 1892 recommended that the Lord Chamberlain's censorship be continued. When Mr Pigott died he was replaced as Examiner by Alexander Redford, a bank manager of no particular intelligence. Redford's principal qualification for the job was that he had been a close friend of the previous incumbent and deputised for him when Pigott was on holiday. Asked in 1909 by what criteria he judged plays, Redford replied, 'I have no critical views of plays. I simply have to maintain standards.'[61]

Shaw greeted the passing of this official with a suitable diatribe. 'It is a frightful thing,' he wrote, 'to see the greatest thinkers, poets and authors of modern Europe, men like Ibsen, Wagner and Tolstoy ... delivered helplessly into the vulgar hands of such a noodle as this despised and incapable old official most notoriously was.'[62] It was a judgement that could reasonably have been applied to most of Pigott's successors. In refusing to allow the subject-matter of *Ghosts* to be discussed within a stage performance, the Lord Chamberlain and the politicians who continued to endorse his theatrical function stifled and suppressed a new drama more thoroughly than at any time in English history. As a result, for more than half a century, the London stage became, artistically speaking, a petrified island, cut off from the major dramatic movements in Europe.

Notes

1. John Johnston, *The Lord Chamberlain's Blue Pencil* (1990), p. 238.
2. Roy Jenkins, interview with author, 20 July 1999. All other

direct quotations from Lord Jenkins are taken from this interview.

3. CAB 128142 CC53 (67). This is a reference to the Cabinet papers for 1967 in the Public Record Office.
4. LC file on *Early Morning* by Edward Bond.
5. Richard Findlater, *Banned* (1967), p. 39.
6. Letter from Peter Rankin to author, 7 September 1999.
7. CAB 128142 CC53 (67).
8. Ned Sherrin, interview with author, 2 September 1999.
9. J. Weeks, *Sex, Politics and Society* (1981), p. 266.
10. R. Crossman, *Diary of a Cabinet Minister* (1976), p. 196.
11. Johnston, op. cit., p. 238.
12. Lord Callaghan, letter to author, 9 June 1999. All other direct quotations from Lord Callaghan come from this source.
13. CAB 128142 CC74 (67).
14. Johnston, op. cit., p. 186.
15. Ibid., p. 117.
16. Peter Rankin, letter to the author, 7 September 1999.
17. Jonas Barish, *The Antitheatrical Prejudice* (University of California Press, 1981), p. 19.
18. Plato, *The Republic* (Penguin Classics, 1987), pp. 421–39.
19. James Turney Allen, *Stage Antiquities of the Greeks and Romans and Their Influence* (1927), p. 134.
20. Barish, op. cit., p. 42.
21. Janet Clare, *Art Made Tongue-tied by Authority: Elizabethan and Jacobean Dramatic Censorship* (1990), p. i.
22. Richard Dutton, *Mastering the Revels* (1991), p. 17.
23. Ibid., p. 22.
24. Ibid., p. 29.
25. Margot Heinemann, *Puritanism and Theatre* (1982), p. 20.
26. Ibid., p. 40.
27. Ibid., p. 9.
28. Valerie Pearl, quoted in Heinemann, op.cit.
29. Christopher Hill, *The World Turned Upside Down* (1972), p. 33.
30. Dutton, op. cit., p. 84.
31. Heinemann, op. cit., pp. 31–2.

32. E.K. Chambers, *The Elizabethan Stage* (1923), vol. 4, pp. 321–2.
33. W.T. McAffrey, 'Place and Patronage in Elizabethen Politics', in S.T. Bindoff, J. Hurstfield and C.H. Williams (eds.), *Elizabethan Government and Society* (1961), pp. 96–8.
34. Dutton, op. cit., p. 178.
35. Ibid., p. 126.
36. Ibid., p. 29.
37. Heinemann, op. cit., p. 39.
38. Ibid., p. 37.
39. Dutton, op. cit., pp. 237–46.
40. Martin Butler, *Theatre and Crisis, 1603–42* (1987), p. 6.
41. Ibid., pp. 23 and 82.
42. Annabel Patterson, *Censorship and Interpretation: the conditions of reading and writing in Early Modern England* (Wisconsin, 1984), p. 11.
43. Glynne Wickham, *Early Stages* (1963), p. 165.
44. Findlater, op. cit., p. 34.
45. Findlater, op. cit., p. 3.
46. J.R. Stephens, *The Censorship of English Drama 1824–1901* (1980), p. 6.
47. Johnston, op. cit., p. 27.
48. J.R. Stephens, op. cit. p. 8.
49. Ibid., p. 10.
50. Samuel Hynes, *The Edwardian Turn of Mind* (1968), p. 60.
51. Stephens, op. cit., p. 38.
52. Stephens, op. cit., p. 69.
53. James Woodfield, *English Theatre in Transition 1889–1914* (1984), p. 3.
54. Stephens, op. cit., p. 82.
55. Michael Egan (ed.) *Ibsen, The Critical Heritage* (1985), p. 14.
56. Stephens, op. cit., p. 36.
57. Woodfield, op. cit., p. 117.
58. *The Weekly Comedy*, 30 November 1889.
59. G. Bernard Shaw, *Collected Letters 1874–1897*, edited by D. Lawrence (London, 1965), p. 329.
60. Woodfield, op. cit., p. 113.

61. Report from the Select Committee on Theatres and Places of Entertainment, 1892, vol. 8, para. 194.
62. G. Bernard Shaw, *Our Theatre in the Nineties* (1931), vol. 3, pp. 52–3.

2

PUTTING WOMEN STRAIGHT

The Sign of the Doll

In the autumn of 1904 a marionette doll could be seen swinging gently from the ceiling of the West End stage set for *The Wife Without a Smile*. The play was a comedy written by that respectable darling of late-Victorian middle-class audiences, Arthur Wing Pinero. The doll caused no scandal at the first performance. No theatre critic objected to what appears to have been an ingenious device by which the orgasmic writhings of sexual intercourse were suggested by the movements of the marionette. It may be that this was a rare instance in which an innocuous stage direction was translated into the indecent gyratory action on stage or that the first audiences had chosen to turn blind eyes to the significance of the doll. Then, on 15 October, Brigadier Surgeon Lieutenant-Colonel J.B.B. Myers read a review of the play in the *Sunday Referee*. The Brigadier deduced to what erotic lengths the marionette was being put and the next day wrote a letter of angry complaint to the Lord Chamberlain, the Earl of Clarendon.

In his original report the Lord Chamberlain's Examiner of Plays had been at pains to describe the function of this doll, or 'erotomer' as *The Times*' theatre critic called it. The toy was used in pursuit of a practical joke played by a retired civil servant, Rippingill. A piece of string had been attached to the springs of the double bed in a room directly above Rippingill's which was occupied by married friends of his. This string was connected, through a hole bored in the ceiling, to the doll that hung in the civil servant's apartment. 'The Doll begins to dance energetically, almost as soon as the man and wife go up to bed. There can be but one inference from the movements of the dancing doll,' Myers wrote, 'in plain language of sexual intercourse taking place. If my surmise be correct could anything be more repugnant to every sense of decency?'[1]

The Lord Chamberlain's Comptroller, Arthur Ellis, on 17 October, promised Myers 'an immediate inquiry'. It may be that the doll's movements were adjusted so that its gesticulations no longer seemed to simulate coital thrustings, or as Johnston puts it, 'agitated in a suggestive manner',[2] for Lord Clarendon commented after his own visit to the play, 'although the doll incident might be indelicately construed, it might also be regarded as a childish accessory.' He did not, however, maintain the courage of his uncharacteristically liberal convictions. When the Bishop of London, as Chairman of the Public Morality Council, begged Clarendon 'to relieve London of what many felt to be a degrading spectacle', the Lord Chamberlain promptly did the decent thing and withdrew his licence for the play to be performed in public.

Bernard Shaw had accused Pinero with lethal aptness in 1895 of having 'no idea beyond that of doing something daring and bringing down the house by running away from the consequences,' as he wrote in *The Saturday Review* on 16 March. Yet the doll and the fuss it engendered were significant. Here were the first signs in the Edwardian period of a playwright's rebellion against the orthodoxies and conventions established by the Victorian Lords Chamberlain and upheld by their successors. From then on, some spirit of adventure would be detected and condemned in plays that addressed questions of sexual behaviour, radical and contemporary politics and religion. But this rebelliousness was most apparent in new drama concerning independent women who defied the Victorian conventions by which they were supposed to love, marry, procreate and run homes in dutiful subservience to husbands.

Victorian legislation on women's rights and that on sexual behaviour had moved in contrary directions. The Victorians had made some timid concessions to the notion of the equality of the sexes, but successive governments had been intent upon regulating sexual behaviour and restricting discussion of it, whether in literature or upon the stage. Middle-class women had been allowed entrance to the professions and universities, and had been given the franchise in some local elections and the right to serve on school boards and as guardians of the poor. Their economic circumstances had been improved by the Married Women's Property Act and the 1857 Divorce Law enabled women to petition for the dissolution of a marriage. Yet despite these liberal tendencies, and sometimes in answer to their 'disturbing' impact, the mid and late-Victorian age revealed characteristic bourgeois anxieties about female sexuality. As a host of predatory females snared men in poems, paintings and novels, and the courtesan of the Parisian drama found herself alluringly transported to the London stage, so there was legislation to control the supposed threats of such licentiousness.

Prostitutes of either sex had been regarded increasingly as a threat to family life and the Contagious Diseases Acts of 1864, 1866 and 1869 were designed to put the prostitute under strict surveillance when she loitered provocatively in the vicinity of military establishments. The Royal Commission on Venereal Diseases conveniently had assigned all blame for infection to women while the men who used them merely succumbed to 'an irregular indulgence of a natural impulse'.[4] The vigour of male sexuality was recognised as a source of potential danger too, but less so; decent married gentlemen stooped to conquer, losing their moral equilibrium when up against the provocation of the roving female. Thomas Malthus's *Essay on the Principle of Population* had encouraged Victorian moralists to warn of the risk of sexual intercourse except within the strict confines of married security.[5] So, there had been a decisive shift in this period from the Georgian relish in the pleasures of procreation to 'civic probity, a realisation of love over sensuality, of the moral law over personal impulse.'[6] People selling their bodies for money, it was implicitly understood, were likely disseminators of the fatal, sexually transmitted disease of syphilis, and the theatre had been required by the Victorian Lord Chamberlain to fulfil a missionary role. 'If the stage was to qualify as a respectable pass-time of organised society it must also set an example. It must not only reflect an idealised picture of social virtues, but must teach a wholesome lesson to fortify the converted and convert the uneducated.'[7]

Novelists too had faced fresh restrictions upon their freedoms. In 1857, the year when William Acton was warning, in his *Functions and Disorders of the Reproductive Organs in Youth, Adult Age and Advanced Life*, that male sexuality was 'a dangerous force to be kept in check', Lord Chief Justice Campbell had inveighed against the poison of noxious books. Brandishing a copy of *La Dame aux camélias*, Campbell spoke in support of the Obscene Publications Bill, which allowed new powers for magistrates and Justices of the Peace to have books destroyed. In 1885 the newly constituted National Vigilance Association had introduced decades of effective agitation to suppress indecent publications. The defensive mood of the Victorian keepers of morality was suggested by the prosecution of Henry Vizetelly under the Obscenity Act. Viztelly, a London publisher, introduced Flaubert, Maupassant, Tolstoy and Dostoevsky to the British public, but he was imprisoned for three months for publishing an insufficiently expurgated version of Zola's *La Terre*.[8]

Edwardian society was remarkable for its fissiparous nature, the distance between its poles, its sense of being in a state of flux. Aircraft and radio telegraphy, the Labour Party, tabloid newspapers and psychoanalysis were disturbing the status quo by 1914. The forces of conservatism, as represented by spirited Tory deference to Victorian conventions of morality and behaviour were increasingly opposed by radicals, liberals and bohemians. The conflict was not simply a matter of class warfare. On each political, social and sexual issue the opposing camps varied in their class composition. The ruling class no longer altogether ruled at all: the overwhelming Liberal election victory of 1906 threatened the security of much that the traditional, conservative ruling class held dear. The two 1910 General Elections, the second caused by Liberal proposals to limit the powers of the House of Lords, precipitated a major constitutional crisis, and there was furious conflict over women's enfranchisement, over independent rule for Ireland, and between unions and employers.

Conservatives sensed a nexus of threats, political, social and cultural in nature, to their conception of how society should be ordered. From 1906 Tories had represented Britain as a decadent and weakening country: there were nascent fears that a new generation of men would lack the right male stuff that had made the Empire, and a neurotic dread of invasion. The fact of Germany's increased nautical power and European hostility to the Boer War undermined British jingoism. A reactionary stage melodrama that envisaged the nightmare of invasion, *An Englishman's Home* by Major Guy du Maurier, was a triumph of the 1909 London theatre season. But artistically, the novels of James Joyce and D.H. Lawrence, the poetry of Ezra Pound, the Manet and Post-Impressionist exhibition at the Grafton Gallery and Epstein's sculptures heralded the modern movement. The moral climate was so fraught and uncertain that James Joyce's *Dubliners* could not be published in 1905 or for a further five years because the publisher feared prosecution for indecency and Asquith's government ignored a joint parliamentary committee's recommendation in 1908 that books of literary merit should be exempted from prosecution for obscenity.

Indeed, it seemed to many, from 1911 until the rumblings of the Great War, that Edwardian Britain was in the first flush of breakdown. The House of Lords was left resentfully at odds with middle-class government after losing its veto upon legislation. Strikes increased yearly in number, gravity and violence, with riots in the Welsh coalfields and Liverpool docks in 1912 which required the intervention of troops. The suffragettes had embarked in 1911 upon militant protest, with a campaign of burning houses and public buildings. The Ulster Unionists were arming to resist the imposition of Home Rule for Ireland. In Samuel Hynes' apocalyptic diagnosis, 'By the summer of 1914 the British Isles were [sic] an armed camp, armed for a war against the workers, a war against women or a war against the Irish.'[9]

Moreover, the suffragettes' militant campaign and the flourishing of socialism – from the Fabians to the Marxist Social Democratic Federation – which by 1914 would be represented in parliament by the Labour Party, were viewed by conservatives as subverting Britain's reliance upon the family as the fundamental moral unit. *The Spectator*, in a 1907 article fearfully discerning a connection between 'Socialism and sexual relations', deduced that 'Most Socialist theorisers have realised that the family is inimical to Socialism, owing to the desire which it creates for the possession of private property, private life and an existence based on individualism. Therefore the family must be destroyed.'[10] Two years later H.G. Wells' novel *Ann Veronica* was condemned by the same journal as a threat to the moral security of the freshly quaking realm. The novel's liberated suffragette knows about birth-control, lives with an older man to whom she is not married, bears his children and comes to no punitive end for these falls from grace. According to *The Spectator*, the book was more than a rallying cry for women's liberation: 'Wells . . . by attacking conventional ideas of female purity and male good faith was undermining not only the institutions of marriage and the family, but also religion, national defence and England itself'. The fundamental anxiety was not for the purity of women but for a threatened social system.'[11] This sort of panic reaction viewed men and women as being engaged in a new and intensifying sex war.

The recommendations of a Royal Commission on Divorce, formed in response to a parliamentary campaign to make the sundering of those marriages not made in heaven easier to effect, were shelved by the government in 1913. But the reformist movement chimed with the views of novelists and playwrights such as Shaw, Granville Barker, St John Hankin, Galsworthy and Bennett, who wanted to expose the miseries inflicted upon women trapped in failed marriages. Bernard Shaw explained how difficult it was to persuade audiences to countenance plays in which women revolted against the governing Victorian beliefs about women's duties in marriage and as objects of male desire. The audiences that flocked to the Edwardian stage were predominantly the children of the Victorian middle and upper-middle classes. The actor-managers leasing or managing the major London theatres faithfully appealed to this constituency. Shaw identified a sub-set of this audience as *petit bourgeois*, whose tastes were in harmony with their so-called social betters. These frequenters of the pit, the gallery or the upper circle 'belonged to that least robust of all our social classes, the class which earns from eighteen to thirty shillings a week in sedentary employment and lives in lonely lodgings or drab homes with nagging relatives.'[12] It was a 'reverence for gentility' that characterised this audience. In their eyes plays such as *A Doll's House* and *Ghosts* were reckoned insults to the security and honesty of their married lives. These audiences sought 'nice plays, with nice dresses, nice drawing-rooms and nice people.' They had no great appetite for the realities of life. 'You can have fights, rescues, conflagrations, trials at law, avalanches, murders and executions,' Shaw wrote. 'But any such realistic treatment of the incidents of sex is quite out of the question.' As a result of these expectations the Edwardian drama 'aimed to project an idealised vision of upper-middle-class decorum, suavity and . . . irreproachable respectability.'

The truth of Shaw's contention is suggested by the example of the popular writer, W. Macqueen Pope. Pope famously recalled the Edwardian theatre of his youth in the star-studded haze of nostalgia that the smug drift and fuzziness of old age often induces. The title of his memoirs, *Carriages at Eleven*, evoked a time when the stalls of West End theatres were stuffed with aristocrats in evening dress and ladies heavy with jewels, snobbery and sumptuousness. His perspective was clouded by the myopia of sentimentality and he refused to acknowledge those symptoms of political and social unrest in Edwardian Britain. 'London in the days of King Edward VII was a city of smiles, the habitation of wealth, of peace, of security and of power,' Macqueen Pope reminisces.[13] 'Those were the days of dignity and of stability. Home life flourished. The great majority were householders.' Arcadian England was 'the centre of the whole world'. The Edwardian theatre, in his complacent view, stood aloof, at several, dignified removes from life or change. 'It disregarded the outside march of progress and it had nothing to do with rush or vulgar clamour.' The morning after a night at the play you would wake with glamorous recall: 'What a nice play, what clever people, how smart the house, what pleasant hours.'[14]

Yet Pope's restricted and partial view of Edwardian theatre was important. He put his faith in the Victorian ideal of 'nice' theatre, into which no cold douches of reality would be injected. Redford, that bank manager who lasted as censor through Edward VII's reign, similarly put his faith in 'intuitive Victorianism' when deciding whether a play should be recommended for licensing. 'He forbade the discussion on public stages of those subjects which in the High Victorian tradition one did not discuss: sex, religion and politics.'[15] Most Edwardian play-goers went to the theatre to escape life not to confront it. They were hot for reassurance, glamour and frivolity.

Meanwhile, Shaw's *The Philanderer* (1907) and *Getting Married* (1908), St. John Hankin's *Last of the de Mullins* (1907), Granville Barker's *The Madras House* (1910) and Elizabeth Robins' *Votes for Women* (1907), which were licensed and performed, variously refused to treat marriage with gravity, regarded sexual attraction as a matter of biology not morality and acknowledged that the issue of the female vote had turned the war of the sexes dangerous. The stage was set, therefore, both in the real world and its counterpart in playhouses, for the drama of the struggle for women's liberation, which entailed challenges to 'the entire social structure, government of men, the bases of morality.'[16] Women in the Edwardian dramas would proclaim their independence by asserting their rights to enjoy sexual relationships outside marriage, rather than be subservient partners within it, as passive vehicles for male desire. They proclaimed their right to abortion. The struggles of such women would be mirrored in the major battles over theatre censorship fought in the first thirty years of the century.

Challenges to Censorship

The impact of Ibsen had encouraged young playwrights for the first time in a century to see the theatre as a forum for controversial debate. Theatre censorship would now polarise radicals and conservatives as never before since 1737. Redford's decision in 1907 to ban two plays, Granville Barker's *Waste* and Edward Garnett's *The Breaking Point*, because they dared allude to abortion and a woman's affair with a married man, inspired a petition from a group of playwrights asking for a meeting with the Prime Minister, Campbell Bannerman to discuss the censorship of plays. Even in the 1950s and 1960s such dramatic action was never taken. Before the meeting took place a remarkable letter of protest was published in *The Times* on 29 October 1907, signed by seventy-one of the major dramatists, poets and novelists of the time. The signatories not only included angry young men of radical disposition. Henry James, W.B. Yeats, J.M. Barrie, Thomas Hardy, Arthur Pinero and Joseph Conrad were among them, as well as Shaw, Granville Barker and Galsworthy. Their protest was against 'the power lodged in the hands of a single official who judges without a public hearing and against whose dictum there is no appeal.'[17]

Asquith did not see the protesters; they had to make do with the Home Secretary, Herbert Gladstone, who met them on 22 February 1908. As a result of the meeting a new select committee to examine theatre censorship was appointed. The theatre managers, both in London and the regions, rallied to support the Lord Chamberlain's power as censor since it provided them with a measure of financial security. They appreciated the fact that plays produced in the regions did not suffer the threat of interference from local councils since the Lord Chamberlain's licence was seen to carry the stamp of royal approval.

The Edwardian ruling class, of which the Lord Chamberlain and his advisers were immaculate examples and executants, believed it faced far more than the challenge of independent women or the dangers resulting from freelance sexual inter-changes. After all, this ruling class included the Church of England's senior clergy, the peerage, the Conservative Party, headmasters of public schools and leading members of the professions. The taking of evidence by the select committee in 1909 revealed what conservatives and traditionalists feared would happen if the stage was freed. 'I think,' said W.S. Gilbert, 'that the stage is not a proper pulpit from which to disseminate doctrines possibly of Anarchism, Socialism and Agnosticism. It is not the proper platform upon which to discuss questions of adultery and free love before a mixed audience composed of persons of all ages, of both sexes . . . of all conditions of life and of various degrees of education.'[18] In other words radical ideas could not be discussed on stage if the audience consisted of women, the young, the working class and the uneducated, for they might be seduced by what they heard. Mr Redford cut a figure pathetic in its incoherence and vagueness when called to give evidence. Asked to explain the principles on which he based his censorship he answered, 'Simply bringing to bear an official point of view and keeping up a standard. There are no principles that can be defined. I follow precedent.'[19]

Playwrights and novelists came to plead the case against the Lord Chamberlain while managers and actors, who had achieved social acceptance in the last decade, urged the retention of the Lord Chamberlain's powers. Henry James testified by proxy, saying he considered 'the situation of the Englishmen of letters ambitious of writing for the stage has less dignity – thanks to the censor's arbitrary rights upon his work – than that of any other man of letters in Europe, and that this fact may well be, or rather must be, deterrent to men of any intellectual independence and self-respect.'[20]

No liberal reform was achieved. The government of 1909 had sufficient difficulties in parliament and theatre censorship was a matter of little general concern. The Lord Chamberlain incorporated guidelines drawn up by the 1909 parliamentary select committee as to what criteria should govern his decision to refuse a play a licence. Any plays which were indecent, 'contained offensive personalities', invidiously represented either actual living persons or the recently dead, did violence 'to the sentiment of religious reverence', or were calculated 'to conduce to crime or vice . . . or to impair relations with any foreign power or to cause a breach of the peace' were not to be allowed.[21] These guidelines served greatly to strengthen the Lord Chamberlain's power; he had been given parliamentary support to outlaw the indecent, the irreligious, the apparently anti-social and it was for him to decide which plays fell within these stigmatised categories. The absoluteness of his power had been confirmed. It is true that the Lord Chamberlain did, through his officers, negotiate to some extent with play producers and investigate complaints made by censorious members of the public about plays in performance. But there was no possible appeal against his decisions, that were made in secret by unnamed officials in the Chamberlain's office.

Every play script submitted for licensing would be read by an Examiner of Plays, of whom there were two from 1930, and several from 1952. The Examiner would write a précis of the play and usually recommend that it be licensed. He would, when necessary, itemise words, phrases, sentences or scenes that he thought should be excised before a licence could be given. Where the Examiner was in doubt about a play his report and list of proposed excisions would be sent to the Lord Chamberlain through the office of the Comptroller or the Assistant Comptroller. In such doubtful cases the Comptroller or Assistant Comptroller would himself read the play and comment upon the Examiner's report before passing on the papers to the Lord Chamberlain. By 1964, when Johnston became Assistant Comptroller, he discovered it was his function 'to endorse – or otherwise – the play-reader's recommendation – before passing it [sic] to the Lord Chamberlain.[22]

Where the Examiner recommended a licence the Lord Chamberlain would normally accept the recommendation automatically. When a ban was proposed the Lord Chamberlain would read the play himself, and, on very rare occasions, refer the matter to the monarch, the Prime Minister, the Archbishop of Canterbury or a cabinet minister for an opinion. In 1909 Redford took it upon himself to license a play called *The Devil* without even referring it to the Lord Chamberlain or the Comptrollers. There was adverse comment in the press about the decision and Redford was questioned about the way in which he had exceeded his authority. Soon after, an Advisory Board was instituted, from which the Lord Chamberlain invited an opinion when uncertain about whether to license a play. But after 1952, when Scarbrough became the Lord Chamberlain, the Board was hardly ever used and faded from existence.

The Edwardian opponents of theatre censorship made one last valiant attempt to check the Lord Chamberlain's powers when an adaptation of Eden Phillpotts' novel, *The Secret Woman*, which had been in print since 1905, was dramatised and refused a licence in 1912 by the new Examiner of Plays, Charles Brookfield. Barrie, Galsworthy, James, Shaw and Wells were among the twenty-four influential signatories to a letter to *The Times*, saying that they had read the novel and considered it 'a worthy work'.[23] The writers complained that censorship had become more rigorous and offered tickets to six free, unlicensed matinees of the dramatisation. Because the performances were free they were beyond the Chamberlain's control. A number of peers attended the production, including Lord Ribblesdale, a member of the select committee in 1909, who confessed a new-found anxiety about theatre censorship. Perhaps enthused by this change of heart, 'theatre critics, musicians, artists, professors, members of parliament and editors' were among sixty peti-tioners to the new King in June.[24] Leading actors and actresses had anticipated this fresh plea and had already despatched their own letter, arguing for the retention of the Lord Chamberlain's control. Sir Charles Hawtrey, Sir Herbert Tree, Gerald du Maurier, Sir John Hare, who shortly afterwards joined the Chamberlain's advisory committee, Mrs Patrick Campbell and Lena Ashwell, anxious that the new-found respectability of the actor was not to be lost by offending the crown, all signed. Nothing more was done; the censor reigned, invigorated.

Yet that xenophobic cultural isolation which had shielded Victorian Britain from the bracing impact of France's new waves in literature and art, or Russia's great novels did not last long in Edwardian Britain. Radical young men and women looked to writers and artists abroad for inspiration and excitement. In contrast the Lord Chamberlain and his advisers continued to display their ignorance of foreign drama and their hostility to it. Their views, however, no longer commanded a universal genuflecting cringe of agreement among Britain's intellectuals and artists. 'They are in revolt against the photo-graphic vision of the nineteenth century,' the critic Roger Fry wrote of the November 1910 exhibition of Manet and the Post-

Impressionists in London.[25] The same words could have been suitably applied to the plays of Ibsen, Strindberg, Pirandello and Chekhov. 'On or about December 1910 human character changed,' Virginia Woolf famously wrote, greeting the modern movement not just in art but literature as well.

The exhibition shocked conservatives who thought that art should be nothing if not faithfully realistic. Sir William Richmond of the Royal Academy wrote to the *Morning Post* confessing how alarmed he had been by these non-representational canvases. 'There came a fierce feeling of terror lest the youth of England, young, promising fellows, might be contaminated there.' Second, less hysterical, thoughts left him oddly buoyed up. 'On reflection I was reassured that the youth of England, being healthy of mind and body, is far too virile to be moved save in resentment against the providers of this unmanly show.'[26] Here was an echo of the conservative fear that England was on the verge of succumbing to moral decadence.

Some ruling-class Edwardians were so possessed by this idea of England being morally corrupted by foreign and radical art that they organised, petitioned and agitated with an intensity outweighing their Victorian predecessors. In 1910 the National Council of Public Morals drew up a manifesto, signed by leading clerics, doctors, MPs and academics and published in *The Times*, warning against those ills which endangered the moral health of England's youth. Sexual morality, although the term was not mentioned, was the main cause for concern. The minds of the young were not just threatened by 'pernicious literature'.[27] The Council was even more perturbed about an education system that had failed to teach the duty to marry and selflessly procreate, conforming to 'our national traditions of marriage and the home', according to *The Times* of 31 May 1911. Its crusade, however, did centre upon literature and a campaign to persuade the government to outlaw indecent literature. The government preferred to follow a line of purposeful inertia.

Pinero's marionette, therefore, proved to be an early sign of the campaigns that playwrights, directors and producers would wage in the cause of sexual freedom, to allow actors and actresses to convey the impact of sexual desire, to use the stage as a medium for confronting those crises and problems which sexuality induced: the problems engendered by prostitution, abortion, adultery, rudimentary forms of birth control, sexually transmitted disease and male homosexuality. Woman was no longer portrayed as the passive, doll-like victim of chauvinsist male society or of a husband to whom social and sexual subservience was the unquestioned norm. The New Woman did not only threaten male supremacy, she was seen as a seductive figure in a radical movement that challenged the traditions of Victorian England. One recurring issue in the arguments over stage censorship is the disturbing allure, and therefore the titillating potency, of the partially unclothed or naked woman on stage. Such a neurotic dread of female power to subvert male assurance remains a durable motif in contemporary English drama. Ruth in Harold Pinter's *The Homecoming*, Alison in John Osborne's *Look Back in Anger* and Kath in Joe Orton's *Entertaining Mr Sloane* conjure her up in differing mid twentieth-century forms, but in each instance as a dangerous, erotic force of nature.

Women Up Against Men 1901–1914

A rich retired prostitute proudly manages an international chain of brothels for gentlemen. A married women impregnated by a backbench politician dies from an abortion. A girl commits suicide after an affair with a married man whose wife has left him. These females who depart from the sexual and social standards middle-class women were expected to observe are challenging figures in the landscape of Edwardian drama. They are characters in three plays by, respectively, George Bernard Shaw, Harley Granville Barker and Edward Garnett, each banned by the Lord Chamberlain in the Edwardian period. In Granville Barker's *Waste* a married woman dies while undergoing an illegal abortion. She has been impregnated by an ambitious and immoral Liberal politician who aspires to achieve the disestablishment of the Church of England. The play was banned in 1907 not simply because it accepted fornication and abortion as facts of life: the censor's discomfort was caused by the fact that Barker's play showed how ambitious, well-heeled politicians might fail to practise the rectitude that they preach, and how easy it was for a woman to be ruined by a sexual encounter while the man could escape untarnished.

The eponymous heroine of Shaw's *Mrs Warren's Profession* caused even more disquiet. There was nothing directly to offend the Edwardian eye or ear. Until the 1920s play texts were remarkable for the purity of their diction. The censor who described the play as 'immoral and otherwise improper for the stage' when it was submitted in 1894 wished only to protect the delicate minds of Edwardian theatre-goers from the seductive force of Shaw's intellect.[28] Even J.T. Grein, who had opposed censorship with such vehemence, was revolted by a private performance of the play in 1902.[29] 'There was a majority of women to listen to that which could only be understood by a minority of men. Nor was the play fit for women's ears ... Even men need not know all the ugliness that lies below the surface of everyday life,' he wrote in his review.[30]

Shaw rejected Grein's prim pussy-footing. He showed that prostitution could pay, that it could sometimes bring financial independence and peace of mind and body. Mrs Warren, who owns a chain of brothels, is regarded as a woman to admire. Shaw dealt with the marriage question by suggesting that it was no more than a form of market in which middle-class women sought money and security for life by union with a man. 'Prostitution is caused, not by female depravity and male licentiousness, but simply by underpaying, undervaluing and overworking women so shamefully that the poorest of them are forced to resort to prostitution to keep body and soul together,' he wrote in his 1902 preface to the play. Prostitutes, if depicted in plays, were not expected to be true to life. They were required to do the decent thing and die, commit suicide, be rejected by their protector or repent their wicked ways. Shaw would have none of that: he argued that prostitution was a question not of morality but of exploitation. 'I wanted to show what was the real character of what is now called the white slave trade and how it was boldly defended morally by the people who defended it,' he wrote to the Lord Chamberlain, Lord Sandhurst, in 1916 when the play was again submitted for licensing and was once more rejected. Prostitution was endemic because 'of a refusal to secure higher wages for virtue than for vice'. The Chamberlain's bulky file for *Mrs Warren's Profession* discloses details of the long campaign to bring the play, to the public stage.

A year later a petition calling for the play to be granted a licence was delivered to Lord Sandhurst, signed by assorted lords, knights, bishops, mayors and MPs. The most respected of Georgian writers, J.M. Barrie, Arnold Bennett, John Galsworthy and G.K. Chesterton among them, and leaders of the theatrical profession such as Ellen Terry, William Archer, Sir Frank Benson, Sir Charles Wyndham and Sir John Martin Harvey, were signatories too. They pointed out that the play was 'a dramatic work of acknowledged excellence by one of our foremost dramatists'. 'The problem with which the play so effectively deals is now recognised to be of extreme gravity,' they said, in allusions to the thriving wartime market in prostitution and the spread of sexually transmitted disease. Lord Sandhurst was unmoved. 'The subject is unsavoury to the last degree,' he minuted in October 1917.[31]

Shaw drew support from some unlikely sources. Beatrice Webb, the Fabian leader, was politically close to Shaw. But she was, despite her socialism, no believer in literature or drama of discussion and disclosure when it came to matters of sexual behaviour. In 1911 she had been a signatory to the National Council of Public Morals manifesto. She had quarrelled publicly with H.G. Wells over his *In the Days of the Comet* and its depiction of sex outside marriage and thought, according to her autobiography, that both Shaw and Granville Barker were 'obsessed with the rabbit-warren aspect of society'.[32] Shaw's *Getting Married* (1908), with its gleeful rejection of conventional ideas about both marriage and divorce, must have alarmed her. Yet Mrs Webb did not object to Shaw's analysis of what incited young women into the business of prostitution. She wrote a letter on 13 March 1918 to Lord Haldane – who had been Asquith's Lord Chancellor in the 1915 wartime coalition of

Liberals and Conservatives, and would hold the same office in Ramsay MacDonald's first brief Labour administration of 1924 – which was accurate and astute.

'I think that many of the Labour people, interested in intellectual questions and moral reform, are beginning to think that the Lord Chamberlain is prejudiced against Bernard Shaw on account of his other opinions,' she wrote to Haldane, adding with silky disingenuousness, 'a surmise which I am sure is not true. But the queer morality which is promulgated by the ordinary conventional Tory dramatist and music-hall artist is permitted to be freely expressed whilst George Bernard Shaw's Puritanism is suppressed.' Mrs Webb hit home: the Lord Chamberlain and his staff were hostile to plays which diagnosed the ills and injustices of society from a socialist or radical perspective. Haldane, in response to Mrs Webb's letter, tried without success to persuade Sandhurst to reconsider his decision on *Mrs Warren's Profession*.

When the Duke of Atholl became Lord Chamberlain in 1921 he did not know what to do: on 19 February 1922 he minuted in the file for the play, 'My opinion is that we should pass it, though I think it is unsavoury.' In a rare, though double-edged example of a Lord Chamberlain being positively influenced by liberal pleadings he wrote, 'I think [the ban] probably does more harm to the censorship lobby unpassed than passed.' But both Lord Buckmaster and Sir Squire Bancroft on the Chamberlain's Advisory Board remained opposed and Atholl did not choose to overrule them. Lord Cromer took a different attitude when he succeeded Atholl. The slightly more liberal attitudes to women and to prostitution may have caused this change of heart. 'It would,' Cromer minuted on 17 August 1924, 'be absurd to go on refusing a licence to this play, ignoring the march of time and the change it brings about in public opinion over facing such questions openly.' This concession to the importunings of what Cromer called 'public opinion' was an exception to the new Chamberlain's iron rules. Lord Cromer's characteristic mode in the 1920s and 1930s was to ignore time's inexorable march with the defiance of Congreve's old Lady

Wishfort surveying the ruin of her beauty in the looking-glass and putting up cosmetic defences against its depredations.

The inveterate fear of the theatre's supposed capacity to act as a seductive agent of immorality and dissent was also exposed when a newly translated version of Sophocles' *Oedipus Rex* was submitted for licensing in 1907. Edward Carson, the Unionist MP who became a member of the Lord Chamberlain's advisory committee, recommended the play for licence on the grounds that it would not 'inculcate immoral teaching in any way'. But Sir John Hare, the elderly actor-manager, advised against allowing the play to be performed. 'I have very grave doubts as to whether the public performance of *Oedipus* might not prove injurious in so much as it may and probably will lead to a great number of plays being written and submitted to the censor appealing to a vitiated public taste solely in the cause of indecency,' he judged. The play was permitted a licence, but only after the advisory committee had considered what moral dangers it might pose for impressionable members of theatre audiences.

In January 1912 *The Times* reported the banning of *The Coronation* by Christopher St John and Charles Thursby, a new play which it accurately described as 'Socialist and anti-military in its tendencies'. *The Times'* reviewer of a private performance a few weeks later concluded that a veto on the play's licensing for public showing was attributable to its anti-monarchical attitudes. That was mere speculation, but certainly by the 1920s the memoranda on plays either banned or sent to the Chamberlain's advisory panel for assessment betray a specific bias against radical social and political drama.

Mrs Webb's reference to the 'queer morality' of Tory drama was apt: farces which relied on innuendo and happily showed married males in hot pursuit of sexual plenty were generally passed by the censor. For two infamous years, 1911–13, the Examiner of Plays was Charles Brookfield, a minor actor and playwright whose philistinism and loathing of serious modern drama must have made him the ideal man for the job. Shortly before he was chosen as the new Examiner he had written an article on theatre in which he lashed out at Shaw, Granville

Barker and Galsworthy. Each of them, he alleged, chose to regard the theatre 'as the heaven-sent trumpet through which he is to bray his views on social problems of his own projection.' Young people were more liable to be harmed by seeing 'a sombre dissertation on the right of a wife to desert a degenerate husband . . . than by the frivolous burlesque of ill-assorted marriages such as one finds in these old French vaudevilles.'[33] Brookfield happened to have written just such a burlesque himself. His play *Dear Old Charlie*, loosely adapted from the French, in which the hero fornicated with his friends' wives, was cited by at least two witnesses to the 1909 Select Committee of Inquiry into Theatre Censorship as 'examples of offensive but uncensored filth'.[34] 'There really cannot be two opinions about the cynical, shameless immorality that underlines the play,' *The Times*' reviewer wrote, in vague echo of that judgement when the play was revived in 1912.[35]

For a final arbiter of what views and behaviour could be put upon the stage the Lord Chamberlain could use a figure as far removed from the public as possible: the sovereign. In 1917 Lord Sandhurst faced the problem of Brieux's *Damaged Goods*, a transgressive drama that dealt with syphilis. The play was being recommended as a suitably moral warning-shot fired in the direction of soldiers at war. The National Campaign for Venereal Diseases, an organisation trying to stem the rising tide of sexually transmitted infections within the fighting services, aspired to achieve a licence for the play, but of course such subjects were not mentioned in polite Edwardian society. The 1913 Royal Commission on Venereal Diseases had played a decisive role in ensuring that no preventive health campaigns were launched and in 1914 Brookfield's successor, Ernest Bendall, had argued that the stage was no place for a play that included 'a detailed interview between a doctor and his patient, who as a sufferer from syphilis is warned against the probable consequences of his contemplated marriage unless he postpones it for at least three years.' How could such matters be discussed in the mixed company of a theatre audience? 'Venereal disease seems to me a subject essentially unfit for description or discussion upon the stage, no matter how good the motive', he judged.

Sir Walter Raleigh, Professor of English at Oxford and a member of the advisory committee, agreed. 'I do not think that the public theatre is the best place for the delivery of this sermon,' he wrote, and he recoiled from the idea that the stage should be allowed to become anything so vulgar as a forum for venting issues of contemporary concern. 'The danger that the theatre should seek out everything that is topical, exciting or scandalous is a danger we face in journalism.' Viscount Buckmaster, exemplifying the close connection between government and the censor, agreed. 'It is better suited to the lecture room of a hospital.' The theatre might have a missionary function, but not if the missionaries candidly discussed the unpleasant facts of life.

Sandhurst, however, seems to have been sufficiently concerned about the application on 14 February 1917 that within six days he had requested and received a verdict on the play from the Archbishop of Canterbury. The Primate, in a typical example of Church of England fence-sitting, came down firmly on the side of uncertainty. 'I could not go so far as to urge you to give sanction to its performance,' he wrote. 'But on the other hand I am inclined on the whole to believe you would be taking a mistaken line if you were to veto it at a moment when the subject with which it deals is freely discussed everywhere, the barriers which used to shut it being rudely broken down.'

The Chamberlain then communicated with Lord Stamford-ham, the monarch's private secretary, saying that he wished to discuss the problem posed by *Damaged Goods* with George V and seek guidance from him. 'I had intended to have asked HM for the honour of a short audience but learning that HM is more than usually overwhelmed I intend to send a memo in the form of a letter to you.' Sandhurst could not see an objection to licensing the play and agreed with the Archbishop of Canterbury. 'The play is now put forward again for licence as a serious effort and practical addition to the propaganda with which it endeavoured to combat venereal disease . . . the play is a very serious work.' But, 'in view of the subject matter', Sandhurst said he did not wish to issue a licence 'without informing His Majesty'. Even after the play had been licensed, the Catholic Federation of the Archdiocese of Westminster, wrote to Examiner of Plays George Street, on 28 April 1917, complaining that a licence had been given to *Damaged Goods*. The Federation also referred Street to 'another very objectionable play' due to be revived at the Kingsway Theatre, having been licensed in 1914. Its name was *Ghosts*.[36]

A Bad Example for the Lower Orders

During the inter-war years the Lord Chamberlain, his advisers and Examiners continued to strike down plays that condoned irregular sexual behaviour or cast figures of authority in a disparaging light. But they also had a new justification for regarding the stage as a focus for social and political dissent from orthodox values. In the general election of 1922 the Labour Party at last emerged as a major political force, with just over four million votes, a hundred thousand more than the Liberals and 1.3 million less than the Conservatives. For the first time middle-class and a sprinkling of upper-class men sat on the Labour benches. The *Daily Herald*, founded in 1912, may not have been a mass circulation newspaper, but it was at least challenging the fixed monopoly of Conservative opinion in the press. Militant and organised labour had already shown a disconcerting willingness to take on management. In January 1924, during the brief period of the first Labour administration, George V implicitly acknowledged that the monarchy had gone into opposition and that the will of the electors ought not be frustrated from Buckingham Palace: '[the new ministers] have different ideas to ours,' he wrote to his mother, 'but they ought to be given a chance and treated fairly.'[37] When it came to theatre censorship the prim George V occasionally succumbed to the temptation to question the Chamberlain's decision to license particular plays.

The twilight of the Edwardian decade was irradiated by a beam of flamboyant, metropolitan decadence. It was as if the naughtiness of the 1890s had returned. 'Up in Regent Street young men, wearing tight suits and nail varnish, were sipping *crème de menthe* in the Café Royal, while down a dark cul-de-sac lurked ... a nightclub profanely named The Cave of the Golden Calf.'[38] In the new jazz age the young, the artistic and the bohemian conspired to make the capital city a centre of wild revelry and hedonism. Noël Coward in his 1920s plays dramatised the lives of not-that-bright young things for whom cocktails, cocaine, opium and adultery were commonplace. Coward wrote from life and close observation. Indeed he was claimed to have been a conduit for decadence, transmitting the phenomenon from 'the Aristocratic Bright Young People to the new middle class'.[39]

London nightlife during the 1914–18 war, with more than 150 nightclubs estimated to exist in Soho alone, had seen high society relishing the chance to end the night with drinking, drugging and dancing to the imported Ragtime music. This four-year period proved a mere prelude to the pleasure-prone antics of the 1920s. That decade ushered in an age of frank excess, for the Licensing Act of 1921 relaxed prohibitions on late-night drinking. Bohemia, that loosely used word to describe the society-people with artistic aspirations and loose morals, flourished. 'In younger London society ... the correct thing to do for intelligent young people with a fixed income and no particular vocation was to call themselves "artists" ... Bohemianism was understood to mean a gay disorderliness of life, cheerful bad manners and no fixed hours or sexual standards.'[40] In the press the modern male youth was regularly denounced for failing to be a real man. The *Daily Express* in 1925 warned that the modern girl's brother was 'weary, anaemic, feminine, bloodless, dolled up like a girl and exquisite.'[41] He sounds like a character straight out of a Noël Coward play.

As for the sisters, 'The shameless abandon with which the new free woman danced, allowing her partner near-sexual closeness of embrace, her immodest dress and coiffure and her profaneness of language were by no means the only charges against her' in the disapproving view of respectable pillars of society.[42] The new woman was not, however, all vacuous frivolity. She could have a mind of her own and go to university. The doors to some professions from which she had been barred were flung open. Greater equality was allowed between the sexes when it came to grounds for divorce. Most important of all, in 1928, an act opposed by Winston Churchill ended the martyrdom of the suffragettes. Women were for the first time allowed to vote, as men could, at 21 instead of 30 and the same qualifications in terms of residence were applied to them as for men.

The Lord Chamberlain read texts of shocking, subversive dramas, with women in the new, more confident phase of emancipation who were little short of outrageous. Their sexual and social independence threatened the orthodoxy that he expected plays to support. Upper-middle-class women behaving badly were to become the bane of the Lord Chamberlain's life when considering plays for licence. Such ladies, far from setting an example when depicted on stage, seduced men young enough to be their sons and committed adultery at the drop of a skirt. They took up with two men at a time and lived in arty sexual triangles. Worst of all they even had sex with the servants. Such women, together with men who outraged the required decencies and decorum of family life, were not to contaminate the stage.

Somerset Maugham had reached the heights of theatrical fame and fashionability when his play *Our Betters* caused the Lord Chamberlain frissons of alarm in 1923. Wilde's comedies had made aristocrats witty and fallible. Maugham now showed the upper classes caught up with decadent, ambitious and adulterous Americans. In *Our Betters* the summer air is thick with social slipping and a liberated woman shamelessly does the indecent thing. Pearl, an American married to a titled Englishman, not only enjoys an extra-marital relationship with a fellow countryman but also seduces a duchess's young gigolo. The aspirant fornicators are reported to be alone in the summerhouse whose door is locked. This shocking incident, as in accounts of catastrophe in Greek drama, is described, not witnessed on stage. George Street, the Examiner, thought that for audiences to see the sinful couple would have been 'much more unpleasant'. He did not see Maugham's intention as maligning the upper classes either. 'The effect is not sympathy with vice but intense scorn of it, not the less because it is made ridiculous as well as odious. If I am right in this it is the reverse of an immoral play.'[43]

The play was sent out to the advisory board whose members did not object to it, perhaps because the American women lead men into temptation. Buckmaster's verdict on the play is significant in its illiberal hedging. 'There can be no sound objection to the introduction of vicious worthless people into drama,' he wrote. But 'if they were used for the purpose of slandering a nation or an individual I should be most unwilling to license a performance.' In other words Maugham's play would have been banned if it could have been taken to impugn the English character, or indeed the American. In this instance Buckmaster saw no such general slurring. As for the incident in the summerhouse, he was prepared to be sophisticated. 'I think the public will not be unduly shocked . . . Indeed if my memory serves me well precisely this incident occurs and is jested about in *The Merry Widow*.' Lord Cromer granted *Our Betters* a licence.

By chance George V read about the play while it was running in London and was shocked. The King's private secretary, Lord Stamfordham, accordingly wrote to Cromer. 'Someone has spoken to the King about a play, *Our Betters*, and if the report is true His Majesty thinks it must be decidedly objectionable and he is inclined to wonder whether it was carefully considered by the censor.' A disparaging report about Maugham's play taken from the low-brow *Daily Graphic* was also enclosed and Stamfordham instructed, 'If you have not read the critique in *The Times* . . . please look at it.' The *Daily Graphic*'s article by 'Cynic' alluded contemptuously to the new, moral character of the age. 'Any censor who endeavours to gratify modern requirements must have so little censoriousness in his composition that the title must become a misnomer. In these days of sophistication the censor of plays must himself be in a tragic position.' The censor was supposed to 'guard the public morals' but what happened when such 'a priceless possession' no longer existed?

Cromer reacted calmly to this challenge to his authority. His letter to Stamfordham on 21 September provides fresh evidence of how far the Lord Chamberlain treated the King as the final arbiter of what could be seen on stage. Cromer offered to send all the relevant documents and the script of the play to the monarch. He declared himself impervious to press criticism and condemned the *Daily Graphic* as a newspaper 'well-known for the regularity of its attacks upon the Lord Chamberlain and his department . . . So long as I take what I consider to be the right and common-sense view of things I remain uninfluenced by newspaper blame or praise.' Stamfordham's reply on 23 September was emollient and jovial. 'His Majesty after reading the newspaper critiques still thinks it might be an unsavoury play, but feels certain criticisms for and against it will be an excellent advertisement and no doubt everyone will take the earliest opportunity of seeing it.' The sovereign subtly impugned the Lord Chamberlain's freedom to censor in accordance with his own assessment of what should be permitted on stage. 'As three of the advisory committee, including a very important opinion like Buckmaster's recommend the sanctioning of the play, you could not have insisted upon censoring it.' The King was, however, wrong. The Lord Chamberlain bore statutory responsibility, the advisory board only advised; it had no authority. Cromer, who wrote a note a few days later saying that he would like to have banned the play if he could, survived as Lord Chamberlain until 1938.

Florence Lancaster, the anti-heroine of Noël Coward's *The Vortex* (1924), agitated Cromer far more than the fornicators in *Our Betters*. Coward, in his mid-twenties, was already reckoned the voice of a frivolous upstart generation that had no respect for its elders. From the vantage point of the Lord Chamberlain it was easy to see *The Vortex* as a class-based attack upon society people, whom Coward cast in no flattering light. Florence, who should have known better by virtue of age and position, was seen in the comfortable grip of a man young enough to be her son but old enough to know better. Her put-upon husband raised no objection and their son took cocaine. Perhaps surprisingly the Senior Examiner of plays, George Street, recommended that the play be given a licence on the grounds that there were people like Florence 'whom it would do good to see how they look to an observer.' The idea of exposing the upper-middle classes did not, however, meet with Lord Cromer's approval. He read the play and was appalled by its implied criticisms of the lower echelons of the high society to which he himself belonged. 'This picture of a frivolous and degenerate set of people gives a wholly false impression of society life and to my mind the time has come to put a stop to the harmful influence of such pictures on the stage,' he wrote on 12 November. [44]

Sir Douglas Dawson, the Lord Chamberlain's elderly Comptroller, was even more outraged by what appeared to him to be if not a call to revolution, then at least an insinuating whisper. 'It is a piece calculated to convey the worst impression of the social conditions under which we live today,' he wrote a day later. 'I often discussed with [Herbert Beerbohm] Tree and [Sir George] Alexander, the power of the stage for useful propaganda on the many thorny problems of life. Especially in these days the importance of this is intensified when class hatred is preached not only to adults at street corners, but to the children in the Sunday schools.' Dawson's comments, written in a blue-blooded flush of indignation, betray fear of the future, fear of a Labour government and of class war. The Lord Chamberlain, in Dawson's view, was bound to protect the public from plays advocating social change or admonishing the Conservatives. Further guidance was required and it had to be taken from the Chamberlain's advisory board. The key report came from the board's most influential member, Viscount Buckmaster. For once Buckmaster took a liberal view, arguing that plays like *The Vortex* 'should be free to criticise not just the feckless, criminal poor but the immoral rich as well.' He outlined the criteria by which the Lord Chamberlain should test all plays submitted to him: a licence should be given to a text 'unless it is brutalising or degrading in character, shocks or pains the moral or religious feelings of reasonable men and women, is likely to disturb international relations, subjects members of the royal family to ridicule or contempt or promotes disorder.'

This judgement constituted a startling departure from Dawson's traditional view that the upper or ruling classes should receive privileged treatment when depicted on stage. Buckmaster conceded that *The Vortex* was 'weak and unpleasant' but he gave the shortest shrift to Dawson's suggestion that Coward was holding up to 'unfair opprobrium the vices of the idle and the rich'. Wealthy people, he said, 'and those who constitute what is vaguely known as society could not claim immunity from criticism of their conduct unless similar exemptions were made for all classes. No one has ever protested against plays disclosing brutalised behaviour on the part of the poor.' Nobody had protested, after all, about a play licensed by the Lord Chamberlain, and then still running, in which 'Trade Union leaders are presented as betraying their cause for money.' He believed 'the follies and vices of prosperous and irresponsible people are just as fit a subject for the stage as the coarser vices of poorer folk.' The crucial test, and here Buckmaster succumbed to the notion that drama can incite to immorality, was whether *The Vortex* would encourage the objectionable conduct it described. He was convinced that it would not lead middle-aged women to take young lovers or young men to sniff cocaine. Sir Squire Bancroft, the retired actor-manager, who found 'this class of play . . . hateful', and H.H. Higgins, a solicitor, were sufficiently impressed by Buckmaster's argument to support his recommendation.

The Lord Chamberlain was, therefore, placed in an embarrassing situation. He and his Comptroller found themselves ranged against the advice of the Senior Examiner and the advisory board. Dawson was so outraged by Buckmaster's report that he penned a message to Cromer which sought to take the sting from the former Lord Chancellor's judgement. 'I regard the insinuation of favour to one class as a misleading opinion of the impartial way in which the board has hitherto exercised its duties,' he wrote. Cromer reacted to the impasse by appealing to the monarch as a court of last resort. The King was sent a copy of the play. According to Johnston, George V did read *The Vortex*, thought it 'disgusting' but believed it could not be prohibited.[45] The letter to Cromer from Lord Stamfordham, however, simply said, 'The King has read the papers', by which he may have meant the advisory committee's reports.

A 'reluctant' Cromer permitted the performance and *The Vortex* caused no revolution in the streets. George Street had observed that there were 'certainly people like its anti-heroine Florence Lancaster' – 'a nymphomaniac mother chasing after young men of a similar age to her drug-addicted son', as Johnston put it in censorious hyperbole.[46] The anxiety generated by this character is most significant. It was not even a small surprise that *The Vortex* should be regarded as a dangerous new play by many conventional play-goers. 'Our parents forbade us to go,' one young member of the audience recalled years later. 'There on stage was a young man taking dope; his mother having an affair with a young man . . . I mean it was absolutely horrifying. But to us it was a revelation.'[47] In old age, when Coward had a love affair with a young man, he was still emphasising *The Vortex*'s morality. 'I disapproved of elderly ladies having young lovers,' he told the *New York Times* in 1970.[48] Perhaps Coward did not practise what he preached, but then he may have had different standards for old men who chase youths.

Within two years Coward was again at loggerheads with Lord Cromer over a play he had submitted for licensing. *This Was a Man* is unknown now, but at the time its impenitent bohemian adulterers provoked more outrage than *The Vortex*. No fast or wicked lady was selected for particular prominence; everyone was caught in a decline-and-fall condition. In the parlance of the Examiner of the Play there was lashings of vice, but no authorial lashing of moral weakness. 'The main intention of the play is to satirise and generally score off the complacent and correct type of Englishmen,' Street reported on 15 September 1926. Such an intention, he conceded, was permissible 'but the means by which it is executed involves an amount of adultery, cynically and light-heartedly treated, which makes the play more than dubious.' Dawson, always eager to keep the theatre straitjacketed in Victorian decorum, had no doubts about the play's capacity to help foment socialist revolution in the nervy aftermath of the General Strike and a Labour government that had been dangerously enamoured of the Russians.

How could Coward defame the better class of people by suggesting they plunged into adultery with as much insouciance as they dived into the sea at the continental resorts where they holidayed. 'Every character in this play, *presumably ladies and gentlemen* [my italics], leads an adulterous life and glories in doing so,' Dawson wrote on 26 September. 'I find no serious "purpose" in the play, unless it be misrepresentation. At a time like this what better propaganda could the Soviet [sic] instigate and finance? It was apropos of just this sort of play that, during my time in Paris, *nice* French people remarked to me, "Would that we had a censor." ' The play was banned, though in the next two years there were productions in New York, Berlin and, of course, Paris. 'The Lord Chamberlain has banned my really very moral play. The whole thing confirms my opinion of stage conditions in our country,' Coward told the *Evening Standard* on 20 October. 'The authorities do not encourage dramatists.'

Perhaps Lord Cromer regretted the leniency of his attitude, for in 1930 he intervened in the rehearsals of Coward's *Private Lives*. The Chamberlain had become concerned about adultery, or rather the specific sort of adultery contemplated by the two attractive young characters, Elyot and Amanda, who, divorced from each other, meet again after marriage to new partners. 'This affair seemed to him altogether too *risqué* for the public standards of morality,' Coward's first biographer, Sheridan Morley, claimed. 'Unless the act was drastically rewritten [Cromer] would regretfully be unable to give permission for *Private Lives* to be performed. Coward was allowed, however, to go to St James's Palace, which housed the Lord Chamberlain's office, and act out the play, reading all the roles himself. Cromer was thereby convinced that *Private Lives* did not amount to an incitement to adultery. [49] The incident usefully shows how hard it can be to assess a play on the basis of a text rather than an actual performance.

Gilda, the heroine of Coward's *Design for Living* and the two men whom she leads a pretty dance to the music of desire, ought to have been an example of the independent, marriage-defying woman of whom Lords Chamberlain disapproved. Indeed it is strange that in 1939 the new Chamberlain, Lord Clarendon, did not take exception to Coward's depiction of attractive but immoral bohemians. Not even the title worried him. Yet thanks to her charms and permissiveness Gilda ends up living happily with two men in a *ménage à trois*. Coward's original idea, wisely jettisoned, had been for the play to be staged 'in a gigantic bed, dealing with life and love in the Schnitzler manner.'[50] But, of course, beds and Schnitzler's play *La Ronde*, had both been banned from the stage. It would be six years before Coward would risk submitting his comedy of chic, high-society bohemians to the Chamberlain, whose then Senior Examiner Henry Game recommended it for licensing 'despite the immorality of its theme'. Perhaps Game was influenced by the fact that the comedy had been welcomed on Broadway five years earlier. He decided that the play was no more than 'an artificial comedy of manners'.[51] Artificiality, however, did not necessarily prevent a play from transgressing codes of behaviour the stage was supposed to uphold. For once the essential frivolity of Coward's characters was of advantage to him in matters of censorship.

There was, though, the veiled question of the relationship between the two men. Nothing was directly said to suggest they were sexually involved with each other, and the discretion of directors and actors ensured that the hidden drama of bisexuality was not realised on stage. It was not until Sean Mathias's adventurous revival of the play at the Donmar Warehouse in 1992 that its full bisexual potential was dramatically realised. Until then it had been implied that Leo and Otto ended up taking turns to have Gilda: the final imposition of a *ménage à trois* was taken as a comic fantasia, an erotic triangle in which the two males never formed actual sexual links. Yet once the play began its run, Mrs E.K. Ruddock wrote to the Assistant Comptroller, Brigadier Norman Gwatkin, on 2 February 1939 from Drayton Gardens in Chelsea to complain about the production. 'Surely one wants to raise the moral tone of England at this time, not lower its standards,' she asked. Gwatkin made an ingenious and unusual defence of the play, arguing that there was 'no erotic and suggestive indecency' in the comedy. The *ménage à trois* was, after all, 'entirely unsuitable for the majority of people in a reasonable world. It is made quite plain that those immediately concerned are bohemians and not particularly good citizens – their lives are centred upon themselves. They are useless members of society except in so far as their artistic products are concerned.'[52] For once a play was not required to set a moral example, 'The principals are objects for compassion rather than disgust, and it may well be argued that the reaction to a play of this description is one of thankfulness that the majority of people need normal lives,' Gwatkin smugly concluded.[53] This view was not, however, typical. The most influential of theatre critics, the *Sunday Times'* James Agate, whose homosexuality was no secret within the theatrical profession, discovered in *Design for Living* a purity of moral purpose. 'Mr Coward sees as clearly as the sternest moralist could wish [that] flouting convention is a form of parasitism,' he wrote in the *Sunday Times* on 29 January 1939. 'Vice should have proceeded out of these vicious babies and possessed us. It did not.'

This specious claim, and the one that Gwatkin had advanced, did not satisfy the moral purity movements and their individual supporters, whose complaints were treated with deferential concern. Writing on behalf of the London Morality Council Howard Tyrer explained the danger of allowing the play to be performed. 'The moral, if you can call it such, seems to be that there are certain people who cannot fit into the ordinary conventions of life and that they must therefore be free to live as they choose, so long as they are not harming anyone else no one has the right to object to what they do,' he claimed. This explication was far more accurate and discerning than Gwatkin's or Agate's. But of course moral campaigners resented any influential condoning of such behaviour. A month later the Public Morality Council, buttressed by the Bishop of London, two other bishops, two suffragans, five or six Misses and a couple of dowagers, launched a more significant protest to the Chamberlain. Their argument was familiar: the play was 'descriptive of people with no morals' and might, therefore, 'injuriously affect persons whose minds were impressionable'. Worse, 'The executive felt that the play had no real justification as representing life in this country and noticed the absence of any really healthy leading character in the play.' Theatre-going apparently, in the Council's view, was supposed to work as a form of cleansing fluid for the spirit, which left the moral fibre of audiences supple but not indecently stretched.

August Strindberg's *Miss Julie*, submitted for licensing in 1927, was reckoned to portray a far more dangerous type of woman than Coward's Gilda. As far as the Lord Chamberlain was concerned the eponymous heroine represented the worst sort of liberated female; she betrayed her class and breeding by stooping sexually to conquer one of the servants. The actor-producer Milton Rosmer, writing from the avant-garde Festival Theatre Cambridge in 1927, noted correctly that the play was recognised as 'a masterpiece ... all over Europe'. That recognition was not universal. Because of the ruling of the Swedish censor the first complete text was not staged there until 1949 and the English censors were only a little less fearful. *Miss Julie* did not receive a licence for public performance until 1938 for a production at the London Mask Theatre, then run by J.B. Priestley. 'There is the sordid and disgusting atmosphere which makes the immorality of the play glaring and crude,' Cromer wrote on 3 October 1925. Even worse, 'there is the very questionable theme in these days of the relations between masters and servants which this play tends to undermine.'[54] The phrase 'in these days' is redolent of an underlying, upper-class sense of social unease, of the same fear that Dawson manifested when reacting to Noël Coward's *This Was a Man* or *The Vortex*.

Miss Julie was an imbroglio of social upheaval and dislocation, a seductive vision in disturbed times that had to be prohibited. The Advisory Board's Viscount Ullswater, when asked to give his view of the play, made the point briskly. 'The character of Julie, quite impossible in life ... is represented as governed by an all-conquering lust for a manservant. This is the main-spring of the piece and I think inadmissible.' Other advisers to the Chamberlain reacted with revulsion not to what was said or shown, but to what was implied. 'The whole sordid and beastly atmosphere makes the thing worse,' Street wrote. 'I have been at some pains to wade through this filthy piece,' complained the retired actor-manager Sir Johnston Forbes-Robertson, appointed to the advisory board at the age of 73. 'No doctoring can do away with the loathsome atmosphere of this piece.' So Strindberg's grim depiction of the sex and class war was kept from the stage.

New plays in which male sexuality threatened the decorum of family life or alternatives to marriage were depicted in a favourable light were equally denounced, censored or even prohibited. Pirandello's *Six Characters in Search of an Author* (1922) proved a case in point. Bernard Shaw was so taken with the play that he was instrumental in arranging for a club performance at the Kingsway Theatre in February 1922 that was well received by the critics. When it came to licensing, though, there was the problem of the re-enactment of the scene suggesting an incestuous relationship of the father and the stepdaughter. Months earlier a first licence had reluctantly been given to Shelley's *The Cenci*. 'I regret that people would desire the public performance of this unspeakable horror,' Buckmaster had written. 'It can teach no lesson. It can give no warning or instruction . . . It can only sicken, terrify and distress. None of these considerations, however, give a real reason for refusing a licence. I can only add that I wish sincerely it were otherwise.' When it came to *Six Characters* Buckmaster failed to apply this reasoning process to a similar theatrical circumstance. 'To base a scene upon the horror of a boy seeing his father and mother in a sexual relationship sickens and disgusts me and I assume it would sicken and disgust a normal audience,' he judged in December 1924.[55]

The prime objection, though, had to do with what Lord Cromer took to be a grossly transgressive portrayal of family life. 'No amount of supposed unreality . . . can disguise the objectionable fact that a stepfather goes to a brothel, that he nearly has intercourse with his own stepdaughter; that he is fortunately saved from this repulsive act by his maltreated wife,' Cromer judged. In vain did Street suggest, 'the events are not supposed to have happened, but to be a pseudo-play within a play and the interest of the whole is not in the incidents but in the mystical or metaphysical theses.' The reaction of Cromer and the members of his advisory committee to Pirandello emphasised how the censor opposed the idea that the theatre could be used to depict and analyse sexual relations. The mere allusion to quasi-incest provoked moral panic. No one cared a jot about Street's metaphysics.

'It is plain filthiness', the elderly and out-of-touch Sir Squire Bancroft wrote from The Athenæum. His comments betrayed the xenophobia and Ango-Saxon superiority of which there had been a distinct strain among critics and commentators since the mid-nineteenth century. 'This play, I think, comes from Vienna,' Bancroft continued in airy ignorance. 'The sooner it is sent back there, the better. The story they [sic] tell is to my mind extremely abominable . . . To grant a licence for this play would in my opinion be to sanction the performance of a degrading spectacle.' The fact that nothing salacious was actually depicted on stage passed him by, as it did his colleagues. 'The core of the play deals with a subject that is quite unpleasant,' Cromer judged. His report on the play also provides illuminating evidence of how far the Lord Chamberlain was influenced by the views of the leaders of the Church of England when making his judgements about a play's admissibility to the stage. 'It is moreover the sort of theme to which the ecclesiastical and other authorities are taking exception.'

Lewis Casson, the actor and director, wanted his wife, Sybil Thorndike, the leading classical actress of her generation, to take the role of the stepdaughter. Nigel Playfair, who was then presiding over avant-garde seasons at the Lyric Theatre Hammersmith wished for the chance to present the play. Both men appealed for a licence to be given; they did so in vain. The Lord Chamberlain was never much taken by the avant-garde. By August 1925 Cromer had become sensitive to newspaper criticism of the ban. 'The press tell us that this country will be the laughing-stock of the world if this play is allowed to be performed.' He argued interestingly, however, that because the stepfather 'nearly' indulged in sexual intercourse with his stepdaughter at a brothel, though not in a scene shown on stage, 'the horror of whole . . . gives a shock to every member of the audience.' There was no question of contemporary playwrights being permitted the freedoms enjoyed by ancient Greek dramatists to deal with the ramifications of incestuous desire or to present acts of extreme physical violence in the manner of Shakespeare and Jacobean playwrights. Yet when Cromer was invited by the theatre producer Barry Jackson to see the play at the Arts Theatre for a members-only performance he found his misgivings unfounded. The sense of moral outrage induced in the Lord Chamberlain and his readers by the account of the brothel incident was not aroused by the enactment of the scene. 'Although to my mind it remains a very disagreeable play,' he wrote on 23 May 1928, 'I felt bound to confess that it is quite inoffensively acted and consequently I have agreed to issue a licence.' What he had seen in the lurid fantasising of his mind's eye was soothed by the reticence of the performers.

Fear of Women

The spectacle of scantily clad young women on stage became a renewed source of concern and anxiety to the Lords Chamberlain and the vigorous Edwardian organisations crusading to enforce conventional forms of morality. Such stage spectacles were disturbing reminders of the erotic power of young women to seduce man against his better judgement. The century before, Queen Victoria herself had taken an anxious interest in the matter of ballet girls who danced in Offenbach's *Vert-Vert* at the St James's Theatre in 1874. Their skirts were very short and the Lord Chamberlain ordered that inches be added to them. The sovereign's private secretary wrote to the Lord Chamberlain to convey the royal satisfaction that attempts were being made 'to curb the licence of the stage'.[56] Despite defiance of the old morality by Edwardian radicals, both on stage and off, the first significant censorship battle over female flesh did not occur until 1915.

War usually proves a great liberator of sexual inhibitions and during the First World War London nightlife thrived in the new nightclubs, where young hedonists danced to the Apache and the Bunny Hug. The theatre-world, where the demarcation lines of class were not observed and in whose ranks were plenty of bohemians and sexual non-conformists, was a centre for this new cult of pleasure.

That the busy members of the Alliance of Honour should have time or inclination, in the middle of a world war, to bother the Lord Chamberlain with complaints about a naked female foot and upper thigh, may seem strange. Nevertheless the Alliance complained about an item in the Ambassador's Theatre's revue, *My Lady's Undress* (1915), and their objection was treated with gravity.

The squadron of bishops, earls, knights, baronets, professors and clerics, who led the Alliance complained in a letter to the Bishop of London, their patron. They appear to have been anxious about the effect that the sight of the thigh, as waved by the French actress Madamoiselle Alice Delysia, would have upon male minds. 'Towards the end of the disrobing scene [done behind a scene], the bottom of the chemise was coyly raised and later on the upper thigh was partially exposed by a lowering of the stocking – all to the apparent delight of the Burglar,' the Alliance explained. The Lord Chamberlain, Lord Sandhurst, reacted to this protest by despatching his Comptroller to the scene of the offending flesh. Madamoiselle Alicia Delysia was seen, according to a report from the Comptroller, dressed in 'chemise and drawers the latter cut very full, with black silk stockings apparently worn over flesh-coloured tights'. Twice she showed 'a supposed bare leg above the top of her stockings'. Once she pointed to her drawers, asked to be excused while she removed them, loosened them down to her knees and went behind a screen. White garments, apparently those shed by Mademoiselle Delysia, were then draped over the top of the screen.[57] A prowling burglar tore them down to reveal a fully dressed actress.

This act of titillation was too much for the Alliance of Honour. Why, one male member of the audience had murmured 'Rough luck' as though to console the burglar. The Lord Chamberlain, sympathising with the complaint, banned

Madamoiselle Delysia from revealing her thigh, even though it was covered by flesh-coloured stockings. She was not even allowed to loosen her drawers in view of the audience or explain to the audience that she was about to disrobe. The incident reveals an interesting fear not of female nudity, but of its imagined impact upon male members of the audience. The Alliance, in appealing to Lord Sandhurst, also exposed its xenophobia: Madame Delysia was, in its view, one of those 'continental players who may have sought sanctuary in this country'.

The close, prurient scrutiny of the female did not abate. The post-First World War woman was liable to be seen in skirts that revealed areas of leg hitherto kept from view or 'new sack-like blouses and jumpers' that the *Sunday Express* described as 'startlingly low'. Short hair on woman was now regarded as a sign of 'female independence' from the old rules of femininity. As early as March 1919 *The Bystander* magazine began to joke about the 'scantiness of women's dresses. The Peace celebrations of that year were remarkable for the way that skirts went up – 'shorter and shorter'.[58] The extent to which this new female look was regarded as indecorous can be gauged by the reaction of the octogenarian Victorian actress Dame Genevieve Ward when she met one of her young female protégés in the early 1920s: 'One of her pet aversions is the present fashion for open necks on day dresses – she says that every woman's chest nowadays looks like raw beef – so I am always very careful to muffle up my throat when I go to see her.'[59]

Naked or minimally dressed women, without the protection of 'an opaque controlling brassière', were believed to pose such a threat to strait-laced morality that in April 1940, when Britain was in danger of invasion, Lord Clarendon decided to fight the Germans by keeping the British theatre well-dressed. To cast off clothes in playhouses was tantamount to surrender, yet ever since war had been declared there had been 'greater displays of nudity and more impropriety of gesture and speech'. Accordingly Clarendon convened a conference of Home Office civil servants, policemen and county councillors, with every single branch of the entertainment industry invited to send a representative. It was very much a men-only occasion, with men deciding how much other men could see of women on stage. The officers of morality brooded manfully over the threat of nudity and dirty jokes on stage. If the Nazis invaded Britain it was essential that they should not be obliged to deal with naked women on stage or men telling *risqué* jokes. A communiqué was issued after the meeting, confirming that the British theatre would maintain 'a decent level of propriety'. This did not mean that naked women were to be banished from the stage: they could appear scantily clad, provided they wore that 'controlling' brassière and tights. Nudity was allowed provided the nude was 'motionless and expressionless' in an 'artistic' pose, and the lighting had to be 'subdued'. All the director of a strip show had to do was to lower the lights a fraction. Who could argue about the artistry of a pose?[60]

Young women, with or without 'opaque controlling brassièr-es' were reckoned far more dangerous when depicted on stage as active seducers of innocent young men. A few plays devoted themselves to young women fired by the freer spirit of a time when contraception and birth control were beginning to allow women sexual adventure without fear of conception. These scripts caused infinite trouble. One of the most bulging of the Lord Chamberlain's files relates to *Fata Morgana*, by the Hungarian, Ernest Vadja. 'The trouble is that of a sexually experienced married woman [Madam Fay] seducing an eight-een-year-old [man],' Street wrote on 15 September 1924, and recommended Cromer should read the play himself. In assessing *Fata Morgana* the Lord Chamberlain fell victim to the deceptive reassurance of stage directions. 'The dubious part is artistically done and I do not consider I should be justified in withholding a licence,' he ruled on 26 August. The play's première at the Ambassador's Theatre passed without problems. Then on 17 September the London Council for Promotion of Public Morality sent in an anxious report. The author of the letter appeared to have watched the play's seduction scene with voyeuristic prurience. His attention was rivetted by Matilda, the play's married thirty-year-old sexual adventuress, whom, he observed, 'very skilfully manoeuvres her dress to display both legs [in flesh-coloured tights] above the knees.' The right hand of George, the eighteen-year-old, 'fondles her right leg above the knee', a dangerous zone in those days, 'as if he would like to put his hand further up.' That last 'as if' surely betrays how lubriciously engaged by the scene the writer was.[61]

An erogenous zone, extending from above the knee as far up as the traditional no-go area, was declared. One enraged Lord Chamberlain, the Westminster Catholic Federation, two chief constables, two detectives from Portsmouth CID, not to mention Dame Beatrix Hudson Lyall, a member of the London Morality Council and a doctor's wife in the Mother's Union, all became caught up in a battle to declare this zone out of bounds for theatre audiences. These respectable complainants were discomfited by the erotic unseemliness of the female knee and the upper thigh. But they were more agitated by the spectacle of a young married woman shamelessly seducing a youth young enough to be her brother. Men, particularly young ones, were not supposed to be portrayed on stage as passive victims of female desire let alone of married women. A complainant from the London Morality Council was insidious and misleading; he pretended there was no distinction between an erotic action simulated on stage and one committed in public. 'I have no hesitation in stating that if these incidents were enacted in streets or parks, the participants would be promptly and rightly brought before the magisterial bench to be dealt with for infringing the laws relating to indecency,' he observed accurately, but with no relevance to the issue at hand.

The views of these moral purity organisations were treated with respect by the Lord Chamberlain, since their ruling boards were thick with bishops and aristocrats. The Lord Chamberlain's Comptroller, G.A. Crichton, at once wrote to the Westminster Catholic Federation assuring the organisation that the complaint would be considered and went to inspect the offending play. 'Once you get over the plot,' Crichton explained helpfully to Cromer in his report on 8 November, '. . . it could not have been acted more moderately. There was certainly no excess of abandon . . . There was not the slightest sign in the house that the audience considered it anything extra special.' Yet 'certain modifications of dress and business' were insisted upon. The roving hand was restrained, the flash of thigh prohibited. This was not enough for a Mrs Munro Faure, who wrote to Lord Cromer on 14 November and again the next day, accusing him of allowing the youth of the nation to be corrupted by 'alien influences'. Dame Beatrix, the Mother's Union member and the vigilant Mrs Munro Faure rained down letters of protest upon an anxious Cromer during the next few months. Another member of Cromer's staff visited the play on 17 February 1925 and found no fondling of legs. There was a flash of the actress's upper thigh, 'but this was probably unintentional . . . It is a case of a boy's first love and his action, throughout, though passionate when she kisses him does not suggest sexual desire.'

Cromer was roused to fury. 'I have seen the manager and producer of the play today and told them that unless my injunctions are obeyed at once the licence will be withdrawn,' he wrote. Yet when the play went off on tour in April 1925, Cromer was greeted with a further battery of complaints about the passionately consenting couple. He required chief constables in all the cities to which the play toured to send detectives out to watch the performance. Detective Inspector A. Mowat reported to the assistant chief constable of Glasgow's Criminal Investigation Department that the 'scene in which Matilda and George make love to each other seated or lying on a sofa which [sic] is in my opinion very suggestive of immorality.' By the time the play reached Portsmouth in May, George was reduced to 'caressing Matilda and sinking to one knee'. He drew his right hand down from 'the upper part of the front of Matilda's body and over her thigh and leg which is covered only by a silk stocking.' The two detectives watching this performance thought this incident 'objectionable' but the audience 'applauded' the scene. Public opinion, it seems from the case of *Fatana Morgana*, was quite willing to see a little love-play and flesh.

John van Druten's *Young Woodley* (1928), first given private performances at the Arts Club Theatre, involved a more controversial form of sexual contact between married woman and youth. *Young Woodley* is a seventeen-year-old public schoolboy who falls in love with a housemaster's wife. How could any respectable playwright depict such a woman in the grip both of eros and a pupil? An apprehensive Lord Cromer revealed his fear of *Young Woodley*'s subversive quality. 'As a play I consider that its effects might be most harmful. Many schoolboys seeing it might call it rot and leave it at that. But no parents with boys at school would take this view. The majority of parents would be up at arms at this sort of play being permitted.' The advisory board endorsed Cromer's judgement. Lord Buckmaster submitted that the stage should idealise and encourage, rather than question received morality. 'I dislike this play intensely,' he minuted. 'Boys at school are sometimes vicious and the conversations may be unclean but that is no reason why it [sic] should be dramatised.' Schoolmasters would legitimately argue that their 'task' had been made more difficult if the play was licensed.

However, when Cromer saw a performance of the play, directed by Basil Dean, at the Arts Theatre's private performance in January 1928, he found himself won over by 'the delicate and admirable way in which it was presented'. He may have been influenced by enthusiastic reviews in the national press as well. There was no erotic contact on stage, but the incident of seduction still posed a problem. Basil Dean tried to influence Cromer by raising the matter publicly. 'If the censorship were to be liberal-minded in this matter after the way the play has been received it would be a gesture of strength rather than of weakness,' he wrote in an article in the *Daily Telegraph* on 16 February. Cromer's prime concern, he recorded later, was that one of the schoolboys in *Young Woodley* remarked that he would not have minded 'being boots in a girl's school for a bit'. This was an allusion to a contemporary court case at a famous schoool 'where a German boot-boy was reported to have deflowered a number of pupils in a capacious boot cupboard.'[62] Cromer, illustrating the close relation between government and Lord Chamberlain when a play's production might cause political problems, sent *Young Woodley* to Lord Eustace Percy, the President of the Board of Education. The minister expressed qualified approval. 'Needless to say I don't like it. But from my own point of view I do not think it is worth while refusing a licence – in fact I think more harm is done by the vague knowledge that a play about a public school has been suppressed,' he commented. The play was licensed, caused ripples of shock, but no scandal.

Even when playwrights resorted to farce in efforts to escape the Chamberlain's reluctance to allow plays which made a mockery of traditional sexual morality the blue pencil struck out words and scene. Ben Travers' 1925 farce, *Cuckoo in the Nest*, exploited bedroom farce to criticise the rigours and unfairness of the divorce laws. A man was required innocently to remove his trousers; a woman was to be seen wearing no more than a négligé and an unmarried couple slept in the same bed because there were no single ones available. 'There is some business of his taking off his trousers and putting a towel around him which carried the thing too far and had better be cut out,' Street gravely wrote. The Senior Examiner appeared not to realise that Travers' motive in writing the farce was serious. In old age the playwright explained, '[The play] was a comment on the contemporary state of the divorce laws. It had always been taken for granted that any unmarried couple who spent a night together in an hotel must, incontestably, be guilty of adultery.'[63] Street did concede that 'nothing really offensive to morals' was included, but 'in the present temper of criticism the play might be objected to and I do not advise the Lord Chamberlain to license it without reading an act or two.' Travers had his own ideas about to whom the 'present temper of criticism' referred: 'The genial Major [Gordon, the Comptroller] confided to me that the Lord Chamberlain had to check up on the second act because bedroom scenes in plays were frowned upon in certain quarters. The certain quarters could only mean Buckingham Palace where Queen Mary was now in stately residence.'

Lord Cromer was convinced that the ridiculous bedroom scene had to be treated with gravity. 'Even if the trousers incident were to be completely eliminated the whole bedroom scene with the lady in a négligé and in bed may be open to strong objections from some quarters although there may be nothing offensive to morals,' he ruled. The Lord Chamberlain's timorousness may have had something to do not only with the King and Queen, but also with the appointment the previous year of Sir William Joyson-Hicks, a fanatical moral purity campaigner, as Home Secretary in Baldwin's second Conservative Cabinet. Joyson-Hicks had even taken steps to see whether a private performance of Eugene O'Neill's *Desire Under the Elms* in 1927 could be prosecuted. Cromer sent out *Cuckoo* to his advisory committee. Viscount Ullswater, a former speaker of the House of Commons, expressed lofty disapproval of Travers. Yes, he found the play humorous, but since when was humour necessarily elevating in the manner required by the Chamberlain's rules? 'I have read act two which I find very amusing but I think it goes too far,' he wrote. 'The whole point is "Will Peter be driven to bed with Margaret?" and the audience are kept in suspense as to how far he will go without actually doing so.' Such a situation was, 'although very funnily expressed, unhealthy and undesirable and open to very serious objection.' Had there not been enough bedroom scenes? 'We shall soon be having them in the WC.' Changes were accordingly required in the second act. But when Major Gordon went along to rehearsals he was almost disarmed.

'There is really nothing unclean in it and I cannot see that any objection can be taken to the bedroom scene in act two by anyone. There is never any question of the man or the lady being on "intimate terms" and nothing to lead an audience to think that he is ever likely to get into the same bed with her,' according to the Major. According to Gordon the farce scaled the heights of respectability. It dealt only with 'the discomfort and consequent antics and adventures of the man because there is no bed for him.' A 'reluctant' Lord Chamberlain then gave the play a licence provided that the man was not seen removing his trousers. The producer accepted this veto. Decency and decorum had been defended to the hilt. A blow for sexual inequality had been taken too, at male expense. Women at least could be seen scantily clad on stage, provided the upper thigh was shielded from view and the lighting was dimmish, but a man could not even take off his trousers, whether or not his underpants were opaque.

True to this spirit of prudery, Travers was threatened with even more fatuous censorship when his wartime farce *She Follows Me About* was submitted to the Lord Chamberlain. Nudity was once more the problem, but this time in the form of photographs. Henry Game had read the play on April Fool's Day 1943 and written a report which contains the vintage, headmasterly comment, 'There is no doubt that Mr Travers has at times allowed his sense of humour to run away with him.' The humour which had sent Travers streaking beyond the perimeters of decorum concerned two girls on a seaside holiday who take pictures of each other in the nude. If that were not a shocking enough affront to respectability, the girls make use of a camera left on the beach by a bathing vicar. On 6 April the Comptroller Gordon read the script and was less disapproving. 'I thought this quite the funniest Ben Travers I have either read or seen.' He disagreed with Game: 'I don't think the censor will or should take exception to Luffe [the vicar]. He is too farcical to resemble any real type of parson and as a man he is a sympathetic and sturdy little man as Mr Game suggests.'

Nevertheless Travers and Bill Linnit, his producer, were summoned to Windsor Castle to see an official in the Lord Chamberlain's office. They had been told that the play would not be licensed, Travers recorded, unless 'my offensive lines' were cut. In the 1950s, in *Vale of Laughter*, he made use of this incident at the hands of 'a punctilious and slightly ridiculous representative of the Lord Chamberlain' to affirm his belief in the 'good sense and equity of the censorship'.[64] In great old age he came to his senses and changed his mind. 'Two extracts from the long argument that took place,' he wrote, 'will serve to illustrate the preposterous fatuities which plagued the playwright under the censorship and the type of individual involved.' After reluctantly agreeing to pass the word 'bottom' as in 'He slapped my bottom', the censor seized upon a word that he said suffered 'an utterly unspeakable double meaning'. The word in question turned out to be 'cock'. Travers, the prime English farceur of the first half of the century concluded in his memoirs, 'What makes the production worth recording is that it provided the prime example I have ever known of the exasperatingly antiquated puerility of those appointed to enact censorship of the plays on behalf of the Lord Chamberlain.' It was a cry of outrage that would be raised by a flock of young playwrights a decade later when the battle to rid the stage of the Lord Chamberlain began in bitter earnest.

Notes

1. LC file on *The Wife Without a Smile* by Arthur Pinero.
2. John Johnston, *The Lord Chamberlain's Blue Pencil* (1990), p. 42.
3. Samuel Hynes, *The Edwardian Turn of Mind* (1968), p. 173.
4. Roy Porter and Lesley Hall, *The Facts of Life, 1650–1950* (1995), p. 127.
5. Ibid., p. 126.
6. Ibid., p. 126.
7. Hugh Hunt in C. Leech, T.W. Craik, and L. Potter (eds), *Revels History of Drama* (1996), vol 7, p. 6.
8. Geoffrey Robertson, *Obscenity* (1979), p. 31.
9. Hynes, op. cit., p. 353.
10. Ibid., p. 116.
11. Ibid., p. 295.
12. G. Bernard Shaw, *Three Plays for Puritans* (Penguin, 1956), p. viii.
13. William MacQueen Pope, *Carriages at Eleven* (1948), p. 1.
14. MacQueen Pope, op. cit., p. 221.
15. Hynes, op. cit., p. 216.
16. Ibid., p. 174.
17. *The Times*, 29 October 1907.
18. Report of Joint Select Committee, 1909, para 3421.
19. Ibid., para 194.
20. Richard Findlater, *Banned* (1967), p. 105.
21. James Woodfield, *English Theatre in Transition, 1881–1914* (1994), p. 126.
22. Johnston, op. cit., p. 20.
23. *The Times*, 14 February 1912.
24. Hynes, op. cit., p. 250.

25. *The Nation*, 19 November 1911.
26. *Morning Post*, 16 November 1910.
27. Hynes, op. cit., pp. 285–6 for details of the manifesto.
28. G. Bernard Shaw, *Plays Pleasant and Unpleasant*, (Penguin) p. 181 (preface to *Mrs Warren's Profession*).
29. Woodfield, op. cit., p. 175.
30. J.T. Grein, *Dramatic Criticism, 1902–3*, (1904) p. 7.
31. All these quotations are taken from LC file on *Mrs Warren's Profession*.
32. Beatrice Webb, *Our Partnership* (1948), p. 447.
33. Charles Brookfield in *National Review*, No 345, November 1911, p. 429.
34. Hynes, op. cit., p. 239.
35. Findlater, op. cit., p. 117.
36. LC files on *Damaged Goods* by Brieux and *Ghosts* by Henrik Ibsen.
37. Harold Nicolson, *George V* (1952), p. 389.
38. Philip Hoare, *Wilde's Last Stand* (1997), p. 5.
39. Hoare, op. cit., p. 229.
40. Robert Graves and Alan Hodges, *The Long Weekend* (1971), p. 130.
41. Ibid., p. 124.
42. Ibid., p. 38.
43. LC file on *Our Betters* by Somerset Maugham.
44. LC file on *The Vortex* by Noel Coward.
45. Johnston, op. cit., p. 86.
46. Ibid.
47. John Lahr, *Coward the Playwright* (1982), p. 25.
48. Ibid.
49. Sheridan Morley's Introduction to *Coward, Collected Plays III* (London, 1999).
50. Ibid.
51. Hoare, op. cit., p. 292.
52. LC file on *Design for Living* by Noel Coward.
53. Ibid.
54. LC file on *Miss Julie* by Augustus Strindberg.
55. LC file on *Six Characters in Search of an Author* by Luigi Pirandello.

56. John Russell Stephens, *The Censorship of English Drama* (1989), p. 135.
57. LC file on *My Lady's Undress*. The correspondence from the Alliance is contained here.
58. Graves and Hodges, op. cit., pp. 36–7.
59. Elizabeth Fagan, *From the Wings* (1924), p. 3.
60. Johnston, op. cit., pp. 126–7.
61. LC file on *Fata Morgana* by Ernest Vadja.
62. Johnston, op. cit., p. 140.
63. Ben Travers, *Sitting on a Gate* (1978), pp. 91–2.
64. Findlater, op. cit., p. 144.

3

HOMOSEXUAL RELATIONS

Better a Cannibal than a Queer

For several centuries there has been more than meets the innocent eye to the relationship between the English theatre and homosexuality. The ties are ancient, close, equivocal and sometimes furtive. In the twentieth century, until 1958, the Lord Chamberlain officially maintained a total ban on the discussion of homosexuality or the depiction of a homosexual on the British stage. It was a ban that could be artfully circumvented but any recognised allusions to homosexuality were excised. No character identified by word, action, deportment or costume as homosexual or lesbian was permitted to strut his or her dangerous stuff upon the stage. As a source of theatrical material they were reckoned more dangerous than mass-murderers or war criminals. One example illustrates the situation.

On 29 May 1958, Lt-Colonel St Vincent Troubridge, the Assistant Examiner reporting on Tennessee Williams' *Suddenly Last Summer*, due to be performed at the Arts Theatre Club and refused a licence, expressed a typical sense of revulsion. 'There was a great fuss in New York about the references to cannibalism at the end of this play, but the Lord Chamberlain will find more objectionable the indications that the dead man was a homosexual.'[1] Presumably cannibalism was a practice to which the average theatre-goer was not reckoned susceptible. Homosexuality, on the other hand, when the taboo became a subject of press, television and radio discussion in the 1950s, was often described as akin to an incurable sexually transmitted disease that far too many young men could be persuaded to catch. Lord Hailsham, the Conservative politician who was fanatically opposed to homosexual acts, had even described homosexuality as a 'proselytising religion'.[2] Yet before 1958 was over the Lord Chamberlain, Lord Scarbrough, announced that since homosexuality had become 'much talked about' it would be 'ostrich-like behaviour' not to allow mention of the subject on stage. Only 'serious' plays would be allowed, presumably because homosexuals were considered an improper subject for laughter.

'Unnecessary' homosexuals, those whose presence was not demanded by the action, would be outlawed as well.[3] Yet despite these prescriptive words playwrights for more than thirty years had been smuggling homosexual characters onto stage in plays that the Lord Chamberlain had licensed. There had even been plays about homosexuality that achieved a licence for performance. By evasiveness, allusion, ambiguity and innuendo, unrecognised by some audience members, easily identified by others, the homosexual had been a frequent, if shady presence upon the stage. The game had been to pretend he was not there. It is important to understand how and why this flouting of the veto had been achieved.

The Lord Chamberlain was not alone in his fear of homosexuality in the twentieth century. He reflected the pervasive belief that homosexuality was an unmentionable debauchery, unfit for discussion either in public or in polite society. This attitude had ancient origins. In Elizabethan England there was not a single man who would or could have called himself homosexual since it was not until the 1870s that the word was coined by a Hungarian doctor. The word was then used to describe a form of sexual behaviour rather than the sort of individual who practised it. In the sixteenth century, sodomy was, according to at least one contentious historian of the 1980s, Alan Bray, reckoned a conceivable source of temptation for any debauched human being and liable to lead to the world's disorder and breakdown.[4] Elizabethan and Jacobean Playhouses were known as meeting places, or even what gay men today might describe as cruising grounds, for men who wished to have sex with other males. John Stubbes in his mid-sixteenth-century *Anatomie of Abuses* condemned the underhand sexual contracts that were informally sealed at the theatre. 'These goodly pageants being ended, every mate sorts to his mate, everyone brings another homeward of their way very friendly, and in their secret conclaves covertly they play the sodomites or worse.'[5] Stubbes was not the only appalled observer. Edward Guilpin in his sixteenth century book of satires *Skialetheia* identified the sodomite as one 'who is at every play and every night sups with his ingles'.[6] He sounds like a late-twentieth-century equivalent of the regular gay London first-nighter, of a certain age, accompanied by his kept young man. Bray also discovers actors and their patrons in the court circles 'linked by sexual relations'.[7]

Bray's assessment of Elizabethan attitudes to sexual relations between males may be exaggerated. Some varieties of male homosexual attachment were expressed in Elizabethan poetry and even approved, thanks to the powerful example set by classical Greek and Roman texts, though not in the precise terms that we understand them. The form of these attachments, which include 'heroic friendship', passionate relations between men and youths, 'playful androgyny', 'and an emergent homosexual subjectivity in Shakespeare sonnets' echo strangely across the centuries in some of the controversial plays about male relations in twentieth-century plays.[8] Some of these, where the play-texts' hints, ambiguities and signs insufficiently disguised homosexual desire or relationships, fell victim to censorship.

It was the disclosures at Oscar Wilde's trial and the Victorian eagerness to categorise and regulate sexual behaviour that led to the defining of a supposedly distinct type of being, the homosexual. 'The sodomist had been a temporary aberration, the homosexual was now a species.'[9] Wilde became the modern founding father of homosexuality. The symptoms of 'effeminacy, leisure, idleness, immorality, luxury, insouciance, decadence and aestheticism' which he was thought to exemplify signposted the twentieth-century search for what homosexuality entailed.[10] Before Wilde's trial 'the effeminate dandy' was usually 'a heterosexual dandy'. After it, effeminacy and homosexuality were bonded. In 'good form' Edwardian society homosexuality would 'be mentioned with contempt in the smoking room, but never in the drawing room' where women were present.[11] The homosexual had by then been defined in terms of physical weakness, effeminate characteristics and a decadence associated with drug-taking. In the Edwardian age and well into the post-war world these characteristics were taken as indicators of homosexuality.

The waves of revulsion and moral horror vociferously expressed in newspapers after Wilde's conviction gave way to the convention of public silence, a willed secrecy calculated to ensure homosexuality once more became the love that could not speak its details. 'The only time that the problem [of homosexual relations] comes out into the open is when a local or Sunday paper reports a recent court case in which the law has punished some individual for being homosexual,' the sociologist Gordon Westwood wrote in his 1952 book *Society and the Homosexual*, published just before the 'problem' began to be discussed in the open terrain of the national newspapers. Patrick Higgins, who studied weekly issues of that scandalising smut-sheet, the *News of the World*, between 1932 and 1959, could find only six references to homosexuals or homosexuality. 'The *News of the World* resorted to euphemisms that conveyed to readers familiar with the paper's long-practised code to tell them exactly what was going on.'[12] Assize Court judges adopted comparable behaviour. During a case heard in November 1954 seventeen Rotherham men were charged with forty-one homosexual offences. The prosecuting counsel gave a grim warning to the jury, when he referred to the twenty-one-year-old man who had created this daisy-chain of gay activity, 'There are no words which sufficiently describe the way he conducted himself. The acts he performed with these men are too disgusting for words and I do not propose describing them.'[13]

Candour in the newspapers during the first half of the twentieth century, even on the subject of heterosexual relations, was checked by the survival of Victorian notions of propriety. In 1943 the Newspaper Proprietors' Association ruined the valuable wartime campaign by the Ministries of Health and

Information to provide facts through the display of advertisements in the press about the sexually transmitted diseases gonorrhoea and syphilis. The words 'on or near the sex organs' were removed from a sentence about ulcers and 'from the sex organs' from a reference to discharges. As a result there were many examples of people writing to the Ministry of Health, fearful that ulcers or sores on parts of the body far removed from the sexual areas were infected with gonorrhoea or syphilis. *The Lancet*, condemning the Association's censorship, recalled that only a year earlier 'advice to the public about washing the hands after evacuation of the bowel had to be withdrawn because the papers could not bring themselves to print "water closet".'[14] As late as 1954 the Prime Minister, Sir Winston Churchill, suggested to his Cabinet how the increasingly prevalent reporting of homosexual court cases could be prevented. A new check to freedom of speech was his answer: a discreet arrangement whereby a pliable backbench Conservative MP 'would be encouraged to introduce a bill to restrict press reports of trials for homosexuality'.[15] The idea was shelved as an impractical form of press censorship.

Yet in spite of the silence engulfing homosexuality there had been homosexual underworlds, meeting places and subcultures in London and other major cities since the late-Victorian period. Theatre bars and those close to theatres, public lavatories and railway termini were known as meeting places for those in pursuit of sexual liaisons. A homosexual brothel was famously discovered in Cleveland Street in 1889. Behind the scenes, fingers of suspicion were pointed at aristocrats. Victorian public schools of the mid-nineteenth century were conduits for adolescent homosexuality and, as the liberal historian Noel Annan put it, 'acted as a hothouse for its growth'.[16] The romantic friendship between Victorian males hovered on the verge of homoeroticism and sometimes tumbled over into the real thing. Intellectual coteries of homosexual dons were in colourful evidence from the turn of the century at Oxford and Cambridge. A.C. Benson observed the open homoerotic behaviour at King's College feast of 1909 with disapproval. 'The public fondling and caressing of each other, friends and lovers sitting with arms enlaced, struck me as curious, beautiful in a way, but rather dangerous.'[17]

Within the Bloomsbury Group, that Edwardian coterie of liberal, upper-middle-class intellectuals, Lytton Strachey and Maynard Keynes candidly discussed their sexual relations with each other and Bloomsbury women. London's West End in the First World War became, according to press reports and personal recollections, a pleasure-drome for those homosexuals who let their inhibitions go. The theatre-world, with its traditions of permissiveness, was a natural arena for the bohemian and the sexual outsider. The Cave of Harmony, opened in 1917 by the actress Elsa Lanchester, who married the gay Charles Laughton, rallied 'the theatrical, the bohemian and the homosexual'.[18] The aesthete or dandy undergraduates of 1920s Oxbridge were predominantly homosexual and often progressed to the literary and theatrical worlds. They created their own discreet cliques. In all these groups and groupings secrecy was a matter of course; code-words and secret signs became the mode of communicating over the heads of the ignorant. For risk of physical violence and blackmail was always a threat.

Male to male sexual transactions, based on a trade between the affluent and impoverished, the middle and working classes, flourished riskily. A number of 1930s trials in London had 'revealed the existence of a highly organised [homosexual] blackmailing racket, operated by a former actor, Harry Raymond, with about forty blackmailing agents.'[19] Young men in the military service rented out bits of their body at a price. Navy week in Portsmouth was, according to Quentin Crisp's enraptured recollection, 'the Mecca of the homosexual world'.[20] Conscription from 1939 and National Service after it, and the necessary removal of young men from female company, was conducive to homosexual behaviour and to the establishment of many homosexual identities. Men's attraction to men was no longer such an intensely cultivated secret.

The playwright Rodney Ackland delightedly recalled the feast of homosexual plenty that came under cover of the Second World War blackout, when inhibitions were tossed aside. The clubs and bars in London where men seeking men would gather increased in number. Ackland's lost play, *Cupid and Mars*, staged at the Arts Theatre in the late 1940s, was inspired by his own wartime cavortings in the capital. [21] Terence Rattigan, who had concealed his sexuality well beyond the point of necessary discretion became, in the disapproving words of one of his heterosexual biographers, 'more abandoned'. In 1941, when an air-gunnery leader, Rattigan, and one of his former lovers, felt free to 'indulge' themselves. The pair went 'for a run ashore' and ended up in 'a particularly notorious public convenience . . . fairly pullulating with activity.' [22]

Frith Banbury, the theatre director, recalled the increased profile of gay nightlife during the war in new bars and pubs. 'Young men were separated from their nearest and dearest and the neighbours and were free to indulge their tastes. And in the war, gay [London] clubs, like the Rockingham and Boeuf sur le Toit, were more uninhibited.' [23] John Gielgud, Noël Coward, Terence Rattigan, Ivor Novello and Binkie Beaumont were major theatrical figures in the West End of the inter-war years. In theatrical circles their sexuality was no secret. They were icons of glamour, if not of a specifically male sort, and though they did not belong to a single, social set or clique, they would have encouraged a false notion that homosexuals held power and influence in the London theatre. No wonder perhaps that Henry Game, the Lord Chamberlain's Chief Examiner, when recommending in July 1946 that a licence be refused to a play about Oscar Wilde, wrote that, 'During the period between the two world wars, a mistaken toleration gave a deplorable stimulus to the practice of abnormalities, and the censorship is undoubtedly right in making perversion taboo as a dramatic theme.' [24]

The taboo upon discussing homosexuality was, however, soon to end. The Kinsey Report of 1948 laid out evidence that homosexual activity was far more prevalent than sheltered minds would have imagined. More disturbingly Kinsey subverted the very idea of sexuality as something fixed. His research indicated that homosexuality was sometimes practised by men who categorised themselves as heterosexual. The McCarthyite witch-hunt against communists and homosexuals in the American public service, launched with fanfares of hysteria in 1950, had been inspired by a disturbing Congressional report. This report identified the homosexual as a new, sub-class of human; a man who took part in same-sex relations was emotionally unstable, a potential traitor or security risk. The defection to Russia of the British diplomats Guy Burgess and Donald Maclean prompted the American press to ask questions about the two men's sexual lifestyle. British newspapers concentrated their reports on the American government's purge of communists in the public service, rather than on homosexuals.

The increasing number of reports of homosexual offences in the national press helped foster a notion that the youth of Britain were being seduced as never before by the temptations of Sodom and Gomorrah. The change in the method of compiling statistics after 1949, counting offences on the basis of charges not convictions, bolstered the view that Britain was beset by moral decline.[25] The two trials in 1953 and 1954, involving an obscure young peer, Lord Montagu of Beaulieu, the diplomatic correspondent of the *Daily Mail*, Peter Wilde-blood, an assistant film director, Kenneth Hume, two teenage Boy Scouts and two working-class airmen, could not have been better calculated to inflame public anxiety. There were nineteen charges of buggery, attempted buggery and gross indecency. Inflammatory matters, concerning homosexual relations with minors were involved. There had not been a more prurient and detailed press coverage since Oscar Wilde had tumbled from glory in 1895.

The Director of Public Prosecutions for England and Wales from 1944–64, Sir Theobald Mathew, put his heart, soul and powers into hunting down homosexuals and bringing some of them to court. He believed that homosexuality was like a chronic disease; once you succumbed to its germ you were infected for life. Matthew had launched a long campaign to prosecute homosexuals in 'positions of authority and trust' who had had relations with boys or young men in their care. By 1952 the national press and judiciary were so exercised by such cases, and the discovery of incidents of homosexual abuse of adolescents in care, that they began to suggest the country was gripped by an epidemic of homosexuality.[26] A demonisation of homosexuals was under way.

The *Sunday Pictorial* took a lead in defying the tradition of regarding homosexuality as unmentionable. 'Evil Men' was the title of the first instalment, with a subhead asking, 'Is it true that male degenerates infest the West End of London and the social centres of many provincial cities?'[27] Well, yes it was, apparently. 'Apart from jokes about "cissies" and "fairies" on stage, one taboo obstinately survived, for newspapers did not talk about homosexuals,' Hugh Cudlipp, the *Pictorial*'s editor wrote in his autobiography years later, when trying to justify his, obsessive witch-hunt tactics. The editor was particularly concerned to root out homosexuals from the civil service and from schools.[28] It was, however, the arrest of Sir John Gielgud on the night of 21 October 1953, for persistently importuning males in a Westminster public convenience, that brought the subject of homosexuality out into the open. The second Montagu trial did not begin until December 1953. Here was evidence to support the traditional conviction that pansies sprouted like weeds within the hothouse theatre world.

At the time Gielgud was second only to Olivier in fame and reputation as a stage actor. He was close to the pinnacle of his career and about to open in a play by the then fashionable writer N.C. Hunter at the Haymarket Theatre, with Sybil Thorndike and Ralph Richardson as his co-stars. He had recently been knighted, belatedly it was thought, because George VI was said to have opposed the honouring of a man known to be homosexual. Philip Hope-Wallace, the theatre critic, used to tell the story of how George VI had snubbed Gielgud when he was presented to the monarch at a first-night theatre opening. The fine and warning handed down to Sir John did not serve to end the controversy; it accentuated it. Every newspaper reported the case, attitudes were vengefully polarised. Traditional moralists, led by High Court judges, bigotted newspaper columnists, politicians, bishops and particularly old aristocrats in the House of Lords, spoke out against the supposed epidemic of homosexuality that was attacking the vulnerable moral fibre of the young British male. 'It is now a widespread disease. It has penetrated every phase of life. It infests politics, literature, Church,' wrote the *Sunday Express* columnist John Gordon, an elderly, emotionally disturbed Scotsman obsessed with homosexuality. 'It is time the community decided to sanitise itself. For if we do not root out this ... it will bring us down,' he suggested in a fearful echo of Heinrich Himmler, speaking on 18 February 1937 about the menace of homosexuals, a menace that the Nazis would seek to end by extermination in the death-camps. [29]

Members of the judiciary took up Gordon's appeal. 'This type of offence seems like a disease sweeping through the community. As far as the law is concerned, it must be stamped out,' Mr Justice Stable said in December 1953 when handing down a judgement. [30] A small but distinct minority of Equity, the actors' union, tried to lobby to have Gielgud expelled on the grounds that he had brought disgrace upon his profession. Such a measure, the agitation for which was led by a serial adulterer, would if successful have terminated Gielgud's career at a savage stroke. To assuage this groundswell of public anxiety, the Home Secretary, Sir David Maxwell Fyffe, decided that a Royal Commission on Prostitution, chaired by Sir John Wolfenden, should also consider the greater menace of homosexuality. Three years later, on 4 September 1957, the report was published with a recommendation intended to sweep away all sight of homosexuals and homosexuality: two consenting adult males over twenty-one should, in a private place, be able to behave in a way henceforth beyond the prosecuting arm of the law.

In view of the fact that there had been such a strictly observed taboo on the public discussion of homosexuality until the 1950s it may seem strange that the Wolfenden report was so concerned to emphasise the word 'private'. It was as if there were a likelihood that homosexual acts might take place in public view. But then 1950s moralists and commentators, among them the psychiatrist D.J. West and the sociologist Gordon Westwood, were intent upon suggesting how far homosexuality was already an *open* secret. They provided warnings for the ignorant that homosexuals were not necessarily identifiable on the basis of effeminacy; the homosexual might look like an ordinary man. 'In the larger towns it is difficult to understand how a man can avoid meeting the problem, unless he is determined to turn a blind eye to it on every occasion. It is only necessary to visit any public lavatory in London to observe how numerous such practices must be. Nor is London unique in this matter.'[31] Both in the capital city and other major towns you could notice and recognise, if you so chose, 'a few notorious bars or clubs patronised by the exhibitionistic set who like to flaunt themselves in public. They dress in the latest fancy fashions and cultivate loud, pseudo-feminine mannerisms.'[32] In other words homosexuals were both seen and not seen. The effeminate homosexual, who could sometimes be written off as a drag-artist, posed far less serious problems than the sort who could not be straightforwardly identified as such. In vain did psychiatrists warn against popular misconceptions. 'The popular idea that all male homosexuals have effeminate body-build, girlish outlook and mannerisms . . . is a complete misconception.'[33] Also misconceived, in the midst of the panic of the period, were the notions that homosexuals were small in stature with 'excess fat, wide hips, smooth skin, narrow shoulders . . . a boyish face . . . an inability to whistle.' 'The ordinary man,' Westwood suggested, thought of a homosexual as an 'effeminate overdressed man with a high-pitched voice and a peculiar walk.'[34]

Westwood's conception of the 'blind eye' of authority could more accurately be termed the blurred or self-censoring eye, a symptom of the half-closed mind. Such a mind was reluctant to come to censorious judgement about the evidence that played before it. We need to be aware of such an attitude when trying to understand how homosexual characters, and indeed homosexuality, managed to infiltrate some of the plays that the Lord Chamberlain licensed. This 'evidence' was conveyed in a sequence of codes and signs, in literary devices of ambiguity and allusion. An anomalous situation was thereby achieved: homosexuals and the subject of homosexuality sneaked upon the stage from the 1920s, but unrecognised by the Lords Chamberlain or

Examiners of Plays. Sometimes even a play adorned by a flagrantly effeminate or camp character would achieve a licence. Presumably, it was believed at St James's Palace that such effeminacy was not necessarily a symptom of homosexuality, and in general terms the Lords Chamberlain were surely right. For even in the 1920s, the rigid demarcation lines between male and female had begun to dissolve.

The bohemian bright young things about London, both before and after the First World War proclaimed the changes in dress and attitude. 'Men wore lounge suits and soft collars, while women's mannish tailored suits with ties, shorter skirts and masculine hats were practical, announcing fierce determination rather than acquiescent feminity.'[35] Bohemia itself was reckoned synonymous with lax standards of morality and sexual liberation. The young dandies who arrived at Oxford and Cambridge after the war were in self-conscious revolt against the masculine values of their fathers. Their dominating concern was with the traditionally feminine 'style ... refinement and fantasy'.[36] Coward's *Semi-Monde* (1926), which he did not submit to the Lord Chamberlain, because he knew its obvious homosexual coupling would cause it to be banned, was prophetic of the bisexually orientated *Design for Living*. The young characters in *Semi-Monde*, lesbian, gay and heterosexual swing both ways with all the ease of a pendulum. Homosexuality could be a chimera: now you saw it, now you did not. Uncertainty was in the air.

The actor Robert Flemyng, recalling the theatre of his youth in the 1930s, observed, 'Gerald du Maurier [the famous actor-manager] ... probably should have been gay – he was a very effeminate man – but of course he wasn't and was consequently violently anti-gay.'[37] Frederick Lonsdale's *Spring Cleaning* (1925) introduced an 'effeminate' boy of twenty-two whose camp chatter made him sound like an early incarnation of a 1990s fashion queen.[38] There would be many more such camp characters decorating licensed plays before 1968. A play such as Noël Coward's *The Vortex* (1924), as we have seen, suffered censorship problems. But these problems had nothing to do with the fact that the play's hero might be gay or that subsidiary character has the diction of an old queen about town. These oblique references were acceptable to the censor. Noël Coward was, after all, the apotheosis of camp. You could not have banned Coward from playing Nicky on the grounds that the character became effeminate when he took the role. Furthermore, playwrights sometimes deceived, by disguising homosexuality under the protective sheath of a masculine manner.

Michel Foucault's complex interpretation of the multifold forms of silence, the diverse ways of not speaking that which is forbidden, also helps explains the survival of homosexual material on a stage which banished such subversive stuff. 'There is not one but many silences. Silence – the thing one declines to say or is forbidden to name – is less the absolute limit of discourse . . . than an element that functions alongside the things said. There is no binary division to be made between what one says and what one does not say; we must try to determine the different ways of not saying such things.' The plays that today we would regard as incontrovertibly about homosexuality, were licensed because their authors practised a form of silence, of not saying. Homosexual elements in the play could either be interpreted as something less minatory than homosexuality, or the blurred eye of authority would not, or could not, detect any conclusive sexual nuances. Innocence and lack of sophistication characterised the West End theatre-world in the inter-war years and for the first decade after. The homosexual and lesbian were not necessarily noticed, except in stereotypical form. 'It took me a long time to realise Binkie was gay. I didn't really know about it. In the late 1940s and early 1950s I wasn't terribly aware,' recalls the veteran actress Faith Brook, looking back on her years as a leading young actress in her twenties. 'But I remember my mother thinking my dad [the stage and film actor Clive Brook] was being seduced by Binkie Beaumont, the producer.' By the time she played the lesbian lead in Sartre's *Huis Clos* in a 1955 London club performance, she was more knowing. 'Then I got a lot of lesbian advances over the years. I was unaware at first. Lesbianism wasn't really discussed. We found it silly and funny – the women with Eton crops and mannish suits. They really advertised. I'm afraid we sniggered. Until *The Killing of Sister George* in the 1960s we did not take lesbianism on.'[39]

Playing the Homosexual Game

J.R. Ackerley's *Prisoners of War* (1925), performed at a London theatre club, was the first British play this century to deal with what was clearly a case of homosexual passion, disguised as a flawed attempt at friendship between two young soldiers. There was no difficulty in achieving a licence when a transfer to the West End was contemplated. George Street, the Chief Examiner, was at pains to stress that nothing improper occurred in *Prisoners of War.* Yet on the grapevines of communication, in the coteries of London society where homosexuals socialised, it was termed a homosexual play. Stephen Spender recalled his excitement as he and Christopher Isherwood, sunning themselves on Reugen Island speculated about this bold piece of theatre.'[40] But even if Ackerley had been bold, there were plenty of heterosexuals unable to gather what was being conveyed. 'Its faithfulness and fine feeling left one with something of that exaltation that the great tragedies leave,' wrote the heterosexual Jack Squire, that ever-reactionary model of bluff, cricket-playing heartiness, in his magazine *London Mercury.*[41] Here is a microcosm of the process that allowed homosexuality to be both present and absent from the stage, according to the attitude and awareness of the spectator. The theatre was not the exclusive beneficiary of this mode of half-seeing and varied understanding. Some First World War poetry, written by Wilfred Owen, Ivor Gurney, Robert Nicols, Herbert Read and even Robert Graves, seem to us now to collapse exclusive distinctions between the homosexual, homo-erotic and the fraternal or comradely, while wistfully celebrating brave, beautiful youths lost to war. In their own time they were not interpreted as homosexual or apparently even symptomatic of forbidden sexual longings. Yet Paul Fussell, writing from the perspective of an academic in the 1970s, observes 'No-one turning from the poetry of the Second World War back to that of the first can fail to notice there the unique physical tenderness, the readiness to admire openly the bodily beauty of young men, the unapologetic recognition that men may be in love with each other.'[42]

A public school classical education would probably have

included exposure to Virgil's second, homoerotic *Eclogue*. There had also been a pre-war tradition of poetry from Manley Hopkins and Walt Whitman to A.E. Housman, which celebrated male beauty and would later be recognised as homoerotic. But though there were realisations and perceptions about the nature of such poetry, it did not lead to open or frank discussion of such desires. Even Geoffrey Dearmer, who served as Chief Examiner from 1946–53, was a First World War poet who wrote at least one homoerotic poem, 'The Dead Turk': 'he seemed to lie, carved from the earth, in beauty without stain'.

Street thought Ackerley's melodramatically inclined drama was 'an extraordinarily strong and moving work . . . It is also one of the most painful plays I have read.' This was not, though, because Ackerley drew aside the veils of reticence, beneath which could be found a young soldier, obsessively and unrequitedly in love with a brother officer; Street quite missed the point. The Examiner interpreted *Prisoners of War* as 'a study of the deterioration in character and mentality due to hopelessness' suffered by a young English captain. The Examiner did recognise the pervasive 'jealousies and animosities', but he did not realise what caused the Captain's breakdown: a homosexual passion that is never recognised, let alone acknowledged by the sufferer. 'Captain Conrad has formed a sentimental sort of friendship with Second Lieutenant Grayle – a caddish young man,' he wrote. 'The end of their friendship more and more comes to upset Conrad.' The use of the word 'sentimental' reveals the Victorian cast of Street's mind.

The notion of 'sentimental friendship' absolved all thought of forbidden physical acts. It was more in keeping with that Victorian concept and practice of passionate, platonic male comradeliness. Yet the censor was not unaware of what implications could, in theory, be read into the relationship of Conrad and Grayle. 'There was no suggestion in the eulogies I read in the press of any unfitness in the play for public representation. The sentimental friendships and jealousies between the officers have no sinister suggestions in any coarse sense,' he judged. The Examiner's assessment provides another example of the creative use of silence, of being unable or choosing not to decypher the codes and signs. Since the actors had played with appropriate male reticence, no critic had chosen to jump to the right conclusions. Street, critics and journalists, of whatever sexual persuasion or none, conspired in the practice of ignoring the implications of what they saw.

Virtually all national newspapers were Conservative in their political convictions and upholders of traditional social values. The leading theatre reviewers, in the inter-war years, did not themselves necessarily share these beliefs, but none was noted for a particular liberality of view. It is significant that the few liberal newspapers of the period, the *Manchester Guardian*, the *News Chronicle* and the *Observer*, all employed critics who did not make any particular mark on theatre-goers. W.A. Darlington, the *Telegraph*'s critic from 1920–68, James Agate, the most highly regarded of reviewers, in the *Sunday Times*, and A.V. Cookman, whose name was not attached to to his notices in *The Times*, were all influential. Even Agate, the only known homosexual critic, misinterpreted what was going on and came to inaccurate conclusions, wilfully misread Ackerley's message or resorted to the saving grace of euphemism. 'It jumps to the eyes that the problem is not one of depression but repression,' he wrote in the *Sunday Times*. Agate's metaphoric reference to eyes is interesting: he implies that Ackerley's intention is obvious, at least to him, but he cannot speak in plain terms. The *New Statesman* critic also detected the swirling undercurrents of homosexual desire engulfing Ackerley's wretched hero. He reviewed the play in pointed tandem with Michael Arlen's adaptation of his novel *The Green Hat*, in which a young man dotes obsessively on his sister's lover. But he too did not resort to using the dangerous word homosexual.

An even greater degree of ignorance was revealed by Phyllis Whitworth, director of the society at the Three Hundred Club, where *Prisoners of War* was due to be presented. She called Ackerley to a meeting in January 1925 to tell him she had heard *Prisoners of War* was 'being talked about in London clubs [perhaps discreetly homosexual ones] as "the new homosexual play" ... She had reread the play and realised that it was open to misconstruction.'[43] Ackerley rebelled against the minor alterations she nervously required of him saying 'that since Mrs Whitworth had read the play several times without recognising its homosexual elements until someone pointed it out to her, it was safe to assume that her lady subscribers would be similarly insulated by their innocence.' This incident exemplifies nicely the manner in which discretion, ignorance and a wilful refusal to believe the evidence of one's eyes allowed certain plays about homosexuality to escape the censor's net. Street's use of the words 'sinister' and 'coarse' was, true to the periphrastic mode of the period, acknowledging the existence of homosexuality while refusing to name or define it as such. Yet Street's ability not to see still strikes one as remarkable, for his generation had been reared in a late-Victorian age which had freshly discovered homosexuality as a focus of moral alarm and sought to penalise it anew. Besides, there were also what would now be taken as clear signs in the stage directions that more than comradely feelings were involved. After she had reread the offending play Mrs Whitworth wished to have two of these directions excised. The Examiner must have failed to recognise their significance.

The play struck all the London theatre critics, when revived in 1994 at London's New End Theatre, as an account of homosexual passion, and all the more poignant because the lover could neither express nor confess his desires. The original stage directions, however, convey explicit meaning to us now. Captain Conrad struggles to achieve a perfect friendship with the handsome Lieutenant Grayle, who is barely out of his teens but wholly aware of what is happening to his smitten admirer. 'Look out someone might come,' warns Grayle, the curls of whose head the captain 'affectionately strokes'. Other stage directions appear even more obvious to our more sophisticated minds. A couple of other soldiers go further, the one linking his finger to his friend's 'dangling hand' and 'the poetry in him is released'. When I interviewed Robert Harris, who played Grayle in the original stage production, he was in his late eighties, but in possession of his mental faculties. I read him out some of these stage directions. Harris, who was homosexual, listened and said he had never realised that the play was blatantly gay.[44] I do not think his memory had forsaken him after more than sixty years, for there would have been real and enduring shock-value in acting out such a play at a club theatre in the 1920s.

It is far more likely that one of Foucault's silences was observed during rehearsals. The author, director and actors would have let the sexual subtext remain latent in the production so that the actors' reticence and decorum saved them. There would have been signs of male comradeliness, not of sexual desire. In the 1990s John Gielgud could still recall the impact of that production upon him and wondered how it was that it could be passed by the Lord Chamberlain. 'I was present at a first-night Sunday club performance of . . . *Prisoners of War* which was built around the gradual decline into madness caused by the homosexual struggle of an imprisoned officer. The audience was greatly impressed . . . I wonder how the Lord Chamberlain's office consented to permit a licence.'[45] Gielgud's bewilderment may have to do with the fact that he had quite forgotten how actors in plays of that period dealt with the signs of gay desire and how homosexuals happily decyphered the codes. 'All today I have carried about with me an inward sense of home sickness for that land where I would be – that Elysium, forever deluding me with its mirage in the desert of my frustrated and distorted desires,' wrote the poet Siegfried Sassoon in his diary, after seeing the play. There were covert messages for those whose antennae were able to receive the muffled messages. Even in the privacy of his diary the unhappily homosexual Sassoon did not choose or dare to speak of his sexuality except in these doom-laden, romantic terms of evasion. It was the language of discretion in which plays about homosexuality had to be written and performed if they were to reach the public stage.

Effeminate and camp males generally appear to have been regarded as a virtual third gender that posed no threat to men. Such characters caused confusion in the Lord Chamberlain's department. In his 1929 operetta, *Bitter Sweet*, Noël Coward could not more blatantly have set a posse of flamboyant queens to strut their dandyish stuff upon the stage, or so it seems today.

The codes and innuendoes could hardly be easier to unscramble. 'Four over-exquisitely dressed young men enter. They all wear in their immaculate button-holes green carnations,' says the stage direction. 'Vernon Craft, a poet, Cedric Ballantyne, a painter, Lord Henry Jade, a dilettante and Bertram Sellick, a playwright.' If that were not sufficient indication, their first bantering repartee surely is:

BERTIE: It's entirely Vernon's fault that we are so entrancingly late.

VERNON: My silk socks were two poems this evening, and they refused to scan.

HENRY: It's going to be inexpressibly dreary, I can feel it in my bones.

CEDRIC: Don't be so absurd, Henry. Your whole charm lies in the fact that you have no bones.

The song that they then sing, 'We all Wore a Green Carnation', underlines what the words have already implied. 'Blasé boys are we, exquisitely free/ From the dreary and quite absurd/ Moral views of the common herd.' The first refrain begins, 'Pretty boys, witty boys too, too, too/ Lazy to fight stagnation/ Haughty boys, naughty boys, all we do/ Is to pursue sensation./ The world our eccentricity condones./ A note of quaint variety/ We're certain to provide./ We dress in very decorative tones . . . We believe in Art, though we're poles apart/ From the fools who are thrilled by Greuze./ We like Beardsley and Green Chartreuse.' The second two refrains colour the gay picture further. 'Our figures sleek and willowy/ Our lips incarnadine/ May worry the majority a bit./ Art is our inspiration/ And as we the reason for the "Nineties" being gay,/ We all wear a green carnation./ . . . We feel we're rather Grecian,/ As our manners indicate/ Our sense of moral values isn't strong./ For ultimate completion/ We shall really have to wait/ Until the day of judgement comes along.'[46]

The wearing of the Wildean green carnation, the camp extravagance of the language and costume, the well-worn air of affectation, the studied adoption of aestheticism, their dilettante posing and relish for *fine de siècle* decadence are all signals of homosexuality. The point is more crudely made with reference to their Grecian and eccentric mode of life and the adjectives with which the boys describe themselves: pretty, witty, haughty, naughty, jaded, willowy and with 'incarnadine lips' complete the gay and effeminate picture. Yet Street remained in the dark, as if his eyes were wilfully closed to the main event of these signals. 'The "green carnation" young men might be offensively bisexual, but that is not indicated,' he wrote in his report on 19 June 1928. 'There is very little to quarrel with. Noël Coward is in a sentimental not salicious mood.' Perhaps Street even thought the chorus of young men was a group of posers, in the sense that the Marquis of Queensberry had originally accused Wilde of *posing* as a sodomite. A year later the homosexual John van Druten, whose *Young Woodley* caused the censor such trouble in 1928, revealingly complained, 'One of the most surprising phenomena which I have recently observed in the theatre, is the portrayal especially in farce, revue or musical comedy, of effeminate men mincing and wilting in what the public regards as "Nancy" attitudes; to the shrieking delight of an audience – and this while any attempted mention, even, of homosexuality is utterly taboo in the serious theatre.'[47] In other words effeminacy was an almost acceptable face of homosexuality, since it was not regarded as a threat to anyone.

There were other forms of indirectness. Dodie Smith, one of the most popular exponents of comfortable middle-class comedy in the 1930s, included a scene in her 1935 hit *Call it a Day* in which a charming young interior designer tries to befriend an even younger one, offering him a partnership in his business. This scene was replete with undercover meaning. 'I say it's jolly queer when you come to think of it,' the young designer says 'that we do get on. We've hardly a thing in common.' The New York producers picked up what the Lord Chamberlain preferred not to see and the scene was removed in its entirety.[48] Frith Banbury recalled Miss Smith saying with pride that she had written the first homosexual scene in twentieth-century English theatre. Seven years later a similar though more troublesome problem was raised by the proposed production of Mordaunt Shairp's play *The Green Bay Tree*, in which Julian, a good-looking, epicene young man, struggles unmanfully to give up living with his rich middle-aged protector, Mr Dulcimer, and to embark on marriage. Street wrote favourably about the play in his report of November 1932, detecting no serious trace of the dangerous subject. 'Its essence is the struggle for a young man's soul and its method is largely implication and suggestion,' he reported. If this assessment implies a scrupulously veiled homosexual affair, then Street was concerned to dispel such an idea. 'There is no suggestion of physical homosexuality and, indeed, the play is inconsistent with it,' he concluded. The reference to pederasty was a sign of the censor's ignorance, since Julian was obviously intended to be over twenty-one.

If Street had any lingering doubts these were dispersed after seeing *The Green Bay Tree* on stage. 'I saw this play last night,' he wrote in February 1933, 'and was confirmed in the opinion I formed when reading it. There is no suggestion of physical homosexuality in it and indeed the play is inconsistent with it [sic]. The few critics who took the opposite view were, I think, influenced by a desire to appear knowing or by the unfortunate fact that homosexuality is in the air very much at present, or at least in the theatrical air. It's true that Mr Dulcimer does not care for women and wants to have this very agreeable young man about the place, but that is a very different matter.' Once again the censor refused to make the appropriate deductions about the personalities and drives of the two main characters and tried to disregard reviewers who had been aware of the play's innuendoes and codes.

The *Observer*'s illiberal critic, Ivor Brown, reviewed the production and confessed himself tired of laughing at 'effeminate men with all the mincing movements of their kind. [Dulcimer] is there as the objectively studied specimen of a rare and unhappy species.' Brown, in his periphrastic and contemptuous allusions to 'effeminate men' seems to be hinting that Dulcimer is homosexual as well as effete. Alan Sinfield has recently claimed in the introduction to his book, *The Wilde Century* that it was not until the middle of the twentieth century that 'effeminacy and queerness became virtually synonymous.' But Brown's knowing reference to Dulcimer and the treatment of the effete Bobbie Williams in Frederick Lonsdale's *Spring Cleaning* (1926), disparaged as 'fairy' and 'powder puff' suggests that effeminacy was recognised as one of the possible, though not definitive indicators of homosexuality earlier than the century's meridian.[49] Playwrights used a form of coded short-hand in their stage directions that would suggest to directors or actors that a character nursing concealed homosexual desires was required. When young men were described in stage directions as sensitive, nervous, neurotic, or artistic, flamboyant, and well-dressed the playwright was hinting the character were homosexual.

The Chamberlain, Lord Clarendon, was even more appalled by lesbianism. His Chief Examiner referred to it in terms far more oblique and muted than those he applied to *The Green Bay Tree*. 'This is a horribly unpleasant play,' Street wrote of Lillian Hellman's *The Children's Hour* (1934). 'It is so obviously impossible to licence it that I can spare the Lord Chamberlain a mass of details. Plays with not a tenth of the lesbian element of this one have been banned.' Yet lesbian acts were not illegal. The trouble with *The Children's Hour* had nothing to do with action on stage. It had to do with words, and what limpid words. 'I love you that way – maybe the way they said I love you,' one young teacher tells another, after the malign animus of schoolgirls' rumouring has precipitated their departure from the profession.[50] There was nothing more blatant than that.

Ten years later Binkie Beaumont, who ran the most powerful and prolific play-producing company in the West End, tried to persuade the Lord Chamberlain that the play could and should be produced. *The Children's Hour* had already been given a club performance at the Gate and Gwatkin had seen it. He was impressed by 'a most powerful piece of theatre'. But Gwatkin reminded Beaumont in a letter, on 27 March 1946, that the human manifestations of 'unnatural vice' could not be presented on stage; that Miss Hellman had shown lesbianism to be a 'deplorable' way of life was no excuse. Four years later when Peter Cotes presented the play at his New Boltons Theatre Club, critics of some of the most reactionary newspapers united in surprising praise. 'I came away last night wishing there could be grades of censorship in the theatre or in the cinema, so that adults if not children might see plays of this adult quality without having to join a club,' wrote the *Daily Mail* critic. 'Why ban this play? It has the uplifting and cleansing quality of tragedy,' asked the *Evening Standard*'s Beverley Baxter, an elderly, reactionary critic who led a double life, also being a Conservative MP. This reference to 'cleansing' may have had something to do with the final abject and unemployed state in which the two supposed lesbian teachers are finally seen.

The Lord Chamberlain's opposition to the play was enduring and implacable. His officials believed that to stage Hellman's play would precicipitate a deluge of dramas about homosexuality. On 30 November 1950, after the producer Tom Arnold had written to the Lord Chamberlain begging that the play be licensed, Gwatkin, then Assistant Comptroller, scribbled a note on an envelope to Terence Nugent, the Comptroller. Licensing the play would, in Gwatkin's fearful estimate, 'lead to a spate of similar plays and make it difficult to say no to the male counterpart which I consider a far greater and more dangerous evil.' Here was a faint but distinct echo of that fear about *Oedipus Rex* in 1909, when it was argued that the licensing of the Sophocles play would set a precedent for other dramatists who would write coarsely on similar themes. In 1951 a deputation visited Lord Clarendon, who felt himself 'under heavy pressure from some shades of public opinion to try and persuade him to allow this subject on the stage, or at least this play, on the grounds that, according to the law, the act of lesbianism [sic] was not an offence; the play brought out the tragedy of the condition and in no way encouraged it.'[51] Clarendon 'once again decided to seek the views of a wider audience'. This so-called 'audience', probably chosen from the Lord Chamberlain's associates, duly recommended that no plays about lesbianism should be permitted. 'Unlike homosexuality between men, it was believed to be confined to a much smaller circle and harm might be done by arousing the curiosity of adolescent girls.'[52] Here again the Lord Chamberlain succumbed to the Victorian belief that the theatre was forever liable to become a school for moral depravity.

The censors' view of homosexuality is encapsulated in an undated memorandum in the file for *The Children's Hour*. It was written in the early fifties, perhaps by Gwatkin as the basis for Clarendon's statement to the deputation and says, 'The main reason for lifting the ban is that the general public is much more outspoken and broadminded than it was, and that to ventilate [sic] vice and its tragedies would be to the general social advantage.' Clarendon retorted that women could not be subjected to such plain-speaking or plain-showing. 'I am, however, advised from other quarters that the ban on this type of play should be retained, the argument being that the subject will be very distasteful and embarrassing in mixed company of all ages and also that the introduction of these new vices might start an unfortunate train of thought in the previously innocent.' Accordingly when Lord Scarbrough, who succeeded Clarendon in 1952, agreed to see Hellman in 1953, and she told him the play was 'moral in that it ventilated an evil and its dreadful results', he would only reply that there had been such 'strong support from a very wide field of advisers' that he would continue to maintain the ban. Gwatkin himself suggested to Peter Cotes, who wanted to produce the play in the West End, that the ban could be circumvented by substituting the lesbian desires of the teachers for 'some more normal vice such as dope or men'. Hellman, whom Clarendon conceded was 'a nice woman', even agreed in May 1955 to remove the play's muted confession of lesbian love at its closure, but she drew the line at a more 'normal vice'. This concession was not sufficient: Lord Scarbrough still would not permit the licensing of *The Children's Hour*. The play did not receive a licence until 1960, nearly three decades after it was written.

The Slide and Fall: Homosexuals Take the Stage

The impact of the Second World War and of the Kinsey Report took quite a while to register with the Lord Chamberlain. When Tennessee Williams' *A Streetcar Named Desire* was submitted for licensing by Binkie Beaumont in 1948, with Laurence Olivier directing his wife Vivien Leigh as the doomed

Blanche du Bois, a single sentence threatened to bring the production to a halt. 'I think we ought to keep the homosexual part out of it. This rule used to be rigid. If we allow a gradual slide like nudity, I think we forge a stick to beat ourselves with,' the Comptroller, Sir Terence Nugent, recommended in an almost illiterate memorandum on 30 June 1948.[53] What homosexual part was this? Blanche had recalled her early marriage to a very young poet, and a day when she came into a room 'which wasn't empty, but had two people in it . . . the boy I had married and the older man who had been his friend for years.' Since Blanche expresses disgust when she catches her husband alone in a room with another man, and since her husband commits suicide soon after, by placing a gun in his mouth, the censor was probably alerted to the homosexual innuendoes. Even a suggestion that the word 'man' be excised or 'someone else' be added was felt to be insufficient. The Lord Chamberlain was, though, prepared to be helpful and offered an inventive change to Williams' text. 'The Lord Chamberlain is of the opinion that this passage should be altered, making the young husband found with a negress, instead of another man,' William Conway, the general manager of Beaumont's office was informed on 12 July 1948. There was no production that year.

On 30 March 1949 Gwatkin noted that Beaumont had rejected the censor's racist suggestion. 'They claim,' Gwatkin wrote, 'that the shock to Blanche would not be adequate if she found her young husband in bed with a negro and want to imply – for those who wish to see it – that the man was homosexual.' The censor rejected Tennessee Williams' suggestion that the sentence be cut down to, 'but had two people in it . . . the boy I had married and . . . afterwards we pretended that nothing had happened'. So the reference to Blanche's appearance in the room was cut and the play first showed its shocking, public face on tour in Manchester. 'Off stage we are left in no doubt there is also a lavatory,' the *Sunday Pictorial* reported in a lubricious article on 2 October 1949. This was an amazing revelation. For lavatories were not allowed anywhere near the stage. Indeed four years later, in 1953, the, censor, when licensing Graham Greene's *The Living Room*, stipulated that the noise of a flushing lavatory would have to be silenced. 'The Lord Chamberlain ... objects in principle to the pulling of lavatory plugs and all that that stands for. In this respect he feels that he would always have ... as he always has to have majority feeling behind him.'[54]

The decision to excise Williams' discreet reference to homosexuality was surprising, in light of the Lord Chamberlain's pre-war acceptance of grey areas, and ambiguity in which effeminacy, aestheticism, bachelors, theatrical and artistic folk, and close attachments in single-sex communities could sometimes be allowed. In the same period William Douglas-Home's *Now Barabbas* (1947), which was approved for licensing after its private club première, resorts to a particularly obvious sort of coding. Young Richards in prison sports 'very long hair elaborately arranged', which the authorities have generously left uncut. He also used to be a 'chorus boy'.[55] His attachment to another prisoner is transparently homoerotic, an adjective that had no currency then. Similarly Travers Otway's *The Hidden Years* (1947), where adolescent schoolboys are caught up in an innocent but homoerotic crush, was given a licence. The fact that these plays were set within all-male societies may have relaxed the Chamberlain's anxieties.

Streetcar duly opened to expressions of disgust from some theatre critics. J.C. Trewin, in his *Observer* review on 13 October 1949, looked down upon the play, in the manner of Lady Bracknell showing the door to a tradesman selling socialist literature. 'A tedious and squalid anecdote,' he called it. A year later he dismissed the play as if it were a salacious trifle '[It] will go into the same box as *His Chinese Bride* and a score of other half-forgotten drama from the twice-nightly Hippodromes of my youth.'[56] The Public Morality Council expressed its outrage and worried questions were asked in the House of Commons. 'The spirit of daring which [Williams] introduced into the London drama was in many quarters received with a venomous opposition, unparalleled since Clement Scott's denunciation of *Ghosts*,' according to the *Sunday Times* theatre critic, Harold Hobson, reminiscing thirty-five years later. 'Like *Ghosts*, it was widely spoken of as 'a nasty vulgar, play' and many theatre-goers walked out of the performance in noisy disgust . . . The reaction was sheer, half-witted moral horror.'[57] Hobson was just as scathing when he reviewed the play's première in the *Sunday Times*. He believed the Lord Chamberlain's censorship to be morally bankrupt, for in obeisance to Victorian values it permitted certain forms of immorality to be depicted on stage, provided that the treatment was frivolous and without serious intent. It allowed plays that upheld the age-old, often upper-class and male heterosexual mode of dealing with fornication. Hobson, who until the end of his career as a theatre critic usually maintained his approval of theatre censorship and remained an impenitent homophobe, sharply pointed out that the Lord Chamberlain succumbed to double standards, allowing light-hearted endorsements of immorality but not serious ones.

'In musical comedies and farces girls who behave like Blanche du Bois are common enough and they end not in an asylum, but in Park Lane. They are glamorised by bright lights, dazzling clothes and catchy songs. Against these entertainments no protest is ever made. No-one in general enjoys *Oklahoma* more than I do, but I am amazed that those who are so shocked by *Streetcar* can apparently listen to the song "I Just Can't Say No" without offence.'[58] One Baroness Ravensdale, who belonged to the Public Morality Council, anticipated a notorious remark made during the trial of *Lady Chatterley's Lover* when she said, 'The play is thoroughly indecent and we should be ashamed that children and servants are allowed to sit in the theatre and see it.'[59] Princess Alice, wife of the Duke of Gloucester, cancelled a visit, on the grounds that the play was not 'the kind of entertainment she would enjoy'. Yet in the early 1950s, when homosexual panic raged far beyond the palace of St James, the Lord Chamberlain did not require the excision of characters in Agatha Christie's works who were coded as homosexual. According to the stage directions there was 'a neurotic young man with long hair' who wore 'a woven artistic tie' and 'a young woman of manly type'. The actors playing these roles duly obliged by playing the characters as respectively and respectably effeminate and butch. The sexuality of the characters never figured.[60]

The acceptable way for a playwright to deal with homosexuality, and the moral panic and prejudice it engendered, was to appear to suggest that innocent heterosexuals, who appeared gay but were not, might be caught up in the process or be exploited by blackmailers. Philip King's *Serious Charge* (1953) was licensed and produced at St Martin's Theatre and turned into a film. The word homosexual is not used and melodrama is produced from a false charge of homosexuality, made by an angelic-looking seventeen-year-old choirboy. The object of his false charge is an unmarried, thirty-year-old vicar with a mother in residence and a passion for interior design, that most suspicious of male hobbies, who naturally suffers a whispering and smearing campaign. 'We are in no doubt at any time that the vicar is innocent of the "serious charge",' Heriot comfortably reported. 'Therefore, though the forbidden topic of homosexuality shadows this play it does so in an inoffensive manner.' Scarbrough, who also read *Serious Charge*, reluctantly agreed. 'I am not convinced by the retort that because the accusation was untrue no question of propriety can arise,' Scarbrough judged, in a vintage display of primness. 'I think on the whole no great harm will be done.' In so saying he betrayed the increasing confusion about how to distinguish a real homosexual from the ordinary man in the street.

The Lord Chamberlain floundered in what were beginning to be recognised as grey areas of ambiguity. He and his Readers had to voyage into uncertain terrain, without maps and compasses, to gather the sexual lie of the land. It was hard to draw a clear, moral line in the misty environs where homosexual desire might be discerned. The signs, symptoms and signals had to be recognised and unscrambled. In 1958, Ronald Hill, the Lord Chamberlain's Assistant Secretary, was sent down to see a performance of the drag revue, *We're No ladies*, and could not even tell what constituted gay innuendo and what did not. [61]

Rodney Ackland's *The Pink Room* (1952), set in a bohemian drinking club on the eve of Labour's 1945 election victory was a radical, anti-heroic work, whose structure and organisation bore no relation to the artifices of the conventional West End drawing-room drama. But where the *Serious Charge* disconcerted the Lord Chamberlain, *The Pink Room* did not. Ackland included three characters who could be recognised as homosexual. There is a film director who seems concerned to forge a friendship with a handsome GI. The director's neglect of his 'secretary', Cyril Clatworthy, 'a sensitive young man', causes plenty of resentment. A bewigged female critic with her companion in tow might be diagnosed as lesbian. But the film director played in 1952 by the masculine Austin Trevor helped conceal what was going on. Not until the Lord Chamberlain's regime had ended and Ackland rewrote the play as *Absolute Hell* could the characters' sexuality be made apparent.[62]

By the time Williams' *Cat on a Hot Tin Roof* was submitted for licensing in 1955 homosexuality had become the subject of even more anxious public discussion. The Wolfenden Committee was sitting. Homosexuals had been repeatedly stigmatised as a threat to heterosexual and family life. The old association between homosexuality and the theatre acquired ominous new significance, as did the signs and codes by which homosexual characters were represented on stage. Williams' *Cat* was the first modern play to deal in specific terms about homosexuality, the agonies of concealment and self-loathing it often induced. There was no pussy-footing about the dread of Sodom. Williams' married footballing hero was, however, designed to look and sound like a fully-functioning heterosexual who was being falsely accused. That did not matter. The Lord Chamberlain felt that the problem posed by the play concerned sexual candour, not sexual identity. Indeed Williams insisted, when answering a charge by the American critic Walter Kerr, 'Brick's sexual adjustment was and always must remain a heterosexual one.[63]

The Chief Examiner, Charles Heriot, reacted with characteristic rudeness to Williams' latest play. 'Once again Mr Williams vomits up the recurring theme of his not too subconscious,' he reported on 2 November 1955. 'This is the fourth play (and there are sure to be others) where we are confronted by the gentlewoman debased, sunk in her private dreams as a remedy for her sexual frustration and overall the author's horror, disgust and rage against the sexual act.'[64] Heriot travestied Williams' feelings about sexual desire, but he did agree with the playwright's assessment of Brick's erotic feelings. 'As far as I can judge the homosexual element is false – that is to say we are to believe Brick when he says that his wife and relations dreamed it up. I think, therefore, with a lot of cuts, the Lord Chamberlain might consider granting a licence for this bogus play.' In November 1955 Lord Scarbrough himself supported Heriot's imaginative suggestion, by which all mention of homosexuality could be eliminated without affecting the play at all.

Scarbrough maintained his personal watch over playwrights who let the faintest whiff of homosexual desire course through their plays. The Chamberlain and his Chief Examiner reacted to Jean Genet's *The Maids* (1956) as had those Victorian critics and commentators who had deplored the idea of 'mixed audiences' watching *Ghosts*. Scarbrough read *The Maids* after Heriot had described it as 'a horrible deeply decadent and morbid play, quite unsuited . . . to public performance before mixed audience.' In his judgement on the play, Scarbrough wrote on 13 January 1957, 'Running through the whole play is a suggestion of lesbianism, not easy to follow, not directly described and in the main left to be inferred.' In the past, where playwrights had left audiences to jump to the right conclusion, the Lord Chamberlain had often overlooked or appeared not to recognise the signs of homosexuality. On this occasion Scarbrough was fearful of the very reticence that had saved gay plays from being banned. *The Maids*' 'unwholesome' characteristics would be more pronounced 'were it to be effectively acted.' He felt that Genet's very ambivalence 'invests those other characteristics [of the play] with a depravity which makes the play unsuitable for public performance.'

In view of the Chamberlain's renewed anxiety about homosexuality, producers played their cards furtively when attempting to win licences for gay-related plays. 'A wall of secrecy has been built around [*Cat on a Hot Tin Roof*'s] possible production,' Robert Muller, the *Daily Mail* theatre critic wrote on 14 April 1956. 'No one admits to having obtained the British rights or having submitted it to the censor. Already *Tea and Sympathy*, *The Children's Hour*, *The Maids* (by Jean Genet) and

South have been refused licences.' Binkie Beaumont and Donald Albery, supported by Stephen Arlen and Ian Hunter, decided to challenge the Lord Chamberlain's edict upon the licensing of plays that dealt directly with the subject. They deftly exploited that loophole through which numerous classic plays banned by the censor had been eased onto the London stage. The Comedy Theatre became the New Watergate Club and three banned plays, *Cat on a Hot Tin Roof*, *Tea and Sympathy* and Arthur Miller's *A View From the Bridge*, were all presented there for members of the club. The first serious challenge to the Lord Chamberlain's authority had been made.

The Lord Chamberlain's file for *Tea and Sympathy* reveals, however, that a remarkable and disreputable change of mind characterised the censor's attitude to the New Watergate season. Sir Terence Nugent, the genial Comptroller, replied in 1953 to a request from Binkie Beaumont in relation to *Tea and Sympathy*, that it 'would be a waste of time' for the script to be submitted. On 6 January 1955 Nugent again told Beaumont that he believed the Lord Chamberlain would not consider the play 'unless the homosexual references are deleted'. *Tea and Sympathy* concerns a heterosexual teenager at boarding school, falsely stigmatised by his fellow pupils because his long hair and artistic tastes are thought to signify homosexuality. To have removed the homosexual references would have been to sacrifice the play's essence. On 9 February, however, Nugent made a suggestion at a meeting with Beaumont and the owner of the play's rights, Mrs Mary Frank, that in the light of subsequent events showed how the Lord Chamberlain's department double-crossed the producer. In a memorandum to Lord Scarbrough, Nugent wrote, 'I said [to Beaumont] that of course if they put the play on at the Arts Theatre or any other theatre club in London I was sure the Lord Chamberlain would be only too pleased to see it.'[65] Nugent was signalling the Chamberlain's willingness to allow a members-only performance of the play. Intimate and non-commercial venues had, as we have seen, frequently been temporarily turned into club theatres. But Beaumont, instead of going to the Arts Theatre, tried to be daring and chose the Comedy. The New Watergate Club was an immediate success, became a commerical enterprise and within two years enrolled a huge membership of 68,000 on a basis 'of little more than mailing list requirements'.[66] It was, therefore, stretching the definition of a members-only theatre club.

October 1955 was chosen for the Watergate première of Miller's *A View From the Bridge*, starring Antony Quayle. The Lord Chamberlain had earlier refused the play a licence unless Beaumont excised a brief parody of homosexual desire: Eddie Cabone, the middle-aged longshoreman sexually attracted to his niece, forces his lips upon Rudolpho, the young man with whom the girl is in love. Scarbrough might have been able to allow the speech in which Eddie accuses Rudolpho of being homosexual. But this kiss, although intended as a mocking insult and slur upon Rudolpho's heterosexuality rather than an expression of repressed homosexual desire, was an image that could not be permitted. A few critics subsequently identified Cabone as a closet homosexual, though there is little evidence to support such a conclusion.[67] Beaumont had refused the cut, and Scarbrough withheld the licence.

The decision was ill-considered. It made Scarbrough appear petty-minded and absurd, even to those who did not have strong feelings about theatre censorship. Moreover, the Lord Chamberlain ranged the two most powerful theatre producers in opposition to him. Articulate enemies of stage censorship seized the chance that Scarbrough's decision allowed them to call for the termination of the Lord Chamberlain's powers. 'Do we still need the censor?' asked Richard Findlater in the *Evening Standard* on 19 October 1956. Of more significance was the fact that the season at the Comedy was a commercial and critical triumph. 'It seems to me that our venerable institution of the Revels is under stronger attack at the moment than at any time since Percy Smith's bill [in 1949 to repeal the Chamberlain's powers],' Assistant Examiner St Vincent Troubridge wrote to Norman Gwatkin on 30 April 1957. 'It's the constantly recurring provocation of that damned Comedy'.[68] Harold Hobson, however, second only to Kenneth Tynan in influence as a theatre critic, gave Scarbrough the weight of his support.

Before *A View From the Bridge* was staged at the Watergate, Hobson wrote an article in which he claimed, 'The reason that more good plays are being written in America than in England is not that America has no Lord Chamberlain. It is quite simply that America has more good dramatists.'[69] This assertion does not merely smack of disingenuousness, it reeks of it.

The battle between producers and censor intensified. Beaumont visited Nugent on 25 October 1956 to inform the Lord Chamberlain that the commercial popularity of *A View from the Bridge* was so great that he and Albery 'might have to consider finding another theatre under the Watergate umbrella to stage *Tea and Sympathy*.' Nugent rightly perceived a danger: if two major theatres in the West End were permitted to put on plays for club audiences, and if these plays proved popular with the public, the force and efficiency of the censorship system would be seriously jeopardised. Nugent resorted to threat and intimidation. 'I did say that I was sure the Lord Chamberlain did not want to be forced into handing over the matter to the law officers. I saw only two possible results of that action – either the logical end of the censorship or the end of the private theatre club. [Beaumont and Albery] both honestly deplored either possibility.' In response to Nugent's threat the two producers pointed out 'that [homosexuality] was no longer a hidden subject, but mentioned in practically every paper, frequently by the BBC, in literature, quite a number of drawing rooms and quite unconcernedly by the young.' Nugent retorted that such a view was at variance with the soundings which the Lord Chamberlain had taken 'a great deal of trouble' to achieve. Beaumont, according to Nugent's own memorandum, 'suggested nicely that the sort of people the Lord Chamberlain asked were as likely to agree to licensing such plays as the House of Lords were to agree to the nationalisation of lands.' The two producers then laid down a challenge: 'Was it not more in the public interest to show good deterrent plays on a subject of great national and moral importance than to let them read juicy details on Sunday in the *News of the World*?' The two producers never went ahead with their plan to find another theatre.

The retreat by Albery and Beaumont in the face of Nugent's

threat was not surprising. Many producers were both reaction-
ary and conservative and relished the fact that the Lord
Chamberlain's licence maintained the ancient connection
between crown and playhouse. When a decade later the Select
Committee on Theatre Censorship took evidence from the
Society of West End Theatre Producers, Emile Littler, then
president, and Peter Saunders, who presented Agatha Christie's
The Mousetrap, argued for the retention of censorship. After
Beaumont launched the New Watergate season he did not
further challenge the Lord Chamberlain. 'The whole Tennent
empire (a theatre production company run by Beaumont) got
terribly worried about the idea of abolishing the censor,' Peter
Hall judged. As a young man Hall worked for Beaumont, and
was responsible for directing adaptations of two homosexual
novels – Gide's *The Immoralist* and Julian Green's *South* – and
Cat on a Hot Tin Roof. 'Those were terrible times with
blackmailing of homosexuals. The whole Tennent operation
was very fine and the amazing thing was that it was a
homosexual club [in its highest echelons], apart from Ralph
Richardson who looked the other way. They were worried
about what would happen if the flood-gates opened. Homosexuality would open the cupboard and all subjects discussed.
Homosexuality and censorship went together.'[70] Peter Wood,
who also worked for Beaumont, supports Hall's contention that
H.M. Tennent was possessed by conservatism and a fear of
provoking establishment anger. In view of Beaumont's uncharacteristically aggressive decision to challenge the Lord Chamberlain's veto upon plays involving homosexuality he cannot
altogether be written off as a conformist theatre producer.

The New Watergate season did serve to put pressure upon
Lord Scarbrough. On 4 June 1957 he went to see the Home
Secretary, R.A. Butler, a man whose mild liberal tendencies
were rarely translated into political action, to discuss theatre
clubs. The Lord Chamberlain expressed his view that the New
Watergate 'had created a position in which the law and the
censorship was becoming rather farcical.'[71] In a 1958 letter to
Charles Killick, Chairman of the Theatres National Committee,
Scarbrough explained that he intended to relax, though not to

repeal, his rules on plays about homosexuality. The subject was still to be handled with care, as though an infectious object which required the wearing of face-masks and plastic gloves in its potentially contaminating presence. Only plays which were 'sincere and serious' in their treatment of homosexuality would be permitted and only when it was impossible to avoid the subject, or as Scarbrough put it, 'references are necessary to the plot'. But dialogue was not to be 'salacious or offensive', presumably to heterosexuals. 'Violently homosexual plays', a weird concept never elucidated, or those where homosexuals sought to embrace each other, would continue to be exiled from the stage. The theatrical spectacle of homosexuals laying hands on each other, or lips on lips, or much worse, would have to wait decades.

Scarbrough's change of heart was simply explained. In the past he had felt that 'to permit references or plays dealing with that subject would inevitably introduce some young people to a subject that otherwise they might never come into contact with,' he admitted. Too much sexual knowledge was danger-ous; silence acted as a form of prophylactic. But now, he conceded in a memorandum on his 1952 meeting with Butler, homosexuality had entered public discourse and 'become, unfortunately, one of the problems of life.'[72] So in the future sober homosexual characters, not the camp, outrageous sort who would raise cheap laughs in the gallery or elsewhere, could walk responsibly into the life of plays. Audiences would be reassured to know that homosexuals had not been disreputably thrust into the action for the sake of cheap thrills or to cause offence to decent, natural people. When these homosexuals spoke, though only to move the plot forward, they would, in theory, sound just like the man next door.

Scarbrough's new guide-lines did not presage any radical change. The Lord Chamberlain and his censors continued to react to homosexuality in play-texts like a maiden lady exposed to a determined flasher. Yet there were frissons of liberality. Homosexual characters, as long as they were neither flamboyant nor funny could take the stage. Shelagh Delaney's *A Taste of Honey* achieved a licence months before Scarbrough's letter to

Killick. Delaney said she had written the play because she had despised Terence Rattigan's *Variation on a Theme* (1956) and thought she could write a better play. The implication was that Delaney had been irritated by Rattigan's discreet pussy-footing on the subject of homosexuality. *A Taste of Honey* broke new theatrical ground by introducing a young, effeminate gay man whose homosexuality was discussed not implied. 'The play is balanced on a knife edge. It is the perfect borderline case,' Heriot wrote in his report on 5 May 1958, 'since it is concerned with the forbidden subject in a way that no-one, I believe, could take exception to.'[73] This is the only case I have discovered of Heriot taking a liberal line on homosexuality and subduing his own prejudices to show due impartiality. 'This is a surprisingly good play, though God knows it's not to my taste. But the people are strangely real and the problem of Geoff is delicately conveyed.' Heriot's conjecture that no-one could take exception to the play was dramatically disproved when Sir Norman Gwatkin did so. 'I've read it and I think it's revolting, quite apart from the homosexual bits . . . To me it has no saving grace whatsoever,' he minuted and laid down a challenge: 'If we pass muck like this, it does give our critics something to go on.' In this instance it looks as if Scarbrough intervened and overruled the crapulous Gwatkin and accepted Heriot's recommendation.

The last playwright to suffer the long-standing blacket veto was Jeremy Kingston, deputy theatre critic of *The Times*. His play *No Concern of Mine* was presented in 1958, well away from the West End at the unfashionable Westminster Theatre near Victoria Station. Kingston recalled that he was instructed by his producers, Robert Fox and the actor Robert Morley, to eliminate all traces from the play of the gay desires felt by a young drama student for his sister's boyfriend. By the time he came to write his play the old sexual innocence of the heterosexual play-goer had been superseded. Homosexuality was out in the open. 'It's perhaps scarcely possible now to appreciate how fidgety the times were in the 1950s,' Kingston recollects. 'There was the increasing call for changes in the law to do with homosexuality, but oddly enough there was a feeling that censorship and self-censorship was actually stricter than before. Before the war, perhaps, so few of the general public thought about it that playwrights could mention it almost more openly than they could when everyone was looking out for signs and references.'[74] It was a stroke of irony that the Lord Chamberlain's new rule was announced on the day that *No Concern of Mine* had its première.

The Lord Chamberlain did, however, keep to his old-fashioned word in banning all characters frankly identified as comic homosexuals. A short note to the producers of *Beyond the Fringe* reveals the practice. This 1960 revue, in which Alan Bennett, Peter Cook, Dudley Moore and Jonathan Miller reintroduced political satire to the English stage, required the Lord Chamberlain to use a terse injunction to the show's producer about a parody of an advertisement for cigarette smoking. 'I am desired by the Lord Chamberlain to say . . . that his Lordship's objection to "Bollard . . . the man's cigarette" is that it is obviously intended to be played by two homosexuals as evidenced by the stage direction, "Enter two dreadful queens." I am to say that if you will let the Lord Chamberlain have an undertaking that all homosexual gestures and business will be omitted and the piece played as between two aesthetic young men, and if the word "darling" be omitted where it occurs as being a feminine endearment, he will allow the piece.'[75] But there were also signs that the Examiners sometimes read scripts hastily or without unscrambling the screamingly obvious codes by which playwrights signalled the requirement of a stereotypically gay character. *Fings Ain't Wot They Used T'Be* (1959) the musical about low-life Soho, transferred from Stratford East to the West End where it enjoyed a long run. Not until February 1961 was the Chamberlain alerted to 'queer goings on' in the musical; he should have realised before. The text referred to 'Horace, a queer interior decorator. He is dressed in a pair of tight-fitting white trousers, green jacket, purple pull-over and bow-tie. He walks and behaves mincingly.'[76] 'The interior decorator is not to be played as a homosexual and his remark "Excuse me dear, red plush, that's very camp, that is," is to be omitted,' came the stern command.[77] Yet the fashion-conscious

queen in Lonsdale's *Spring Clean* thirty-six years earlier was just
as obviously effeminate.

Joan Henry's *Look on Tempests* (1960) was the first play openly
dealing with homosexuality to receive a licence under the new
regulations. There was no problem posed by an identifiably gay
character taking the stage since there was no such person in the
cast. The play's homosexual, around whom the action agonis-
ingly revolved, was never seen, since he happened to be at the
Old Bailey, charged with having committed homosexual acts.
So much for the new candour. In view of the restrictive framing
of the new Scarbrough rules it was understandable that initially
few playwrights rushed to put homosexuality on stage. Writers
like Rattigan and Coward were ageing and content for their
characters to talk the language of the closet.

In a 1965 essay, 'The Royal Smut Hound', Tynan took up
his lethal cudgels and subjected the Lord Chamberlain's dictat
on homosexuality to withering ridicule: 'These ludicrous bans
have now been lifted,' the critic noted in reference to *Cat on a
Hot Tin Roof* and *A View from the Bridge*, 'but the censor still
forbids all theatrical representations of queer characters who
follow their sexual leanings without being tragically punished or
revealing any sense of guilt.'[78] Tynan's assessment was to the
point. By 1964 the Lord Chamberlain, Comptrollers and
Examiners still differed about what should be allowed and what
banned. When it came to homosexuality they were more
confused than ever. The differences over *A Taste of Honey* had
been an omen of difficulties to come. The subject was out in the
open, but the question of just what that openness should allow
confounded them, as the case of Mr Sloane confirmed.

Joe Orton's *Entertaining Mr Sloane* (1964) signalled its
intentions to homosexual cognoscenti and the sophisticated. In
style, though not in content, the play was oblique and
ambiguous. Orton did not beat about the bush, but his diction
was veiled in the euphemism of lower-middle-class pseudo-
gentility. For his time, though, Orton was a homosexual radical.
He refused to accept that gay desire was inherently problematic
or dangerous. In Mr Sloane he created a psychopathic hero who
was quite happy to use his body as both bartering and battering

ram for reasons of financial and practical advantage. There was no missing the lines of thought or action. The text could not have been better devised to cause bemusement at St James's Palace. The Assistant Examiner who read the text noticed 'the thread of homosexuality which runs strongly through the play', observing, 'there is no attempt to deal with the subject of homosexuality in a serious manner'. But despite these apparent sticking points he still recommended the play for licence, subject to a number of cuts, some of which were examples of Orton's happy exploitation of gay innuendo.[79]

Sir John Johnston, the Assistant Comptroller, then reviewed those passages recommended for censoring and passed almost all of them. He permitted the use of some language that would have been banned a few years earlier, but most surprisingly he allowed a flotilla of gay innuendoes to sail on through. At a stroke of his most conservative pen, or for lack of it, the first play in which homosexuality was a simple if sexy fact of life, was allowed to take the stage. This was no case of a closed or half-shut mind: Johnston's attention had already been drawn to what in those days would have been termed Orton's proclivities. Yet he did not seek to blue-pencil Sloane's insinuating remarks to the sexually enthralled Ed, a youth propositioning an adult man in Orton's portrayal of homosexual seduction. Johnston sanctioned: 'He was an expert on the adolescent male body'; 'he wanted to photo me for certain interesting features I had that he wanted the exclusive right of preserving'; and 'Do you wear leather . . . next to the skin? Leather without . . . ah . . . pants?' The purity of stage diction had been further sullied. The prim and precious attitude to the stage representation of homosexuals and homosexuality had been jettisoned, a mere six years after it had been supposedly revised.

Perhaps Cobbold was adjusting his standards to suit the spirit of the times. The passing of the Obscene Publications Act of 1959 and the failure of the state's prosecution of D.H. Lawrence's *Lady Chatterley's Lover* were indicative of more liberal attitudes both in parliament and among the public. The BBC's early 1960s satire show, *That Was the Week That Was*, in its iconoclastic blasting of politicians and revered figures of authority, had shown the extent of this new liberality. The release of Jack Clayton's 1959 film *Room at the Top*, with its outburst of candour in dealing with sex and the working class, heralded the end of English cinema's long and almost untrammelled age of gentility and conservatism. When the ultra-conservative theatre producer Henry Sherek complained in the press and on radio during 1961 about his 'embarrassment at the filth the Lord Chamberlain allowed to go on in the theatre', Norman Gwatkin struck a rare note of realism. 'The Lord Chamberlain cannot, even if he wished to do so, forever travel in a horse carriage; he is now in a motor car and many people are trying to force him into a space-ship,' he wrote to Sherek. 'You would probably be surprised to know how much we cut out in words and how we warn about business, but since the evidence at the trial of *Lady Chatterley* I am beginning to wonder who one is trying to protect.'[80]

The Lord Chamberlain's censors had begun to lose their old sense of assurance. But not until John Osborne's *A Patriot for Me* (1965) did serious battle begin over the right to represent homosexuality upon the stage. It was then that a battle of wills and wiles was joined, involving the Labour government, law officers, directors, writers and the Chairman of the Arts Council. Lord Cobbold was no politician. His conservatism blinkered his perspective so that he failed to read the writing on the wall. His notions of what could be seen or said on stage were too out-dated and repressive to be accepted by the Labour government. Having had a meeting about theatre censorship with the Solicitor-General Dingle Foot in 1965, in which they discussed Edward Bond's *Saved*, Cobbold wrote in a haughty memorandum to his senior staff, marked confidential, 'I said the Lord Chamberlain would be very willing to co-operate with Her Majesty's government on this subject provided always that Her Majesty's government were [sic] willing to co-operate with the Lord Chamberlain.'

He had got above himself or rather his role. He had forgotten that his function, in terms of the professional theatre, was to fulfil the Lord Chamberlain's duties as acts of parliament stipulated, not to treat the government as if he were its equal in power. By so behaving he fortunately hastened the Lord Chamberlain's long-overdue downfall as theatre censor. Roy Jenkins, however, claimed that Cobbold was strongly in favour of terminating his responsibilities for the theatre. Even after the act that achieved this, whenever the two men met, Cobbold was always friendly and frequently expressed his appreciation of Jenkins' efforts in terminating the censorship. Jenkins did, however, concede that there was a possibility that the former Lord Chamberlain's expressions of cordiality may have been made in the face of the inevitable.[81] In any case Cobbold made it plain during the second and third readings of the Theatres Bill that he strongly believed in some measure of theatre censorship, although feeling that the Lord Chamberlain should not administer it.

John Osborne's *A Patriot for Me* gave Cobbold his first real taste of defeat. He wanted the Royal Court prosecuted for artfully circumventing the censorship system by presenting the play for club members: 'club' membership was so easily available in this instance that it seemed as if the censor's ban on the play meant nothing. But the government refused to allow any such prosecution: the system by which the Lord Chamberlain licensed and censored plays was becoming unworkable. The advent of a Labour government had bolstered the campaign led by a younger generation of directors and playwrights to be rid of censorship. Cobbold, piqued that his autocratic powers had been successfully defied, went on insisting that the censorship laws could not be evaded.

The Lord Chamberlain's huge file for *A Patriot for Me* makes clear how eager Cobbold and his staff were for the Royal Court to be prosecuted for its subterfuge in presenting the unlicensed play for 'club' members. In this first major test of the 1958 Scarbrough rules the Lord Chamberlain simply ignored them. The 1958 concession had been extended to serious, sincere treatment of homosexuality, while ruling out the salacious and offensive. Osborne's play adhered to the spirit and meaning of all those adjectives. Almost no one believed that Cobbold was correct in ruling that *A Patriot for Me* had to be banned for defying the prescriptive definitions. Osborne's account was based on a real-life story, of the downfall of Alfred Redl, homosexual Jewish officer in the last phase of the Austro-Hungarian Empire before the First World War. Osborne not only dared to show Redl in bed and embracing a man, but the play's centrepiece was a drag-ball for army officers and their many admirers. The extent to which Heriot, as Chief Examiner, had by 1965 forfeited any semblance of objectivity and disinterest when assessing plays, may be gauged by his report on *A Patriot for Me*. The long-serving Examiner no longer bothered to conceal his hatred of Osborne's views as well as his plays. An odd and inappropriate bias had begun to protrude from his reports. He was at personal war with the creators of the 'Theatre Revolution' of the 1950s, detonated by *Look Back in Anger*, but founded upon Beckett's *Waiting for Godot*, a year earlier.

'Mr Osborne's overweening conceit and blatant anti-authoritarianism cause him to write in a deliberately provocative way. He almost never misses a chance to be offensive,' Heriot wrote, as if Osborne was some upstart public schoolboy who would not subscribe to the institution's hallowed rules. Johnston, when he read the play, wanted the excision of not only the transvestite drag-ball but also the scene showing Redl in bed with a waiter. 'It starts with a semi-naked man in bed and Redl in a dressing gown,' Johnston recorded, 'and continues with physical embraces between men.' The redundant emphasis of the word 'physical' betrayed his distaste. Ronald Hill, the Lord Chamberlain's homophobic Assistant Secretary, warned, 'This play looks to me like the Pansies' Charter of Freedom and is bound to be a *cause célèbre.*' Yet it would be difficult to imagine a play less set upon gay liberation. *A Patriot for Me* viewed gay men with pitying contempt, as victims of a life-flaw and a life-force, not to mention society's condemnation, which often made their lives a misery. 'I cannot conceive of any play less sentimental towards homosexuality, more cold-eyed and ruthless in its exposure of the horrors of life with a particular kind of homosexuality,' Lord Annan, who was staunch in his support of homosexual rights, said in the House of Lords on 17 February 1966.

Hill, in his undated memorandum, showed himself anxious to fight a wily campaign against the Royal Court. He urged caution in proceeding and in the process resorted to a strange piece of imagery that spoke volumes about his own disturbed state of mind. Let us be careful, he said, that 'if we disallow the play we don't hand ourselves over bound hand and foot to these people.' Instead of the Lord Chamberlain's usual form of letter he recommended that it be said the play was being banned because of the 'proselytising and corrupting' force of the 'Pansies ball'. A year later Hill in another memorandum explained why he felt the scene corrupting. 'By presenting homosexuals in their most attractive guise – dressed as pretty women, [it] will to some degree cause the congregation of homosexuals and provide the reasons whereby the vice [of homosexuality] may be acquired.' Hill betrayed the conviction that homosexuality could be picked up as easily as the common cold. You only had to see men attractively dressed as women and you succumbed. One present-day scrutineer of the *Patriot* files has claimed that Cobbold 'did attempt to accommodate the play . . . he was prepared to allow the theme, characters and general action.' He only wished to cut the entirety of the drag-ball because it 'constituted an alternative social structure'. Here was evidence that homosexuals were already uniting in com-munities.[82] But that is to project back from 1999. The play's director, Anthony Page, Lords Goodman and Harewood, Laurence Olivier and Irene Worth all believed that Cobbold was unfairly obstructive and the Chamberlain, when giving evidence to the parliamentary committee on censorship, agreed with Michael Foot that his excisions would have made 'quite a considerable difference to the play's impact'.[83]

Johnston took Hill's advice to heart. In a memorandum he told Cobbold that Hill's tactic would ensure 'it will not be quite so easy for them to make a case, and if they quote us, some little in our defence will come out.' Johnston's letter to the Royal Court duly noted there were several scenes that 'exploit homosexuality in a manner that may tend to have corrupting influences.' He would not allow such scenes as a 'gay ball at which some of the men are dressed as women (including one as Lady Godiva in a gold lamé jockstrap) and another in which men embrace each other and are seen in bed together.' Johnston did not make it clear whether the gold lamé jockstrap was a cause of objection because it demeaned a member of the aristocracy or because it might make the actor in question appear seductive to homosexuals. In *The Lord Chamberlain's Blue Pencil* Johnston made no reference to his zest in preparing his master's stratagem against the Royal Court. He wrote, 'The Lord Chamberlain continued to keep an open mind pending possible alterations to the script.' But in fact Cobbold's mind was, as usual, closed to all conciliatory tactics.

By June 1965 the Royal Court had wearied of trying to achieve a compromise. Under the aegis of George Devine's English Stage Company the play was to be mounted unlicensed as a club production. 'We got a few things allowed. But we were up against an impasse,' the play's director Antony Page recalled. 'The play could not be done except in club conditions.'[84] William Gaskill, who would succeed Devine and was then a Royal Court associate director, remembered 'visits to the Lord Chamberlain in his dusty little office in St James's Palace, the bandying of arguments about the validity of "shit" or "christ"' as now seeming 'rather quaint and harmless'.[85] More than the use of expletives was at stake. '[The Lord Chamberlain] was limiting not just the scope of what could be shown on the stage, but the strength and vitality of the language.' This assessment, though, makes it misleadingly seem as if a war over 'fuck', 'shit' and 'bastard' defined the limits of the battle. Expletives are not sure symptoms of a strong or vital stage diction, but their excision ensured that modern drama could not accurately convey the language of real life.

The Lord Chamberlain reacted to the Court's defiance with an attempt to invoke the rigours of the law. Johnston was required to inform the Director of Public Prosecutions, Sir Norman Skelhorn, of the Royal Court's defiance. 'The Lord Chamberlain would also wish to emphasise that he . . . is solely concerned to avoid a position where the law can be brought into disrepute by what is no more than a subterfuge,' Johnston wrote to Skelhorn. 'He feels if this production goes unchallenged it may be difficult later to establish any line between what is and what is not a genuine theatre club.'[86] If, though, the

Lord Chamberlain had been seriously concerned to maintain the distinction between a club and public performance he could have given the Royal Court helpful advice, as Nugent had years earlier. But he was out for battle. Hill had taken it upon himself to talk to two members of the DPP's office: 'They both have no doubt that this is an offence against statute [he meant section] 15 of the Theatres Act of 1843 and appears as confident as any lawyer can be confident that a conviction can be secured.' He also revealed that the DPP wanted to prosecute 'in an exemplary way'. A Mr Barry in the DPP's office gave Hill confirmation that the Director had 'instructed him to give us every assistance'.

Cobbold's disingenuous response to this news was, on 30 June 1965, to write from Holyrood Palace saying, after the DPP had taken his decision, 'I should like it to be known . . . we are not moved by any hostility to the Royal Court and that we are more concerned about precedent and implications for the future than this particular instance.' The pace quickened. On 13 July Cobbold wrote to the elderly, unwell Frank Soskice, succeeded as Home Secretary by Jenkins later that year, saying he had had a discussion with Skelhorn, who felt 'there is probably a breach of the law'. Soskice, himself a lawyer, said he would talk to the Attorney-General. Cobbold's hectoring attitude was, in the circumstances, unwise. On 11 February he had been to see Soskice and, according to Johnston, 'expressed doubts about being able to continue much longer because of the organised opposition to the censorship by some theatre companies, including the Royal Shakespeare.'[87] Soskice's procrastinating response had been to say 'he would prefer to let things ride for a while longer'. No wonder: the government had a minute majority of four. There were far more important matters for parliamentary legislation than theatre censorship. 'A further example of the government playing for time,' Johnston unfairly claimed. There was no missing the fact that the Lord Chamberlain was now at logger-heads with the Labour Government.[88]

Soskice's reply should at least have alerted Cobbold to the fact that there was little sympathy in the Labour government for the Lord Chamberlain's theatre operations. As it was Cobbold maintained his angry offensive. There was virtually no opposition to what he was doing; no MP raised complaints about how Cobbold had betrayed the Scarbrough rulings. Then on 4 July 1965 Harold Hobson sensationally turned upon Lord Cobbold. 'One cannot protest too strongly against the double moral standards which prevail in the government of the English theatre,' he complained in his *Sunday Times* review of the play. 'If I did not know it be untrue I should think that the Lord Chamberlain is mad,' he wrote hyperbolically. The censorship system made it permissible to treat a difficult and delicate subject frivolously' but 'any thoughtful consideration is almost automatically penalised'. On 21 July Prime Minister Harold Wilson signalled that the days of the Lord Chamberlain's theatrical duties were probably numbered. Wilson was asked by a backbench Labour MP about government policy in relation to theatre censorship. 'So far as this aspect of national life needs some degree of modernisation, I would have thought there was a pretty strong case here,' Wilson said. It was a subject which the Lord Chancellor might consider now he had 'the necessary machinery' in the new law commission.

Cobbold ought to have understood and heeded the implications of the Prime Minister's words. Six days later Cobbold received a letter from the DPP, giving news of what amounted to a government snub. The law officers, Skelhorn wrote, were convinced a prosecution of the Royal Court 'would stand a good chance of success' but they did not wish to take Cobbold's punitive lead. The DPP put it diplomatically: 'They [the law-officers] are, however, strongly of the opinion that it would be inexpedient to institute such a prosecution in connection with the performance of a play which has attracted a great deal of public interest and a good deal of support and which has been running for some time.' Elwyn Jones, the shrewd Attorney-General, must have realised the government would have created uproar if he sanctioned a prosecution of the Royal Court. A man less inclined to stand upon his dignity than Cobbold would have realised this decision served as a vote of no confidence in him. Cobbold might have concluded that Elwyn Jones believed the decision to ban the play was based on outdated and incorrect assessments about what was fit for the stage. Or he might have felt the law officers were critical of his decision to persuade them to apply the strictest letter of the law in a sensitive case and at a time when the principle of the Chamberlain's control of the theatre was due for review. But no: he told the DPP that he felt 'vindicated', though 'vanquished' would have been a better description. 'So much for government support for the Lord Chamberlain,' Johnston commented ruefully and with far more sense of realism. Cobbold 'naturally had to accept this decision, but he hoped some sort of warning might have been possible.'[89]

In the first extended interview ever given by a Lord Chamberlain on matters of stage censorship, Cobbold spoke to J.W. Lambert in the *Sunday Times* on 11 April 1965. Cobbold was at pains to explain how much in favour of theatre clubs he was. 'They give selective and interested audiences a chance to see experimental work and I think they are very useful to the theatre.' The only exception to this proviso was 'where a management uses them for a different purpose, e.g., to put on for a long run a play a part of which [sic] has been refused a licence.' The Royal Court had never originally intended to run *A Patriot* for a longer season than usual. It was Cobbold who had precipitated the clash. Having been given what amounted to a public warning that the government disagreed with his assessment of the play and the Royal Court's defiance of him, Cobbold still clung defiantly to his judgement of the play. Once *A Patriot for Me* had become a commercial hit, the Royal Court aspired to have the play licensed and produced in the West End. Anthony Page, who remembers Sir John as 'a dry and humourless old stick', pleaded with the Assistant Comptroller for Cobbold to reconsider his decision, arguing that the play's homosexual aspect had caused no outrage.[90] Eric Penn, the Comptroller, behaving as if the play had not even been produced, went to see the play himself and supported Cobbold's original verdict. 'I do not think that the tolerance of homosexuality has yet reached the point where this play in its present form is suitable for public performance,' he wrote on 13 August.

Significant pleaders put the case for licensing. Foremost

among them was the Prime Minister's personal lawyer and Chairman of the Arts Council, Lord Goodman, and Lord Harewood, the Queen's cousin who was then director of the Edinburgh Festival. Cobbold was implacable, but, bizarrely, he did ask the actress Irene Worth for her view of the play. She was an odd choice, being an American citizen and associated with the avant-garde work of the Royal Shakespeare Company. 'I really didn't think it needed to be limited to a subscription audience,' she wrote to him. 'It seemed to me to be written with seriousness, dignity, humanity and to be impartial.' She concluded in a strange echo of Bancroft's apprehensions about *Oedipus Rex* in 1907, that 'passing this play could set a precedent for an avalanche of inferior and tasteless copies.' She implied that a theatrical appetite for plays about homosexuality would be stimulated by Osborne's bleak drama. Yet she was sensible enough to admit, 'I don't honestly feel that Osborne's play should suffer because of that.'[91]

A Patriot for Me did suffer, in the sense that Cobbold continued to refuse to allow it a licence for production in uncensored form. In 1966 Laurence Olivier wanted to present the play at the National Theatre, of which he was the first director. He went to see Cobbold in May 1966 and was met with an obfuscating cloud of negatives. The Lord Chamberlain had been armed by Hill with a paper recording the details of the 'British Medical Association report on homosexuality', which had been submitted to the Wolfenden Committee nine years earlier. This report laid emphasis on the idea that homosexuality was, like influenza, something which you could catch by contact. It was either 'essential' or 'acquired' through 'seduction, initiation, cultural aspirations, depravity – new sensations for jaded appetites'. As far as cultural aspirations were concerned, 'some people adopt homosexual practices because they think such activity denotes superiority of mind.' The author of these fancies was the BMA's assistant secretary, Ernest Claxton, who ended up in the thick of Mary Whitehouse's National Viewers and Listeners Association and urged 'religious conversion' as a 'cure' for homosexuality. Claxton consulted many psychiatrists but quoted only one, who recommended

'Christian doctrine' as an aid to cure. Claxton had dreamed up a mad scheme for putting homosexuals straight which involved treatment centres with a diet of 'Christian inspiration mixed with farm-work, forestry and market-gardening'.[92] It was on such an authority that Cobbold indirectly leaned when refusing Olivier's request.

In the same year that *A Patriot for Me* caused such anguish, Frank Marcus's *The Killing of Sister George*, the first play that dealt with candour about lesbianism, reached the stage. It is instructive to discover how little alarm or concern it caused in comparison with Osborne's play. The Assistant Examiner, Kyrle Fletcher, was disturbed by the 'atmosphere of lesbianism' that permeated a play in which he discerned two masochistic episodes. Alice, 'the slave character' had been forced to 'eat the butt' of the cigar enjoyed by Sister George, an alcoholic lesbian actress in a radio soap opera. The second involved Alice in drinking bathwater. When Heriot read the play he was more shocked. All the characters were lesbians, living in 'a private world' analogous to that of the 'perverts' in *A Patriot for Me*. This led him to conclude, preposterously, that the play 'may well be a trap for the Lord Chamberlain'. A trap? Of what sinister sort? Well, three or four characters are clearly going to a lesbian drag-ball. 'If the Lord Chamberlain licenses this play I can easily imagine the cries of righteous indignation in some quarters that a play about lesbians is permitted, while a play not entirely about perverts is not [licensed].' Poor, dotty Heriot. Johnston read the text and was convinced there was nothing that would corrupt. No one actually proclaimed herself lesbian or made speeches about the trials and tribulations of being sapphic. There was no sighting of lesbians at a shocking lesbian ball, nor were the couple seen in bed. On 2 April 1965 Cobbold, after talking to the Examiners and Johnston, licensed the play without a single cut. 'I still think this is a dangerous play,' whined Heriot on 26 May.[93] No one listened to him. Homosexuals were dangerous, but you could not take lesbians seriously. After all Queen Victoria did not even think they existed.

The liberation of the stage from the Lord Chamberlain's control did not at once provide the stimulus for plays depicting scenes of homosexual passion or intimacy. In 1967 at the Open Space theatre club, *Fortune and Men's Eyes* by the American playwright John Herbert lifted the veils of discretion from the incidence of male rape and same-sex love in American prisons. When it transferred to the West End and was submitted for licensing, the Chamberlain pruned the foul language. The signs of passion, apparent in language rather than action, were not repressed. Perhaps the Lord Chamberlain believed, and rightly, that homosexuality broke out in prisons because there was no alternative source of sexual relief.

That same year, months before the Chamberlain's powers were aborted, Harold Hobson went to see Colin Spencer's *The Ballad of the False Barman* at Hampstead Theatre. He was shocked to the marrow, as his review, 'Where has all the goodness gone', of 1 January 1967, made furiously clear. 'At one point in the second act the whore stands with his back to the audience very close to the front of the stage,' he informed his readers. 'He lowers his trousers and shows us a long and complete view of his naked bottom. Now I do not deny that this may be a source of much pleasure to my homosexual friends. I merely say that to me – and I do not care what Freudian interpretations are put on this remark – it is hideous and disgusting and should be stopped. The licence our stage has arrogated to itself goes far beyond any limits which a decent society should permit. There is today a campaign to get the censorship abolished. What in actual fact is needed is that the Lord Chamberlain should exert over theatre clubs as well as theatres the authority which a recent legal decision has shown that he possesses.' Alas poor Hobson, so disturbed by the sight of naked male buttocks that he called for an invigorated form of censorship. Within a year he would renounce his own recommendation. But it would take three decades before dramatists felt themselves free to depict gay sexual activity on stage.

In 1979 the National Theatre was taken to court in a private prosecution by Mary Whitehouse, the president of the National

Viewers and Listeners Association. The cause of her outrage was a scene of male rape, discreetly done, if such a violent incident can be so managed, in Howard Brenton's *The Romans in Britain*. She had never seen the play. Michael Bogdanov, the director of the play was charged with procuring acts of gross indecency. But the Attorney General intervened to terminate the case. In the 1990s simulated buggery and analingus were at last used as shock tactics on stage. In Tony Kushner's *Angels in America* at the National Theatre, an act of unprotected buggery was mimed in stylised form, with the actors standing decently apart. Shortly afterwards the simulation was far more graphic in *Poor Superman* and *Shopping and Fucking* at the Hampstead and the Royal Court respectively. These detailed simulations were enacted with greater candour than heterosexual acts usually were on stage. Prudery and repression of all things homosexual had died a death in the theatre. In the real world it was different.

In the year 2000 the stage spectacle of two men kissing would have occasioned no comment or interest. In real life such an incident could still lead to the kissers being taken to court. At last the theatre, as far as homosexuality was concerned, had become more gayly civilized than the world beyond it.

Notes

1. LC file on *Suddenly Last Summer*.
2. Tudor Rees (ed.), *They Stand Apart* (London, 1955), p. 22.
3. John Johnston, *The Lord Chamberlain's Blue Pencil* (1990), p. 172.
4. Alan Bray, *Homosexuality in Renaissance England* (1982), p. 26.
5. John Stubbes, *The Anatomie of Abuses* (W.O. Turnbull, 1836), p. 6.
6. Edward Guilpen, *Skialetheia*, The Shakespeare Association Facsmiles, no. 2, 1931.
7. Cited in Bray, op. cit., pp. 54 and 55.
8. Alan Sinfield, *Cultural Politics – Queer Reading* (1994), p. 13.
9. Michel Foucault, *The History of Sexuality* (1988), vol. 1, p. 43.

All further references to Foucault are to his introduction to *The History of Sexuality.*

10. Alan Sinfield, *The Wilde Century,* (1994), p. 3.
11. Noel Annan, *Our Age* (1991), p. 163.
12. Patrick Higgins, *The Heterosexual Dictatorship* (1996), p. 281.
13. Ibid., p. 216.
14. Gordon Westwood, *Society and the Homosexual* (1952), p. 22.
15. Davenport-Hines, *Sex, Death & Punishment* (Fontana, 1991), p. 313.
16. Annan, op. cit., p. 135.
17. David Newsome, *On the Edge of Paradise: A.C. Benson, the Diarist* (1980), p. 276.
18. Philip Hoare, *Wilde's Last Stand* (1997), p. 31.
19. Higgins, op. cit., pp. 102–3.
20. Quentin Crisp, *The Naked Civil Servant* (1968), p. 97.
21. Rodney Ackland, interview with author, September 1990.
22. Michael Darlow, *Terence Rattigan, The Man and his Work* (2000), pp. 142 and 146.
23. Frith Banbury, interview with author, 26 February 1999. All other quotations from Frith Banbury in this chapter come from this interview.
24. LC file on Oscar Wilde.
25. Higgins, op. cit., p. 158.
26. Ibid., p. 173.
27. *Sunday Pictorial,* 25 May 1952.
28. Hugh Cudlipp, *At Your Peril* (1976), p. 317.
29. Richard Plant, *The Pink Triangle* (1987), p. 88.
30. Higgins, op. cit., p. 274.
31. Westwood, op. cit., p. 00.
32. D.J. West, *Homosexuality* (1960), p. 52.
33. Ibid., p. 4.
34. Westwood, op. cit., p. 20.
35. Hoare, op. cit., p. 11.
36. Martin Green, *Children of the Sun* (1997), p. 31.
37. Hoare, op. cit., p. 136.
38. Nicholas de Jongh, *Not in Front of the Audience* (1992), pp. 30–1.

39. Faith Brook, interview with author, February 1999.
40. Peter Parker, *Ackerley* (1989), p. 100.
41. Ibid., p. 98.
42. Paul Fussell, *The Great War and Modern Memory* 1977), pp. 279–80.
43. Parker, op. cit., p. 90.
44. de Jongh, op. cit., p. 25.
45. John Gielgud wrote 2 pages of comments on Johnston (op. cit.) which were sent out to journalists to accompany publication.
46. Noël Coward, *Collected Plays II* (1999), pp. 169–71.
47. John van Druten in Norman Haire (ed.), *Sex and Censorship in the Theatre* (World League for Sexual Reform, 1930), p. 319.
48. Valerie Grove, *Dear Dodie* (1996), p. 000.
49. de Jongh, op. cit., p. 32.
50. Kaier Curtin, *We Can Always Call Them Bulgarians!*, p. 208.
51. Johnston, op. cit., p. 173.
52. Ibid.
53. LC file on *A Streetcar Named Desire*, Tennessee Williams.
54. LC file on *The Living Room*, Graham Greene.
55. Sinfield, *Out on Stage*, op. cit., p. 124.
56. J.C. Trewin, *The Theatre Since 1900* (1951), p. 285.
57. Harold Hobson, *Theatre in Britain* (1984), p. 151.
58. *Sunday Times*, 13 November 1949.
59. Richard Huggett, *Binkie Beaumont* (1989), op. cit., p. 420.
60. Quoted in Dan Rebellato, *1956 And All That: the making of modern British drama* (1999), p. 236.
61. Ibid, pp. 185–90.
62. Charles Duff, *The Lost Summer* (1995), p. 151.
63. J. Klum, *Acting Gay* (1992), p. 294.
64. LC file on *Cat on a Hot Tin Roof*, Tennessee Williams.
65. LC file on *Tea and Sympathy*, Tennessee Williams.
66. Johnston, op. cit., p. 211.
67. Dominic Shellard, *British Theatre Since the War*, p. 150.
68. LC file on *A View From the Bridge*, Arthur Miller.
69. *Sunday Times*, 30 September 1956.
70. Peter Wood, interview with author, 5 April 1998.

71. Johnston, op. cit., p. 212.

72. Ibid., p. 172.

73. LC file on *A Taste of Honey*.

74. Letter to author, 3 November 1987.

75. LC file on *Beyond the Fringe*, various authors.

76. Frank Norman and Lionel Bart, *Fings Ain't Wot They Used T'be* (1959), pp. 153–4.

77. Cited in Sinfield, *Out on Stage: lesbian and gay theatre* (1999), pp. 153–4.

78. Kenneth Tynan, *A View of the English Stage* (1975), p. 32.

79. LC file on *Entertaining Mr Sloane*.

80. Johnston, op. cit., pp. 164–5.

81. Roy Jenkins, interview with author, 6 November 1999.

82. Sinfield, *Out on Stage*, p. 263.

83. Johnston, op. cit., p. 208.

84. De Jongh, op. cit., p. 25.

85. William Gaskill, *A Sense of Direction* (1988), p. 68.

86. Johnston, op. cit., p. 206.

87. Ibid., p. 187.

88. Ibid.

89. Ibid., pp. 203 and 206.

90. De Jongh, op. cit., p. 105–119.

91. Johnston, op. cit., p. 207.

92. Davenport-Hines, op. cit., pp. 320–1.

93. LC file on *Killing of Sister George*, Frank Marcus.

4

PLAYING POLITICS WITH THE STAGE

Defying Dangerous Plays

The House of Lords was full of peers indulging in mutual congratulation on the afternoon of 28 May 1968. They were taking part in the preliminary funeral obsequies for the Lord Chamberlain as Censor Absolute and Extraordinary of the Theatre. These obsequies took the form of the second reading of the Theatres Bill that was designed to end the Lord Chamberlain's duties as licensor and censor of stage plays. Blue-blooded and life peers were giving heart-felt thanks for the way theatre censorship had been administered in the past. That afternoon Lord Cobbold congratulated himself and his predecessors for what they had done for and perhaps to the theatre. Even the liberal-minded Lord Norwich unctuously thanked the Lord Chamberlain and his predecessors for exercising 'this unenviable function with understanding, sensitivity and perception'.[1] Cobbold likened the situation in which the Lord Chamberlain found himself to the unavoidable parting of two close friends who would no longer be meeting. He lamented their separation. The Lord Chamberlain's office, he asserted, had carried out its theatrical duties 'to the benefit of the public and of the theatre'. In a sentence of gargantuan cheek he suggested that if proof were needed of the Lord Chamberlain's valuable works, one had only to look at the strength and vitality of the English theatre.

Cobbold and his predecessors had prevented some of the great plays of the century from being seen on the public stage for years. They had censored on a grand scale; they had hacked, pruned, clipped and cut away essentials and characterising details with prudish philistinism; they had suppressed or truncated plays which dared to be politically motivated or to discuss contemporary political problems or to feature living politicians as characters. Cobbold and his twentieth-century predecessors had played a crucial role in erecting bulwarks of reaction to withstand each successive wave of modern drama, clinging obstinately to Victorian notions of what the theatre should do and be. Yet this impenitent censor, last in a line of ignoble suppressors, had the gall to claim that he and his like had worked for the common and theatrical good. He was claiming to have been a facilitator rather than a destroyer. Waxing extravagant with nostalgia, he recalled, 'Over a period of five years I can count on the finger of one hand the occasions on which discussions, even when they did not result in complete disagreement, have been conducted on anything but friendly and understanding terms.'[2] If it seemed to Cobbold that the theatre directors in the 1960s who were summoned to see him about offending plays were friendly, then it was only because they calculated that charm and affability might prove to be of more influence. If Cobbold believed he was receptive to the problems of theatre directors when they struggled to make him change his mind about intended cuts, then he had scant self-knowledge.

'They were always very patronising. They represented a kind of medieval power. They implied that it was good of them to see you at all,' recalls William Gaskill, who as the Royal Court's artistic director was involved in a succession of battles to save words, sentences, incidents, scenes and whole plays from the Chamberlain's axe.[3] Peter Hall thought the atmosphere at St James's Palace as threatening and unpleasant. Peter Wood found Sir John Johnston remote, patronising and unhelpful. Anthony Page, who battled with Cobbold and Johnston over *A Patriot for Me*, remembered Johnston's inflexible, humourless attitude. In fact Cobbold's references to his own friendliness and understanding were symptomatic of his eagerness to counter the idea that he and his officials were hostile and haughty in their dealings with radical young directors and producers. The House of Lords debate was a typically English occasion, tinged with hypocrisy and humbuggery. The intention was to send the Lord Chamberlain to the blazes in a glow of glory and not to mention the damage he had done to the vitality of the British stage. During this little political ceremony there were no allusions to the way in which Lords Chamberlain had played politics through the centuries, censoring that which embarrassed the government of the day or the monarch. Cobbold himself had continued to act as the government's adjutant, doctoring plays that were critical of friendly foreign governments or leaders, or satirised British politicians. As it represented the interests of the government, or rather the Establishment, the Lord Chamberlain's office was political in a most fundamental sense.

The Jacobean and Caroline censors, according to an analysis of deleted sections of texts and manuscripts of the period, reveal that 'unfavourable presentation of friendly foreign powers or their sovereigns' and 'personal satire on influential people' were justifiable reasons to apply the blue pencil of censorship.[4] The vigour of this politically motivated form of censoring that survived right to 1968 acted as a deterrent to dramatists. In the twentieth century it was not until the 1930s that serious attempts to defy such censorship were made. In that 'low dishonest decade', as Auden called it, *What Made the Iron Grow?*, an assault upon Hitler's anti-Semitic policies was banned. In 1938 the young Terence Rattigan, whose reputation rested primarily upon his adored light comedy, *French Without Tears*, involved the Lord Chamberlain and his staff in more than a year of wrangling and negotiation over his 1938 play, *Follow My Leader*. In the 1950s the upper-middle-class Rattigan was unfairly written off by younger theatre critics as a lightweight and reactionary dramatist. Yet although he had all the airs, graces and income of a grand young gentleman about town in the 1930s, his political sympathies were with the Labour Party. 'One moment he was marching down Whitehall ... with other members of Equity, the next leaving the demonstration to dine at the Savoy Grill.'[5]

Follow My Leader may have disguised its political concern about Nazi expansionism beneath a farcical veneer, but it was likened by the Lord Chamberlain's office to an exploding bombshell. The play was submitted for approval and licensing soon after Austria had been annexed by Hitler in 1938, at a time when Czechoslovakia was assumed to be the next object of Germany's conquering desires. Rattigan did more than touch upon contemporary European politics; he embarked upon a light-hearted though pointed critique of German aggression. The debate about this political farce revealed the Lord Chamberlain in operation as the government's adjutant, executing its guidelines on dealing with foreign powers. Rattigan's allegory deals with Hans Zedesi, a plumber in the mythical country of Moronia, who is acclaimed as the ideal leader, or rather the dumbish mouthpiece of a totalitarian regime. The play does not take Zedesi seriously, nor do the real leaders of the state who use him as their puppet and regard him with suitable contempt. But there's no missing the fact that Zedesi is a caricature of Adolf Hitler.

Henry Game, the Chief Examiner, read the play on 4 July 1938 and was anxious. Even at this late date the Lord Chamberlain, in common with most of Britain, much preferred to cling to the belief that it was wise to treat Hitler as a leader who posed no real threat to Britain. 'This is a most difficult play to deal with,' he wrote, irritated by the insidiousness of Rattigan's technique. 'It is a farce. It satirises the Nazi regime. It burlesques its leaders. But except in its more blatant moments, the satirical effect is achieved more by innumerable minor touches of ridicule than by an obvious and direct method of attack.' He believed, 'the source of inspiration of the author's fun is unmistakable – Germany and the three leading Nazi personalities appear to be burlesques of Hitler, Goering and Goebbels.' Game then revealed the pervasiveness of the government's control of the stage when politics was involved. 'The topical matter could stand, but the personalities are another matter. And in view of the recent letter from the Foreign Office, in which their views on these questions were indicated, I think this play should be sent to them for an opinion. It seems to me that there are some grounds for German objections to the caricaturing of their leading men.' There were also unseemly words to be excised. 'Piddling' might be used in eighteenth-century literature, 'but is now a school-boy phrase and we cut it.' 'God damn' was not allowed either, except where the word God was omitted. 'Pansy', used as an adjective rather than a noun, presented a more difficult problem. It might be allowed – there was room for discussion since the words 'Pansy and cissy have already found their way into a *Times* leader.'

More significant was an unheard-of outbreak of passionate disagreement between the Lord Chamberlain's two Examiners about the play's likely political impact. Geoffrey Dearmer, Game's deputy, disagreed with his superior's report, though diplomatically saying that he agreed with Game 'in substance'. Dearmer rightly regarded himself as one of the more liberal examiners. Before being recruited as a reader he had been 'madly agin [censorship]. The very idea of the censor stank to high heaven. But when I got the job there was no doubt I was up to it.' His attitude changed and he came to see his role as a protector rather than a suppressor. He even recommended Heriot, who was a former amateur actor and subsequently a professional purveyor of malice as an examiner. 'The theatre loved the Lord Chamberlain because the Examiner saved them from the risk of prosecution,' he claimed. 'I was always on the side of the theatre. I cannot imagine a more harmless play than *Miss Julie.*'[6]

It is difficult to assess how liberal Dearmer was, because he wrote so few reports on controversial plays, but he did struggle hard to save *Follow My Leader* from the censor's veto. Dearmer, in his report, described the play as 'a light-hearted burlesque of fascism generally'.[7] He did not believe the three leading characters could be said to resemble Hitler, Goering and Goebbels. 'The authors have taken pains to make Zedesi as unlike Hitler as possible.' Dearmer was eager to battle against the government on the question of censorship as well. 'If the play is sent to the Foreign Office I think reference should be made to plays on the same subject already licensed. (Elmer Rice's) *Judgment Day* was a much more formidable attack and bitter if not savage, whereas this is not. Shaw's *Geneva* deals directly with the subject without making any attempt to disguise the personalities, whereas this play carefully alters them. It is true that *Geneva* is high philosophy and does not ridicule, but does criticise. If this play were banned the authors might complain with reason that preferential treatment is given to the GBS's and Elmer Rice's of the dramatic world. The censor has never been guilty of this.'

This reference to Shaw's uncensored *Geneva*, that opened at the Malvern Festival of 1938, was pertinent. 'The play is a lampoon with Hitler and Mussolini unmistakably on the stage,' Shaw had said to the theatre director H.K. Ayliff.[8] Yet the lampooning nature of *Geneva* did not mean that either Hitler or Mussolini emerged as stage characters to which their real-life originals might object. Shaw admitted that he had engaged in a drama which 'flatters them enormously'. He insisted the two fascist leaders were his satirical version of political abstractions. The critic Desmond McCarthy was stung to the quick by the spectacle of Shaw, the Fabian socialist, anxious that Europe be saved from the catastrophe of a second world war that century, while apparently surrendering his reverence for the principles of liberal humanism: 'The case for the Jew ought of course to have been vigorously put. It was not. Nor was the case of the democrat. [Shaw] has been false to his mission in life ... [*Geneva*] made me ask if it were possible that I had been a fool about Bernard Shaw all my writing life.'[9]

Follow My Leader was sent to the Foreign Office on 4 July, with the warning that it was 'rather tricky' and the admission that even the Lord Chamberlain's readers disagreed about it. Unfortunately the Foreign Office view of the play is missing from the Lord Chamberlain's files. Perhaps it was weeded out. The following day the producer Gilbert Miller was warned that *Follow My Leader* posed the fiercest of censorship problems. 'The bombshell has arrived and exploded with shattering force underneath the new Lord Chamberlain,' he was told. By the end of the month a formal ban was imposed. There was no attempt to conceal the political nature of the decision or who had taken it. The Foreign Office, in a letter of 28 July, said it was 'of the definite opinion the production of this play at this time would not be in the best interests of this country.' Miller retaliated by asking why, if Shaw's *Geneva* had been licensed, should Rattigan's be banned. Had Gwatkin been honest he would have said that Shaw's portrait of Hitler was sufficiently oblique and sympathetic to ensure no offence would be taken by the German embassy. Instead he shrugged off the producer's question. '*Follow My Leader* is a farce in which certain of the German leaders are definitely burlesqued, whereas *Geneva* is a politico-philosophic discussion in which the characters are abstractions rather than personalities,' he replied.

A year later, in July 1939, when war was just a couple of months away, Rattigan's producer submitted a revised version of the play. 'My collaborator (Anthony Goldschmidt) and I have revised the play,' he wrote to Gwatkin on 24 July 1939, 'and would be agreeable [sic] to delete such passages as the Lord Chamberlain or the Foreign Office found objectionable. I really think that [the] Führer would find it very hard to recognise himself in the person of Hans Zedesi, particularly if played by Robertson Hare.' The reference to Hare, a short, bald, bespectacled actor who specialised in the playing of hen-pecked and timorous little men, gives an idea of the farcical motif. Geoffrey Dearmer was convinced that the play could now go on and that the ban was out of date. 'There was a reason for banning the play last year because of its central political situation and the policy of appeasement. Neurasthenia [a mythical country in *Follow My Leader*] and Czechoslovakia were very much alike. The protection of the Neurasthenia minority and the impending invasion [of Czechoslovakia] was much too imminent and likely to happen off the stage to be allowed upon it,' he reported on 29 July. Of course: Dearmer was admitting that plays which treated contemporary events were subject to an automatic ban.

In this, his finest moment as a Chamberlain's Examiner, Dearmer urged that a playwright should not have to be scrupulously two-faced. 'Surely a dramatist may echo by implication the government's and the country's political views. To take the opposite view and ban a play because it makes full use of fascist ideology would be to hand over as a gift to the censor's enemies the most weighty of ammunition. The play is a political farce and any foreign embassy which took exception to it would be suffering from a very far-fetched imagination and a guilty conscience.' When making an astute comparison between *Follow My Leader* and Shaw's *Geneva* with its relatively docile attitude to the fascists he argued, 'One cannot pretend . . . that a dramatist is not entitled to base a light-hearted burlesque on this sort of international events which are now matters of fact . . . the puppet plumber in no way resembles Hitler . . . Is it fair to Rattigan to take the view that GBS's characters are any more philosophic types because his are comparatively favourable to their originals and Rattigan's are not?' Dearmer did not even accept there had been a reason for banning the play a year earlier.

Dearmer's view did not prevail. Henry Game, who did not read the new version of the play, adopted a pose of benevolent even-handedness that did nothing to conceal the political nature of the censorship. 'Plays concerned with the ideology of other countries should be allowed, provided always that the theme is reasonably true and reasonably balanced . . . There would be no objection to the farce had not the author taken – or so it seems to me – too many facts which he has rather thinly travestied.' This argument was misleading. It was because Rattigan had rudely travestied the figure of Hitler that objection had to be made: 'The dictator is a puppet which Hitler is not, the field marshall is a fool which Goering is not. The propaganda minister is inefficient which Goebbels is not. About the only thing that rings true is that the British ambassador practically apologises for having an embassy which could be blown up,' Game judged on 1 August. Again his argument was faulty. If Rattigan's play had been closer to the dangerous truth it would have been regarded with even greater apprehension by the Foreign Office. 'I suppose in common with most people I would rather be sworn at than laughed at – the Germans are notoriously lacking in humour and if they think this play is one which holds not only their ideology up to ridicule but makes absurd caricatures of their leading men, and even their leader, this may cause great offence,' Game wrote.

Today it may seem that Game was improperly concerned about the feelings of Germany and its Nazi leader and that the

censors neglected the interests of the stage and a popular young
dramatist. But it was the Chamberlain's duty to ensure that
political views in plays reflected government policy in relation
to foreign countries. The Chamberlain's office was deferring to
the Foreign Office's wish that no foreign country, or at least a
country with which relations were amicable or sensitive, should
be offended by a stage play. That was the Chamberlain's duty. A
section of the right wing of the Conservative Party was
sympathetic to Hitler, strongly anti-Semitic and believed a
continuing policy of appeasement was in Britain's best interest.
'I'm afraid this is a bit of a teaser,' Gwatkin reported to
Clarendon on 3 August. The play was accordingly sent to the
German embassy by the Lord Chamberlain's office, with a
request that Germany give a view of the script. Herbert Biloni,
whom Gwatkin described as 'a reasonable German', replied in
diplomatic terms, saying that *Follow My Leader* 'contains in its
present camouflaged form without any doubt a lot of allusions
which can't but raise unfriendly feelings in the audience. Thus I
don't think it would be helpful in improving Anglo-German
relations.'

Gwatkin agreed, saying in a memorandum to Clarendon, 'I
had hoped that the play being an absolute farce and all the
characters being the antithesis of what they are in life, that the
German would take the view that the cap didn't fit.' He
proposed, therefore, that the play's political sting should be
removed, particularly the references to the burning of the
Reichstag and to the persecution of Jews. 'No minority talk,' as
he euphemistically put it. At a time when German troops were
massing on the Polish border, the Lord Chamberlain himself,
poised to go north for grouse-shooting, wrote from his country
home to the Comptroller. His letter reeked of anxiety and
irritation. 'Personally I should like to ban all these anti-Nazi
plays, for they cannot help to promote a better atmosphere. On
the other hand a policy of appeasement cannot be said to have
done much good so far,' he wrote in nice understatement. He
was well aware of the precedent of *Geneva* and *Judgment Day*. 'I
do not think I can refuse to license this play having regard to the
fact that *Geneva* and other similar plays have been allowed. For

that would give the authors a chance to complain that *Geneva* and *Judgment Day* air severe criticism of the Nazi system whereas this play is, as you say, a burlesque on the German leader and German ideology.' Clarendon thought the best course would be for Rattigan to be asked to make the alterations proposed by Gwatkin. He even wondered whether it would be a good idea to refer the play back to the Foreign Office.

At the interview Gwatkin and Nugent had with 'the very charming' Rattigan on 10 August, the playwright was told, 'The Lord Chamberlain has naturally to be very careful in not allowing any guying of heads of foreign states.' Perhaps Rattigan was relieved or soothed by Gwatkin's assurance that Nazi Germany was 'always very particular to prevent any objectionable references to the British royal family.' On 20 September when Britain was finally at war with Germany, a letter arrived from Rattigan's agent, A.D. Peters, asking again for permission for the play to be licensed. 'There is no longer any reason why we should be anxious not to hurt Nazi feelings,' the Lord Chamberlain minuted on 23 September. The play was given a licence at last. But, of course, the time for *Follow My Leader*, if there really had been an ideal one for such juvenile 'guying' of those German leaders, had passed. The play lasted just eleven nights, during January 1940, in the West End. 'I just personally *don't* see that you can write a full-length burlesque about, say, the Plague when the Plague is in actual visitation,' James Agate aptly commented in his *Sunday Times* review.[10] 'Its time had gone,' recalled the director Frith Banbury, who was then an actor and one of the members of the cast. The idea that Hitler was a nobody manipulated by powerful Nazi strategists had already been proved spectacularly wrong.[11]

Changing Climates

Between the advent of the Second World War, when *Follow My Leader* sputtered into brief life, and the 1960s, there were no important battles over the political content of plays submitted for licensing. But scrupulous concern for the feelings of fascist leaders, like Hitler and Mussolini, was not replicated when it came to communists. *Shadow of Heroes* by the American writer Robert Ardrey, staged in 1958 with Peggy Ashcroft as its star, was a 'semi-documentary' about the Russian revolution. There were no problems about the impersonation of real-life Hungarian politicians on stage, because the characters 'were nearly all communists and they do not qualify for special protection by the Lord Chamberlain.'[12] Given that it was two centuries since the mocking and humiliation of a Prime Minister and his party had brought the censorship into existence, the Lord Chamberlain was still peculiarly vigilant in his search for any acerbic or mocking reference to the party in power. The petty absolutism of his political censorship is well characterised by Lord Scarbrough's decision in 1954 to ban the song 'Right Hand Man' in the Lyric Hammersmith revue *Light Fantastic*. This sketch, in which a character clearly based upon the Foreign Secretary, Anthony Eden, complains about his long wait to succeed the ancient Winston Churchill as Prime Minister. Lord Scarbrough had once been Eden's parliamentary secretary in the House of Commons and, therefore, may have had additional, personal grounds for ensuring that his old chief was not lightly mocked.[13]

Otherwise, though, no leading British playwright of Shaw's generation, or the one following, aspired to deal with British or European politics in the form of a stage play. In the changed theatrical climate of the 1960s, plays such as *The Representative*, *US* and *Soldiers*, struck the Lord Chamberlain as a threat to relations with friendly countries or as libels upon dead British heroes. He therefore sought advice from the government on particular play-texts, his censorial regime was not independent. It looked to the government of the day for advice.

The Royal Shakespeare Company posed recurrent problems for the Lord Chamberlain once it moved down to London's Aldwych Theatre, and under Peter Hall's direction, presented sensation-causing plays, old and new. The RSC's proposed production of Rolf Hochuth's *The Representative* (1963) drew the Lord Chamberlain, for the first time since the war, into protracted discussions with government about the desirability of allowing such a play to be staged. Hochuth argued that Pope

Pius XII maintained an attitude of scrupulous passivity to the sight of Nazi extermination of the Jews, since he saw in Hitler the man who could free eastern Europe from the grasp of communism and Stalin. Not only was the papal nuncio in London consulted by Cobbold, but also Lord Home and Henry Brooke, respectively the Foreign and Home Secretaries of Harold Macmillan's administration. On this occasion actual evidence existed to support Hochuth's indictment. Cobbold was only concerned that *The Representative* might, in his view, pose problems for Britain's relations with both Germany and the Catholic Church. Besides, Pius XII counted as a recently dead head of state, of the grand sort whom Lords Chamberlain always sought to protect from the posthumous revenge of playwrights.

Heriot, who read the play, was alert to the dangers it posed. He recommended not only that the words 'bugger it', 'balls' and 'crap' should be removed, but also that *The Representative* ought be seen by Gerald O'Hara, the nuncio, who disliked what he read. Cobbold decided to seek the advice of the Home Secretary. He wrote to Brooke on 15 May 1962, saying that he found a decision 'extremely difficult' to make. The play had already been produced in Germany and was scheduled for performance in America. 'It would, therefore, in some ways look stupid to ban or cut. On the other hand the play would undoubtedly give offence to many people and I cannot help feeling that Pius XII is only five years after his death more of a contemporary character than a historical figure.' Cobbold was asking for secret government approval of a vetting and censoring procedure not generally in use since the nineteenth century: beyond the question of plays endangering foreign relations or defaming recently dead political leaders, he was implicitly asking the Home Secretary to support the idea that a play should be banned because its ideas would cause offence to those who saw it. Brooke, one of the most illiberal and reactionary Home Secretaries of the century, gave Cobbold what he wanted. 'On a narrow balance,' he wrote, 'I would myself be disposed to refuse the licence on the grounds that the play deals with the actions of a person who died very recently and that it would unquestionably give offence to large numbers of Her Majesty's subjects.'[14]

Cobbold then had a private conversation both with Brooke and Harold Caccia, the permanent secretary at the Foreign Office. 'He is content,' Cobbold recorded cryptically in a reference to the Home Secretary. The nature of that 'content' may have to do with a rare compromise that Cobbold worked out, presumably with government approval. The condition of a licence being granted was that the Royal Shakespeare Company would give space in *The Representative*'s theatre programme for the Catholic Church to defend itself against the charge that Pius had failed to speak out against Hitler's extermination of millions of Jews. This compromise is symptomatic of a disproportionate fear of theatre's power to upset. Cobbold's consultation with Brooke also reveals how far the Lord Chamberlain remained a servant of the government in his censorship role.

Three years later there was a far more serious clash of views between the RSC and Cobbold. Peter Brook's production of *US* necessitated anxious discussion with the Foreign Office and the American ambassador. 'I would say that by then we felt the Lord Chamberlain couldn't survive and that we had got to go on pushing. We derided him and his office and this made copy in the newspapers,' Hall remembered.[15] 'A piece of hysterically subjective anti-Vietnam war propaganda,' wrote Chief Examiner Heriot of *US* on 28 September 1966. Heriot loathed the script that had been written jointly by Adrian Mitchell, Denis Cannan and Michael Kustow. 'The attitude [of *US*] to America seems to me to be dangerous and insulting to an ally, and since the war in Vietnam is, so to speak, sub judice (would we have permitted a play about the Suez crisis during the crisis?) the piece is not recommended for licence.'[16] Here Heriot gives an insight into the Lord Chamberlain's thinking about plays involving the contemporary political actions of allies. He dutifully blue-pencilled 'an insulting reference to President Johnson', the use of the word 'balls', and 'For Christ's sake'. But his real anxiety was *US*'s attack on American intervention in the Vietnam War.

The Lord Chamberlain's file on *US* detailed a close communication between his department and the Foreign Office about how to deal with the offending drama. Cobbold was concerned to proclaim his independence of government, even while leaning heavily upon it for advice, guidance and succour. He liked to cultivate an air of impartiality even though he took the government's part. Harold Wilson's support of the American administration in bombing North Vietnam had exposed him to criticism from left-wing MPs, but Cobbold supported him and the Foreign Secretary, George Brown, was also asked for his view of the play. On 27 September, with Johnston in attendance, Cobbold had a talk with Sir Paul Gore-Booth, the permanent secretary at the Foreign Office. The Lord Chamberlain minuted that he told Gore-Booth how in his 'preliminary view' he detected a 'strong slant throughout the script on this highly inflammatory topical subject with its international political implications.' The Lord Chamberlain welcomed 'Foreign Office advice'. Implicit in Cobbold's statement was the conviction that a play could jeopardise Anglo-American relations. There appeared, however, to be a danger that, if the government did express public opposition to *US* being performed, it might be seen as Stalinist in its state censorship. The Labour administration regarded theatre censorship as best done in secret.

Cobbold made a show of his determination to resist government pressure if it were applied. 'Whilst the decision rested entirely with me, I said that I would welcome Foreign Office advice on this point,' he wrote, alluding to *US*'s criticism of America's Vietnam policies. He was still able to assure Gore-Booth that if the play finally reached the stage, its distasteful message would be conveyed in the most wholesome of language. 'They need not worry about the obscenities which I should deal with in the normal way.' A copy of the script was then given to Gore-Booth. The Foreign Office permanent secretary telephoned Cobbold the next day, 28 September, and said that his view of the script coincided with the Lord Chamberlain's. But, in mandarin fashion, he warned Cobbold that his view might not prove to be the official Foreign Office line, or presumably that of the Foreign Secretary. He thus conveyed the impression of concern about the script and possible diplomatic ramifications. He explained that 'he was consulting the Secretary of State and there were questions of domestic politics and timing involved.'

Since the joint parliamentary committee on censorship had first met at the end of July the reference to 'domestic politics' may have been a reference to the future of theatre censorship. There would have been high embarrassment if the government was caught putting pressure on the Chamberlain to veto a play, at a time when parliament was considering the idea of ending its system of theatre censorship. Cobbold appeared sensitive about consulting the Foreign Secretary: he was not used to taking instructions or recommendations from Labour politicians. 'I repeated again that the decision was mine and I was only giving them an opportunity to comment,' the Lord Chamberlain minuted. Gore-Booth had asked a potentially sinister question: he wanted to know whether the RSC was subsidised. Implicit in this question lurked the idea that an Arts Council funded theatre, being in receipt of government money, should not cause embarrassment to the Labour administration.

There was no missing the sense of urgency about these communications between the Permanent Under-Secretary to the Foreign Office and the Lord Chamberlain. This was no matter for eminent underlings. Usually censorship problems concerning a controversial play took weeks or even months to resolve. But on this occasion Cobbold wrote a minute in his own hand that same day. Gore-Booth also informed Cobbold that the question of *US* had already been raised with Brown who, 'though he personally thinks this revolting and tiresome stuff, disapproves of government censorship.' Cobbold added in smug parenthetic agreement the words 'As I do.' Perhaps in view of the Foreign Secretary's attitude, Gore-Booth informed Cobbold that the Foreign Office was resolutely determined to be neutral. It did not 'wish to express a view one way or another'. Cobbold replied that he 'entirely accepted this and was only concerned to give them an opportunity of commenting if they wished.' But the Lord Chamberlain's minute does not conceal the fact that the Foreign Office was far from neutral. It relied upon the traditionally disingenuous lean of diplomatic pressure. 'At the appropriate moment [the Foreign Office] will

let the US ambassador know privately about our conversation,'
Cobbold recorded.

If Cobbold licensed the script the Foreign Office would tell
the American ambassador that any opprobrium should be visited
upon the Lord Chamberlain. Cobbold, realising the force of this
remark had suggested to Gore-Booth that he was inclined to
ban *US*. 'I said I had not finally made up my mind, but was
contemplating saying the present script was unacceptable
because so much would be offensive to responsible foreign
opinion and suggesting they revise with this in mind and
resubmit if they wish to.' The allusion to 'responsible foreign
opinion' indicates that Cobbold interpreted 'responsible' as
meaning 'supportive of official American policy'. He was not,
however, sure of himself and that same day sent the script to Sir
Tim Nugent, the former Comptroller.

Nugent sent back a report which displayed the frankly right-
wing convictions endemic in the Lord Chamberlain's office,
and the hatred that the Royal Shakespeare Company inspired in
his department. But he was in political terms shrewd and level-
headed. His report on *US*, unlike Heriot's, did not succumb to
hysteria and rage. 'To ban or not is a purely political question,'
Nugent wrote in his report. 'If the Foreign Office were to say
that they believed the production would impair relations with a
friendly power then such a view would have to be given much
weight.' But, he observed in his worldly fashion 'most of the
anti-American, anti-war stuff' had already been published in
press reports and pamphlets. So 'with all the talk in the papers
about the anti-Vietnam war demos' the play was not 'exactly
new or earth-shaking'. He imagined that RSC audiences were
'usually the same, very left-wing beardies etc, so this play would
be preaching to the converted and I doubt if many recruits
would be won for the anti-Americans.' The act of banning a
play, he reminded Cobbold, 'always gets more publicity . . . and
I think this could probably be explained to that nice and very
sensible US ambassador [David Bruce].'

Nugent's comment about 'left-wing beardies' showed how
far he had lost touch with the contemporary theatre. He and
Cobbold's staff believed that sinister left-wingers, protesting

hippies and peaceniks made up the RSC's audience. In fact the people attending RSC performances tended to be liberal, young and middle-class. The Comptrollers much preferred the kind of theatre dreamed up by respectful, respectable pre-war play-wrights. They were at ease with plays about nice upper-class people who shot animals rather than people and were guilty of not much more than adultery committed offstage. Nugent had, though, recognised the nature of the new-wave theatre and its rejection of the drawing-room drama on which the London stage had depended for sustenance since the 1930s. Charles Marowitz, the American director who came to England in the summer of 1956 and was an editor of the new-wave theatre magazine, *Encore*, put the point well at the time. 'It is pointless to consider the changes in British theatre, in the late 1950s and early 1960s, outside the context of the new left movement of which the theatre was an integral part . . . In retrospect what was "new" about the New Wave was its willingness to face down establishment powers which had ruled the British theatre since before the war.'[17] No wonder, then, that Nugent betrayed his malicious bias. 'Do you think George Browne [sic] will try to get the RSC's subsidy cut?' he asked. 'That would be too good to be true, but he couldn't very well do it unless the play was produced.' The former Comptroller did not even have to justify his hope that one of the two most valuable theatre companies in the country should lose its subsidy. So much for the idea that the Lord Chamberlain was concerned about serious new drama.

Cobbold's next move, fortified by Nugent's recommenda-tions, was to immerse himself in the politics of behind-the-scenes persuasion. He invited George Farmer, the chairman of the RSC's finance subcommittee, together with Peter Hall, the artistic director and Peter Brook, *US*'s director, to visit him at his home on 30 September. According to Cobbold's report of the meeting, he told the RSC delegation that the play had given him 'considerable trouble' and that his initial inclination had been to refuse a licence. Without explaining his reasons for a change of heart or mind he told Farmer that the play would be licensed provided certain cuts in the text were made. He then read the text of a letter to Farmer in which Cobbold expressed his objection to disparaging references to President Johnson and other political figures, some examples of obscenity and one reference to drug addiction. If Peter Hall's own account of this meeting is taken as accurate then the Lord Chamberlain's minute is partial and hypocritical. According to Hall, Cobbold made it clear that while officially notifying the RSC he would license the show, subject to certain cuts, he would also attempt to use his influence to persuade the governors of the company to cancel the production. An ominous question was posed. 'Lord Cobald [sic] asked me whether I thought it right for a major theatre company in receipt of public funds to present something which was critical of a great ally with whom we had a special relationship.' It sounded as if Cobbold believed theatre companies that received public money were disqualified from presenting plays critical of the government. Hall replied by asserting the theatre's independence from its provider of funds. 'If the writers, the directors and other artists involved sincerely believed what they were saying, and had reached their judgements responsibly the short answer had to be yes.' The RSC director believed the theatre had 'every right to be as polemical as the press'.[18] Hall was already well versed in the Chamberlain's tactics when it came to matters of censorship. 'I think we all found in the 1960s that with every play causing problems you would submit it and it was emasculated by the Lord Chamberlain's office. The director would go down and have a chat and end up with a little bit more [left intact]. It was a process of negotiation.'[19] On this occasion, however, relations with America were involved and Cobbold was not amused. 'The Lord Chamberlain pondered . . . He then warned me that he would be having a word with my chairman (Sir Fordham Flower) and that the purpose of this would be to advise the cancellation of the show. He also reminded me that the president of the RSC was Anthony Eden, well-known for his fervent support of American intervention in Vietnam.'[20] This threat to exert pressure by having a word with the chairman of the board of governors of the RSC proved hollow.

Hall noted that Flower 'was outraged at this unofficial

interference, told me to go ahead with the production and discussed the whole problem with the board, getting their full backing.' Eden's feelings were dealt with in the traditional English manner. 'To prevent him being in an embarrassing position when we did the show, Fordie explained the situation to him and gently hastened his retirement (from the RSC Presidency).'[21] In a letter to Cobbold on 5 October, Farmer implied that the Lord Chamberlain had laid a trap for the RSC. At the RSC's meeting with Cobbold, Farmer had been asked for assurances that *US* 'was calculated not to give offence to responsible American opinion'. Farmer might just about have been able to agree to such a request, but Cobbold's letter to Farmer had substituted the word 'liable' for 'calculated'. When Farmer complained about the change of words Cobbold replied that he had never intended to make a distinction between 'liable' and 'calculated'. So in his despatch to the American ambassador on 11 October, that was marked 'Private and Confidential' Cobbold wrote saying he had been assured by the chairman of the RSC 'that [*US*] is not liable to give offence to American opinion'. But in Cobbold's judgement there was 'a risk that some people may see an anti-American slant in it'. The Lord Chamberlain explained why he had decided not to ban the show outright. 'I thought for a time of banning it, but the trouble is that this always causes an enormous hullabaloo and may well do more harm than good.' There was no more talk of censorship. There is no further reference in his files to any meeting with Fordham Flower. It may be that the official, who went through the Lord Chamberlain's censorship files before they were placed in the public domain, may have removed references to further discussions. The improper, bullying tactics had failed to make Hall fall into line.

There remained the business of purging the text of indecent language. *US* dealt with the dirty, murderous business of war, but the script-writers were only allowed to do so in purified or bowdlerised English. 'I see his great black cock sizzling and spitting like a cabab on a skewer,' had to be deleted, not because of the precise language, but because a penis was involved and a black one at that. References to soldiers masturbating were removed; soldiers were only allowed to meditate. Nor were they allowed to be the possessors of 'balls'. When it came to hard-hitting imagery, calculated to disgust or horrify, subtle changes of emphasis had to be made. 'Crawling and swallowing each other's sick' was moderated to 'crawling in one another's sick'. The difference was slight but it is an example of the level on which the RSC and the Lord Chamberlain's office negotiated.

A New Atmosphere

The fracas over Rolf Hochuth's play *Soldiers* endured acrimonious flutters of activity from the autumn of 1966 to April 1967, the last full year of the Lord Chamberlain's jurisdiction over the professional theatre. It ranged the newly fledged National Theatre against its own board of government-appointed directors. In particular the National's chairman, the former Conservative Cabinet minister Oliver Lyttelton, who became Lord Chandos, fought to impose censorship upon his own artistic director, Laurence Olivier, who wanted to present the play. Olivier had been pressed into support for *Soldiers* by his literary manager Kenneth Tynan. The play posed particular problems both in terms of censorship and of theatre politics. It was written by a young German and accused Winston Churchill and his adviser, Lord Cherwell, of 'being deliberate accomplices of the mass-murder caused by the blanket bombing of Dresden.' Worse, *Soldiers* claimed, without a shred of hard evidence, that Churchill had colluded in the assassination by the Secret Service of General Sikorksi, leader of the Polish government in exile. [22] Hochuth, whose attitude to Churchill was tinged with admiration, seemed to concede Sikorksi's despatch was a question of cruel, political calculation. He incorporated into his play a passionate debate about the morality of civilian bombing by the device of introducing the character of a former Bishop of Chichester, who had taken just such a pacifist position during the war.

Tynan's widow, Kathleen, conceded, 'As for the circumstantial evidence of foul play none of it stands up in the light of hindsight.'[23] Perhaps that did not matter to Tynan, the critic turned dramaturg; he was eager to cause uproar. He wanted to stage plays that dragged theatre into the cockpit of politics. Tynan's justification for mounting the play was expressed in an elated memorandum to Olivier on 23 December 1966. 'It's one of the most extraordinary things that has happened to British theatre in my lifetime. For once the theatre will occupy its true place – at the very heart of public life.'[24] This outburst stooped to silliness. The theatre would not be allowed to become a forum of political controversy while the Lord Chamberlain retained control of it. Moreover, Chandos had been Minister of Production in Churchill's War Cabinet and felt personally insulted.

The National's chairman was, he claimed, all for free speech, though not all for free action, when it extended to a few touches of mutual masturbation in Wedekind's *Spring Awakening*, whose production he and his fellow directors had banned two years earlier. Chandos's anxiety centred, he said, upon the seriousness with which the play might be regarded by foreigners if presented at the National Theatre. The Chairman imagined that the choice of venue was all important and influential. 'If we put on this play some poor Italian gentleman might say "Ha-ha, so that's what went on in England during the war". If somebody chooses to put it on at some theatre club in Hampstead, that's a different matter.'[25] Churchill's old Cabinet friend failed, however, to keep a professional sense of proportion and distance. *Soldiers* brought him out in egotism. 'You would have thought that anyone with . . . even common loyalty or good manners, would have refrained from putting up a play to a board whose chairman was a very close friend of Winston and the Prof [Lord Cherwell] who knows all the so-called facts are phoney,' Chandos wrote to a friend.[26] The right of a playwright to play false with known history, as Schiller had done in *Mary Queen of Scots*, or the problems caused when a board of theatre directors interfered with the choices of its artistic supremo did not concern him. When the play was at last produced in 1968 by Michael White, after the Lord Chamberlain's theatre powers had been repealed, a libel action was launched by the pilot of the plane who had alone survived the air crash killing Sikorski, and White ended up having to pay £75,000 in libel damages. Chandos's resolve turned out to be fortuitous for the National, saving it a large financial burden. He had also, to be fair to an autocratic and interfering chairman, supported the idea of building a national theatre all his life. He had feared, wrongly as it turned out, that there would be a furious public reaction if the play was staged. 'Getting a National theatre going has been forty years' work. I wouldn't like Tynan to ruin it in two weeks.'[27]

Soldiers was initially read in 1966 by one of the new Assistant Examiners, Kyrle Fletcher, who did not recognise the burden of the charge against Churchill. Fletcher believed the play dealt with 'ethical, spiritual and military problems of bombing open cities as an instrument of total war.'[28] The one specific problem for the Lord Chamberlain was Hochuth's controversial sugges-tion that General Sikorski's death at Gibraltar was engineered by the British Secret Service, since the Polish Prime Minister in exile constituted a potential threat to Anglo-Russian relations. A second difficulty was raised by the playwright's treatment of Lord Cherwell, Churchill's chief scientific adviser, who in Hochuth's 'seriously biased view', emerged as an advocate of saturation bombing of civilians. Fletcher's only other anxiety was the 'offensive' suggestion that the Royal Navy traditionally relied on 'rum, sodomy and the lash'.

Ronald Hill read the play a few days later and in the privacy of a memorandum dismissed Tynan as if he were a subversive schoolboy plotting to burn down his school. 'I am not surprised [*Soldiers*] has been taken up by Mr Tynan,' he wrote, 'since the latest aspect of the activities of the progressive theatre has been to move from the sphere of calculated political indecency, through the theatre of cruelty, to plays which fictionalise real events in the interests of a policy of antagonism to all in authority.' This glimpse of fury, this sign of what the Lord Chamberlain's officials felt about the modern theatre move-ments, its dramatists and literary managers, is revelatory. It belied Johnston's governing fiction that censors and theatre folk practised mutual admiration in private when they met to haggle over scenes and words. Michael White, who produced *Soldiers* in the West End, had set up a fascinating traffic of plays in the late 1950s and 1960s, from Jack Gelber's *The Connection*, with addicts awaiting their fix, to the homosexual prison drama *Fortune and Men's Eyes*. He looked back in contempt to the modes of theatre censorship and recalled the Lord Chamberlain's officials with distaste. 'When you went to see them it was like being summoned in front of a headmaster. They were all ex-army officers. They weren't friendly. They weren't sympathetic. They were just dogmatic and very, very set in their ways.' Peter Hall was similarly dismissive, remembering their appalling sense of humour. 'They rolled about with mirth when discussing a bit of buggery and then banned it.'[29]

Hill's hatred of plays that were anarchic and opposed to authority would have struck a chord with Robert Walpole and Harold Wilson. But you could not ban a play for such reasons. Hill himself realised this. 'I know that where there is a political context to a play the Lord Chamberlain is at his weakest, since the last thing he can afford to be accused of is political bias.' He, therefore, suggested that Lord Cobbold sabotage the play by taking a different line of attack. Hill argued, not with complete accuracy, that the Chamberlain had 'a mandate from parliament to forbid invidious representation', a mode upon which Hochuth apparently relied. In fact there was a ban upon the representation of living people in stage plays, whether famous or not, with some licence allowed for gently satirical impersonations of the famous in theatre revues. Hill was infuriated that Hochuth had, when dealing with actual historical events and real-life characters, dared to use his imagination. 'The whole of this play is imagination and it is imagination projected as fact through the mouths of the living or very recently dead.' Already, Hill recalled, there had been a production at Hampstead Theatre of *The Case of Robert Oppenheimer*, about the American physicist. Now Hill could see the theatrical future and it did not work as it should.

Dramatists were up to no good, playing around with known facts and without factual evidence imputing base motives to recently dead heroes like Winston Churchill. 'Each play will descend further into scurrility and the Lord Chamberlain will find himself in the position of trying to ration the amount of libel he allows,' he wrote, as if the vague but absolute powers vested in the Lord Chamberlain by the 1843 act were frail armaments. There was, in fact, no question of allowing a defamatory script a licence and Hill knew it. But he was fired by the challenge to the Chamberlain's control of the stage. 'I feel that the growth of this form of play constitutes a very cogent reason why the Lord Chamberlain should either lose the censorship or have his authority endorsed.'

Johnston, who always kept his cool in dealing with plays and playwrights, while Hill succumbed to the pleasures of hyperbolic reaction, was practical. He saw how the play could be legitimately stopped. It was simple. 'Sir Arthur Harris [Commander-in-Chief of Bomber Command] is still alive,' he wrote to Cobbold. 'Therefore quite apart from what the Churchill and Cherwell families might think I believe we should be justified in asking if Harris has any objection to the play.' Cobbold meanwhile took a behind-the-scenes approach. Lord spoke informally to Lord, closed mind to closed mind, and sewed up matters neatly behind closed doors. The Chamberlain wrote to Chandos at his Chelsea home asking, 'I wonder if there is any chance of our having a private and informal word about it if you are in London next week. Would you care to look in and have a drink one evening at my house in St James's?'

This informal exchange of views between the aristocrats resulted in their secretly colluding to frustrate Tynan. It was the first phase of a plan by which the National's board of directors thwarted the agenda of its artistic director (Olivier) and his literary manager. Cobbold came away from the meeting delighted. '[Chandos] is opposed to the NT putting this play on. The board discussed it earlier this week and in the end deferred a decision until they have a complete and definite script,' Cobbold wrote to Johnston. 'Please now write to Tynan and say "The Lord Chamberlain has now read the script and regrets that he is not prepared to make any comment until a final script is formally submitted on behalf of the board of the NT".' Tynan was treading on dangerous ground. He knew that Hochuth's hypothesis about a conspiracy to murder Sikorski would outrage historians. On 16 December 1966 Tynan had written to Isaiah Berlin soliciting his view of Hochuth's theory. Berlin had replied saying the idea was 'highly improbable and intrinsically too unlikely'.[30] By the time the board met Tynan had consulted a number of respected historians and gathered some faint-hearted support for Hochuth's theories. M.R.D. Foot, for example, told Tynan he thought the hypothesis was 'highly improbable . . . but I wouldn't put it past British Intelligence or the Secret Service.'[31] Only David Irving, the revisionist Hitler-admiring historian, gave unequivocal support to Hochuth. Tynan put his case in a memorandum for the board of directors at its January meeting. 'To suppress a serious work on a subject of national and international concern is an act that the board should not lightly undertake.'[32] The excited literary manager was astride cloud nine and was not to be coaxed down to the real world by cold douches of reality. There was something splendid and absurd about his campaign.

When Hochuth's final version of the play was finished, Tynan sent it to Sir Arthur Harris on 30 March, 'asking for permission to proceed'. Harris retaliated, writing to Chandos on 18 April that he found 'the whole thing thoroughly objection-able with references to me'. He felt the play defamed bomber crews who, 'at such bitter cost in casualties, we know saved this country from being the first recipient of the atom bomb and therefore from inevitable defeat.'[33] Harris's objection would have been sufficient to ensure that the Lord Chamberlain refused a licence for the play. *Soldiers* was likely to be libellous. Tynan, being neither diplomat nor boardroom tactician, did not plan his campaign. He did not seek support from the press by highlighting the way that Olivier's authority was being limited by Chandos. Instead he did his high-handed best to antagonise the Lord Chamberlain's office. Tynan's furious response on 10 April, to a letter from Johnston telling him the matter of a licence must rest until the fixing of a production date, was sheer, silly provocation. 'Nothing in the Theatres Act of 1843 stipulates that a theatre manager must guarantee production of a play before the Lord Chamberlain expresses an opinion. Will you kindly fulfil the function laid down for your office in law – namely that of informing us whether or not you will grant a licence for a performance of the play in question.' Tynan raged like Lady Bracknell in trouble at the theatre, 'The reasons for your procrastination are of course perfectly obvious. The implication is that you propose to judge the play by one standard if it is presented as the National and another standard if the National decides against it,' he accused. Tynan was wrong in his surmise.

This is the only example I have discovered in the Lord Chamberlain's files of a supplicant management writing not in the usual terms of humility or cringing deference, but with patronising rudeness. Of course Tynan's tone betrays resentment that his wish to stir a political scandal was being resisted. 'I think Hochuth is the test of our maturity – the test of our willingness to take a central position in the limelight of public affairs,' he said at the time.[34] The Lord Chamberlain, however, was required by acts of parliament to ensure the theatre could not become a focal centre for any serious political debate. Besides, Hill had reminded his superior, section twelve of the 1843 act stipulated that the Lord Chamberlain was only obliged to give his judgement on a script submitted for licensing when the date of a play's production was known. This was a pedantic, unhelpful ruling, expressly designed to frustrate and irritate Tynan.

At the crucial National board meeting on 27 April, Olivier, perhaps fired by the more radical spirits of Tynan and his wife, Joan Plowright, tried to assert the validity of presenting a political play that posed important questions but depended upon a fanciful premise. Plowright recalled asking Olivier what he thought of the play's value and his replying, 'I don't like the bloody thing. But I expect it'll get near to grounds for divorce if you think I'm frightened of doing new stuff. You'll despise me, won't you?'[35] Presumably on the advice of Tynan, Olivier read the board of directors a pointed extract from Aristotle's *Poetics*. 'The poet's function is to describe not the thing that has happened, but a kind of thing that might happen ... what is possible as being probable or necessary.'[36] The board was not impressed by such a hypothesis. Chandos wanted only to face the facts and the defaming of the reputations of famous men.

There was also the threat of direct political fall-out. The National's board was in negotiation with the Conservative-controlled GLC for the building of the new theatre. Chandos argued that the production of *Soldiers* might threaten the chances of obtaining the GLC's crucial finances. When the National's governing board refused to allow Olivier to present the play he made a public statement deploring its censorial action. From the Royal Shakespeare Theatre, Peter Hall supported Olivier, describing the board's decision as a 'black and miserable day for the English theatre'. Both men, though, missed the point. It was the form and scope of theatre censorship which militated against the production of the play upon any professional stage. Cobbold was able to ban *Soldiers* because of the slurs it cast upon Churchill's wartime record. Cobbold could reasonably judge that *Soldiers* threatened 'the preservation of good manners', 'decorum' and 'the public peace' in contravention of the 1843 act. Furthermore, not only Harris was alive and angry about the play. Cherwell's brother, Brigadier Charles Lindemann, although senile was still alive. On 28 September Cobbold received a letter from Lindemann's solicitor saying that the Brigadier 'would be greatly distressed by the presentation on stage in Great Britain of a performance which was a distortion of history and reflection upon the honour, judgement or morals of Lord Cherwell.' *Soldiers*, therefore, had to wait for public performance until 1968, after the Lord Chamberlain ceased to police the country's professional stage. When finally presented at the New Theatre by Michael White there was no outcry at all. The reviews were respectful rather than outraged. No one could quite understand why there had been such a huge, sustained fuss about the play's production. Politically motivated plays could now be staged. Heads of friendly countries could be condemned or ridiculed, Prime Ministers savaged. Yet no such plays were staged in London for the remainder of the century. The art of political satire, as practised on stage, had fallen into desuetude thanks to the Lord Chamberlain.

Notes

1. Hansard, May 1968, House of Lords, vol. 292, 3.
2. Hansard, op. cit., 1062.
3. William Gaskill, interview with author, February 1999.
4. Margot Heinemann, *Puritanism and Theatre* (1982), p. 39.
5. Geoffrey Wansell, *Terence Rattigan* (1995), p. 89.
6. Geoffrey Dearmer, interview with author, 4 April 1993.
7. LC file on *Follow My Leader*, Terence Rattigan.
8. Michael Holroyd, *Bernard Shaw*, vol. III 1918–50 'The Lure of Fantasy', (1991) p. 400.
9. Ibid., pp. 407–8.
10. Wansell, op. cit., p. 103.
11. Charles Duff, *The Lost Summer* (1998), p. 127.
12. Richard Findlater, *Banned* (1967), p. 159.
13. Ibid., p. 158.
14. LC file on *The Representative*, Rolf Hochuth.
15. Peter Hall, interview with author, April 1997.
16. LC file on *US*, Adrian Mitchell, Denis Cannan, Michael Kustow.
17. Charles Marowitz, *Burnt Bridges* (1990), p. 37.
18. Peter Hall, *Making an Exhibition of Myself* (1993), p. 196.
19. Peter Hall, interview with author, April 1997.
20. Hall, op. cit., p. 196.
21. Ibid., p. 197.
22. John Elsom and Nicholas Tomalin, *The History of the National Theatre* (1978), p. 200.
23. Kathleen Tynan, *The Life of Kenneth Tynan*, (1988), p. 251.
24. Kathleen Tynan, op. cit., p. 251.
25. Elsom, op. cit., p. 201.
26. Kathleen Tynan (ed) *Kenneth Tynan Letters* (1994), op. cit., p. 394.
27. Elsom and Tomalin op. cit., p. 201.
28. LC file on *Soldiers*.
29. Michael White, interview with author, 10 October 1999.
30. Tynan, *Letters*, op. cit., p. 374.
31. Ibid., p. 379.
32. Ibid., p. 378.

33. Ibid., p. 394.
34. Kathleen Tynan, *The Life of Kenneth Tynan* (1995), p. 251.
35. Tynan, *Letters*, op. cit., p. 253.
36. Ibid., p. 397.

5

NO FLUSHING, PLEASE,
WE'RE BRITISH

Imagine these scenes staged in a West End theatre some time in the 1990s. A fifteen-year-old girl, neglected by her parents and earning money by prostitution, is seen in bed having sex with a middle-aged man. By chance the police break into the room and the girl ends up in a children's magistrate's court. In the course of the hearing it is learned that the girl has had sex with a sailor, contracted syphilis and gone through an abortion. Such a play was staged in London and the act of under-age intercourse was discussed although not depicted. It all happened a very long time ago. *Pick-Up Girl* by the American writer Elsa Shelley opened at the New Lindsey Theatre Club in London's Notting Hill during 1946, and caused a sensation. The ancient Queen Mary went to see the play on the eve of her seventy-ninth birthday, having discovered an interest in juvenile delinquency. A group of people whom you would never expect to visit fringe club theatres briskly followed the dowager Queen's theatre-going example. After the performance, according to the play's director, Peter Cotes, the Queen confessed that 'she had not enjoyed herself so much for years'.[1] The Home Secretary, Chuter Ede, and several other Labour ministers and 'an impressive list of experts on juvenile delinquency' were soon observed in the audience. In view of *Pick-Up Girl's* success, the play was submitted to the Lord Chamberlain for licensing, since it was to be presented at the Prince of Wales Theatre.

'A very unsavoury theme but handled with all the decency possible,' Henry Game reported. 'I give the authoress the credit for sincerity . . . and despite the sordidness of the story the play has its beauties. The child herself . . . and the Judge . . . show facets of human nature that are admirable and very moving.' The play, he estimated, could not do harm, 'and if it brings home to some people the supreme importance of parental responsibility it can receive a licence.' The Lord Chamberlain, Lord Clarendon, read the play himself and agreed. 'The theme for the play is certainly unsavoury and certainly will make the squeamish squirm. But as it is sincere and brings out the great importance of parental responsibility it can receive a licence.' Norman Gwatkin, who thought *Pick-Up Girl* of great importance, did, however, warn the producer Frederick Piffard that three words were liable to cause such shock or revulsion that they would have to be excised. The words were 'abortion', 'syphilis' and 'miscarriage'. There was also a five-word sentence that had to be cut, perhaps because it left nothing to the imagination: 'They were both wearing nothing.' Another remark alluded discreetly to a sexual activity that was popular in the 1940s but had not then received a general seal of medical or public approval. 'He said I should go do something to myself' referred to masturbation and Clarendon was not allowing it. Information about these vetoes was then leaked to the London evening newspaper, *The Star*, which reported, 'On the West End stage and screen murder, strangulation and criminal lunacy are having a tremendous boom at the moment. The censor does not interfere, provided everything is said *in his West End way* [my italics].' When Peter Cotes subsequently complained about the cuts Clarendon relented and *Pick-Up Girl* was staged in its entirety.

Elsa Shelley's play marked the first phase of change in the censoring of the English stage after the Second World War. There survives a myth that not until the 'theatre revolution' at the Royal Court, the trail blazed by John Osborne's *Look Back in Anger* in 1956, did the Lord Chamberlain begin to contend with a new outspoken school of realism. This theory dramatises and caricatures a process that was evolutionary rather than abrupt. *Pick-Up Girl* caught the censorship process at a point of transition. The requirement that stage plays had to preserve the gentility of speech found in the mixed society of an upper-middle-class drawing room was no longer being so rigidly enforced. The Chamberlain had begun to accept that sexual matters could be discussed on stage provided, as *The Star* said, it was done in his 'West End way'. Williams' *A Street Car Named Desire*, performed in London two years later, was full of Yankee outspokenness. To allow the use of such words as 'syphilis' and 'miscarriage' signalled the willingness of the Lord Chamberlain to admit that the ordinary sexual facts of life could be mentioned if not discussed. The New Lindsey was in the tradition of theatre clubs and societies that, since the late nineteenth century, when *The Cenci* was given a single performance in 1881, had existed to stage productions refused licences by the Lord Chamberlain. The loophole in the Theatre Regulation Act of 1843, that appeared to exempt from the censor's control any play performed privately to those who had paid to join the club or society presenting a performance, was closed, in March 1966 when William Gaskill, artistic director of the Royal Court was found guilty of presenting the play, 'for hire' before it had been licensed. The illiberal Director of Public Prosecutions, Norman Skelhorn, wrote to Lord Cobbold on 3 May 1966, 'The Prosecution will probably have achieved the desired result of causing those responsible to cease from presenting unlicensed plays at the Royal Court Theatre in the way in which they were doing.' Skelhorn was right. Edward Bond's *Early Morning*, also refused a licence, was given a special dress rehearsal to which critics were invited.

Beckett's *Waiting for Godot* (1955) was a truly modernist play in terms of both form and content. It marked the arrival in England of what would come to be called the Theatre of the Absurd, and incidentally challenged the rules of polite stage diction. Here was the desolating calm before the storm of John Osborne. *Look Back in Anger* in 1956, at the newly formed writers' theatre at the Royal Court, led the charge of the new dramatists' brigade. Playwrights from then on chafed against the Lord Chamberlain's rules of theatrical engagement. Yet Beckett and Osborne were not the first post-war harbingers of theatrical change. Both before Peter Hall's arrival as artistic director and during it, the Arts Theatre Club ran daring seasons from the mid-1940s and all through the 1950s, with plays like Sartre's *Huis Clos*, Gide's *The Immoralist* and Julien Green's *South* that would have never been licensed by the censor.

In the first fifty-five years of the century the Lord Chamberlain, his Examiners and Comptrollers had sometimes been repelled or even appalled by the candour of foreign dramatists and their tendency to deal with facts of life which were unmentionable in polite, mixed society. The characteristics of theatrical modernism, the realist, surreal, symbolist, expressionistic and absurd styles as pioneered by Ibsen, Strindberg, Pirandello and Jarry, may have left the censors bemused. But at least these playwrights were foreign; English dramatists, with rare, rebellious exceptions, had been conditioned by the dark ages of censorship to accept its governing codes. The Lord Chamberlain insisted that dramatists give their characters a clean bill of speech, from which expletives, vulgarity and blasphemy had been purged. Dramatis personae spoke in a prescribed tongue of bland primness, detached from most people's realities. The English drama was an offshore island, impervious to the influence of Modernism. 'Since the great Ibsen challenge of the [eighteen] nineties, the English intellectuals have been drifting away from drama,' Kenneth Tynan, the most scathing, influential and left-leaning of post-war theatre critics, wrote in an article on 'West End Apathy' in 1954.[2]

There had been rare, recalcitrant exceptions to the generality of British playwrights who knew their place as docile entertainers. From the end of the Victorian age, when he wrote *Mrs Warren's Profession*, the Irish-born Bernard Shaw eloquently campaigned against the autocratic power of the Lord Chamberlain and his stunting influence upon the theatre. Granville-Barker, whose *Waste* was promptly banned in 1907, and Terence Rattigan, with *Follow My Leader*, were the only other significant playwrights to suffer the censorship of entire plays. Most writers for the theatre, though, knew the English form, which was to keep to the straight and narrow of a polite naturalism. The enthusiasms of these English dramatists might lead them to try to slip through some rude word or scene of impropriety, but in terms of subject matter and the forms in which they expressed themselves they were reassuringly conventional and traditional.

Kenneth Tynan, in his famous 1954 complaint, *West-End Apathy*, surveyed the West End stage and found it decrepit and exhausted with drawing-room comedies. He damned the 'peculiar nullity of our drama's prevalent genre, the Loamshire play.' Loamshire, the sort of place which boasted plenty of stately piles to which the Lord Chamberlain and his wife were invited for weekends, was a place where optimism triumphed. 'Except when someone must sneeze or be murdered the sun invariably shines ... Loamshire is a glibly codified fairy-tale world of no more use to the student of life than a doll's house would be to a student of town-planning. Its vice is to have engulfed the theatre, thereby expelling better minds.'[3] Even in the early 1950s, as the novelist Peter Vansittart recalled, West End playhouses were refuges from modern life 'where black-satined ladies of utmost gentility sold, with trained condescension, expensive chocolates and over-priced though uninformative programmes, and where at matinees, trays of tea and biscuits provided a rattling accompaniment to the next act.'[4]

The English theatre's long engagement with the romance and manners of the upper-crusted was rudely terminated when the New Wave seeped into West End theatre. The experience of the Second World War had hastened if not precipitated the erosion of the symbolic barriers dividing one class from another. Reverence for figures and symbols of authority dwindled in a society for whom deference was no longer instinctive. Britain's slow but remorseless loss of Empire; its declining status as a world power; the impact of a new, sexier youth culture which vividly manifested itself in a growing consumer society; in new popular music, the flash and glamour of young icons of screen and the recording studios, and the accompanying fashions; the increasingly secularised, sexually more liberal English society: all proved subtle but goading incentives for change in artistic behaviour. It was in the 1950s that wild seeds which flowered amidst the libertarian surge of the 1960s were sown.

Change was endemic. 'A confluence of altered moral

attitudes was starting to make the Lord Chamberlain's position increasingly problematic . . . Religious uncertainty exacerbated by the Cold War, the questioning of official attitudes, the diminishing respect for the Establishment . . . the emergence of a rock' n' roll culture; and the dawning of a liberal conscience that demanded access to contraception and the loosening of the laws governing homosexuality all brought into question the value of an institution that failed to permit freedom of expression.'[5] A post-war generation of young English writers, whether novelists or playwrights, were inevitably shaped or at least influenced by these upheavals. Some of them belonged to that generation of non-middle-class youth which had taken advantage of the Butler Education Act of 1944 and gone to university by virtue of state grants in aid, not thanks to their parents' money. The novel, not being policed by any special form of pre-censorship, was far freer to speak its mind. Kingsley Amis, John Braine, John Wain and Alan Sillitoe wrote novels of anger and protest about 'the unsmart reality of life in the provinces'.[6] Well before their time the novel enjoyed freedoms that the stage did not. In 1925 O'Neill's *Desire Under the Elms* was judged 'too horrible for performance', by George Street in a memorandum of 19 March. The play was sent out to the advisory board and when recommending that it be banned Buckmaster wrote, 'If it were turned into a novel it might well rival *Crime and Punishment*. But there's a great difference between book and [performed] play.'[7]

There was renewed criticism of the fact that the stage had to suffer a special form of surveillance against which there was no court of appeal. A theatre revolution is said to have broken out at the first brawling stroke of John Osborne's *Look Back in Anger*. In terms of its form and structure Osborne's play was, however, traditional. Its reputation as a revolutionary piece of work relies more upon its language and power, and how it was interpreted and understood. Jimmy Porter expressed the values and beliefs of the young and upwardly mobile post-war generation set upon challenging the power-structure, conventions and values of class-bound Britain. As such he was anathema to the Lord Chamberlain.

Writers like Coward and Rattigan, who had resorte
ambivalence, understatement and artful concealment of their
true intentions from all but a coterie of the sophisticated and the
cognoscenti, and the conformist ranks of English playwrights
who had prided themselves on their allegiance to all things prim
and proper, to escapism and frivolity, were now superseded by
direct plain-speakers. This new generation of left-wing playwrights, though Osborne himself soon outwore any such
political designation, dispensed with the old conventions. They
would have nothing to do with the theatre's petrified milieu of
the upper-middle-class drawing room; they wrote from per-
spectives of dissent and dismay; they had wild, unlikely hopes;
they aspired to make the playhouse and the play an agent for
social and political change.

While Osborne, Pinter, Arden, Mercer and Charles Wood
became identified and established as the voices of this new
theatre of disaffection, often lauded and applauded by theatre
critics and public alike, the Lord Chamberlain and his advisers
remained bastions of the old order. They tried to stand firm
while buffeted by waves of what they felt to be the new
indecency. In their reports and comments on controversial plays
submitted for licence the Examiners and Comptrollers began to
betray a slightly rattled, bewildered defensiveness.

Edward Bond's *Saved* (1965) was sent by Eric Penn to Tim
Nugent, in retirement in Chelsea Square, with a request for his
comments. 'I've read this revolting play which certainly ought
not be shown on any stage,' Nugent wrote back. On Bond's
depiction of the murder of an infant, smeared with excrement
and stoned to death, he commented, as if unmindful of the far
more graphic scenes of the murder of Lady Macduff's son in
Macbeth or of the Duchess of Malfi's in Webster's play. 'The
scene of the killing of the baby is the most revolting I have ever
read.' The fact that he was so shocked says something about the
docility that censorship had so long imposed on generations of
playwrights.[8] Nugent concluded on a note of wary, weary
caution as if he no longer believed that the censor spoke for
England or confidently reflected its feeling about what could be
said and done on stage. 'I suppose the Lord Chamberlain is not

the arbiter of taste and taste seems to be sadly low today.' He then made an artfully malevolent suggestion, seemingly that he believed the Royal Court was at war with the censors and had no serious belief in Bond's play. 'If the play is banned could not Devine [the artistic director] tone it down considerably and then put it on at his theatre club as an example of the Lord Chamberlain's prudishness, whereas if the play is not banned but merely cut to ribbons he couldn't bring off this childish score of the Lord Chamberlain.'

So no longer could the Lord Chamberlain and his advisers bask untouched in the higher reaches of grandeur. No longer could they remain entirely impervious to people critical of their decisions and standards. Playwrights and producers had to defer them, but the Lord Chamberlain's men did not abandon the seigneurial, patronising manners that directors like Peter Hall and producers such as Michael White resented. The censors even attributed malign motives to particular theatres and producers. This was not surprising, for the campaign against theatre censorship indirectly owed its impetus to the steady development of a system of government-financed theatres, funded by money channelled through the Arts Council. Theatrical experimentation and innovation were given official seals of approval as the result of this system of state aid. The profit motive was no longer the sole or most important criterion. George Devine, the Royal Court's first artistic director, spoke of the 'right to fail'. The producers were happy to see the Lord Chamberlain survive, because the Chamberlain's licence made them think their productions were immune from legal proceedings.

There must have been a little reference book for the Lord Chamberlain's staff, listing banned words and the dates when any forbidden word or phrase was at last permitted. The advent of the theatre revolution required that the Lord Chamberlain begin a new wrestle with dirty words, lots of them. In 1948 Charles Heriot went to see a club performance of a play about Oscar Wilde and listened to the audience's comments in the interval. 'They did not appear to know the difference between criminal libel and sodomy,' he noted fancifully in his report.[9] All the military men in the Lord Chamberlain's department obviously knew more than enough to distinguish between, say, fellatio and cunnilingus. But when it came to contemporary diction they were quite often bemused by words beyond their ken.

'I do not know what "crumpet" is supposed to mean,' Lord Chamberlain Scarbrough complained in a memorandum when Osborne's musical *The World of Paul Slickey* (1957) was causing no end of censorship problems. The dangerous line was simply, 'They'll make it much too hot for us to tackle any crumpet.' Brigadier Sir Norman Gwatkin did not know either, but he had asked Charles Heriot. The omniscient Heriot had reported on 6 April that crumpet was 'a recognised pseudonym for "the female pudenda" and the meaning certainly fits the rhyme and the functions.' No one thought to go out on the streets and discover what 'crumpet' meant in the real world. Scarbrough's response was to agree that the word would have to be changed, though he fancifully suggested 'I doubt if any but the esoterics will recognise anything scandalous about it.' This reference to 'esoterics' suggests that he remained unaware of how commonplace the word was among the classes with whom he had never mixed. American slang continued to pose nagging problems for the out-of-touch gentlemen of the Lord Chamberlain's office. They realised there was more to 'shit' than 'excreta', but *what*, exactly? Heriot gathered it meant 'heroin' to 'American negroes'.[10] When Heriot read *A View From the Bridge* on 17 January 1956 he was left in doubt over the word 'punk'. In English 'it means diseased whore', he observed. 'I do not know its exact meaning in American slang . . . I think we should have this point clarified and if necessary the word altered throughout.' Lord Scarbrough agreed.[11] When it came to that American term 'screw' as used in the sexual sense they reacted as if the only screws about which they knew were the ones used by their odd-job men. 'I'll screw you in that chair', the threat contained in *Tomorrow with Pictures* by Anthony Creighton and Bernard Miller (1960), was disallowed, with the helpful concession, 'The word "nail" would be acceptable.'[12] Heriot also busied himself trying to clean up and tone down the dirty new drama by suggesting odd alterations in outbursts of what now might be described as verbal cleansing. 'Omit "shit" and substitute "educated man",' he had directed mysteriously after reading Jack Gerber's play, *The Connection* (1960), imported from America and produced by the young radical producer Michael White.[13] It was actions such as these that gradually created a climate of opinion in which the Lord Chamberlain and his advisers made themselves laughing-stocks.

Letters sent out to theatre managements from St James's Palace with details of what could not be allowed in submitted play-texts would begin, 'I am desired by the Lord Chamberlain to inform you that he regrets that he must disallow from the above-named play those parts detailed in the annexure to this letter.' This parlance charmingly proclaimed an adherence to antique diction. By the mid-1950s the Lord Chamberlain's men had been forced to become text-cleansing officers, imposing the rules of dramatic hygiene upon scripts full of the likes of 'piss' and 'piss off', thick with 'shit', 'crap' and 'farting', and mention of naughty bits of the body like 'tits', 'balls' and 'arses', Genet's 'spot of sperm' and even 'up your arse', as Harold Pinter unsuccessfully tried to put it in *The Caretaker* (1960). They waded through shocking new theatrical terrain where vulgar words jumped out at them to cause affront. They were obliged to read texts where people talked about 'smoking pot' and being 'pissed': 'pissed off' was allowed in a 1965 revival of *The Caretaker* but 'piss-off' broke the tolerance barrier and was not permitted in Orton's *The Ruffian on the Stair* (1966). The dread words 'anally' and 'orally' had to be removed from Osborne's *Plays for England* (1962) and the phrase 'When you've slept with the bride and groom' had to be changed to 'When you've been on such intimate terms with the bride and groom'. It only required a verbal emphasis for this bowdlerised sentence to become a touch more salacious than Osborne had originally intended.

In retrospect there seems something hopeless about all these emending tactics. The Lord Chamberlain was like a tired old domestic vainly employed with bucket, scrubbing-brush and soap to rid the theatre of vulgar graffiti that kept on reappearing.

The problems proliferated. Where was a line to be drawn? Over what and whom? The boundaries were no longer certain or safe. The slow, seeping nature of social change in the 1960s even bore down upon the Lord Chamberlain. There was no longer a uniform code of values and rules by which the censor and his staff worked. The Examiner's report on Joe Orton's *Entertaining Mr Sloane* (1964), all three pages of it, betrayed signs of anxiety about the informal let alone the vulgar diction. The play was first read by an Assistant Examiner who issued a warning, 'There is no attempt to deal with the subject of homosexuality in a serious manner.'[14] That was true, but this fact bothered no one. Not until the 'serious', though laughter-inducing, drag scene caused *A Patriot for Me* to be banned the following year.

The Examiner wrote, 'There are many cuts which will have to be made.' He listed more than twenty of them. These ranged from 'Why don't you shut your mouth and give your arse a chance?' to 'He was an expert on the adolescent male body', by way of 'You wanted to see if my titties were all my own' and 'You've a whole bloody baker's shop in the oven from the look of that.' But the Examiner's report was itself examined and decorated with the words 'alter', 'warn', 'leave' and 'cut'. Lieutenant-Colonel Sir Eric Penn, the Comptroller, had been through the script reinstating most of the Examiner's excisions. The nuances of censorship were quaint. Penn required the removal of 'bugger' in 'lying little bugger' and inserted a warning that Sloane was not to touch 'the point where he judges her nipple to be', but allowed, as we have already seen, 'He was an expert on the adolescent male body' with its intimation of paedophilia and the hint of multifaceted sexual intercourse in 'he aches at every organ'. Penn also overruled the Assistant Examiner's cutting of Sloane's own scathing put-down to Kathy, 'What a cruel performance you're giving. Like an old tart grinding to her climax.' Lord Cobbold himself then went through the text himself and overruled his Comptroller, cutting 'grinding to her climax' again.

Osborne was an obvious rebel, criticizing, condemning and excoriating in a language of enthusiastic invective. Where Osborne led, riding the surge of the New Wave, plenty more would follow on. '*Look Back in Anger* presents post-war youth as it really is, with special emphasis on the non-U intelligentsia who live in bed-sitters,' wrote the jubilant young Mr Tynan in the *Observer*. The play might be a 'minority taste', he conceded, but the size of that minority was 'roughly 6,733,000 which is the number of people in this country between the ages of twenty and thirty.'[15] In his 1959 retrospect of the decade's theatre he gleefully noted, 'A change, slight but unmistakable, has taken place; the English theatre has been dragged, kicking and screaming into the twentieth century.'[16] Only five years earlier, he had judged, 'a three-power coalition of drawing-room comedy, murder melodrama and barrack-room' virtually dominated the West End, 'united in their determination to prevent the forces of contemporary reality from muscling in on their territory.' Escapism was the ruling theatrical mode. 'Anyone whose knowledge of England is restricted to its popular theatre would have come to the conclusion that its standard of living was the highest on earth.'

The values and attitudes of theatre-goers in the regions tended to be even more reactionary than those in London. Conservative government, took even the most trivial or wildly over-pitched public complaint about the avant-garde dramatists with seriousness. In October 1957, for example, when *Look Back in Anger* was presented at the Torquay Pavilion, the Home Secretary, R.A. Butler, was sent an intemperate letter of rage from a member of the public about Osborne's dialogue. 'It is the conception of a diseased and depraved mentality and the outpouring of a cesspool mind. I am at a loss to understand how this play could reach the English stage. I beg of you in the interests of what is left of sanctity and sanity to give this matter your immediate and earnest attention.' 'Treat officially', noted Butler's private secretary and sent the letter on to the Lord Chamberlain's office. Brigadier Gwatkin replied soothingly, agreeing the play was 'unpleasant'. He claimed inaccurately that 'a considerable number of amendments' had been required and thanked the writer for his view as it helped the Lord Chamberlain 'very much in his difficult task to hear what the public reactions are [sic].'[17]

After Beckett and Osborne, the New Wave playwrights brought to the stage subjects that the Lord Chamberlain believed should be left skulking in the closets where guilty secrets were traditionally hidden. Drug-taking, male homosexuality, sex education, lesbianism, the debunking of patriotism, the mockery of living politicians, the mistreatment of corpses on stage, ritual murder and the atrocities of post-adolescent delinquents formed the theatrical subject matter over which he had to brood.

The Connection, Jack Gelber's play about hard drug addicts waiting for their next fix, was ominous of the provocations laid out in the agenda of the new drama. There may have been half a century between the first performances of *Spring Awakening*, Frank Wedekind's turn of the century portrayal of adolescents in the first throes of sexual desire, and Bill Naughton's *Alfie*, about a wide-boy whose cockiness led him into a world of sexual grab-and-take and illicit abortion. But the frankness of these plays in dealing with sexuality launched them both upon a sea of troubles with the Lord Chamberlain. Plays involving blasphemy and acts of violence, like *Endgame* and *Saved* ensured that theatre censorship became a frequent source of press interest and concern. The exploitation of the revered and influential dead, as in Bond's *Early Morning* with Queen Victoria and Florence Nightingale, or in *Soldiers* with Churchill, might have been calculated to rack the old-fashioned and patriotic hearts of the Lord Chamberlain's staff.

The Examiners, Comptrollers and the Lord Chamberlain, for all the outbursts expressed in their confidential memoranda, believed they were doing their duty to withstand the forces of dissent. Since the Lord Chamberlain and his men were soldiers and administrators with little cultural awareness, they were mystified by modernism. The Theatre of the Absurd, as Martin Esslin termed one of the new trends, left them puzzled, and Artaud's Theatre of Cruelty, with its mystic notion of a magical drama which would shake you to your core, was beyond them. Johnston was so far out in the theatrical dark that he described Artaudian drama as consisting of 'exercises, improvisation and sketches'.[18] Orton would have been amused to discover that

Johnston considered his plays as belonging to the Artaudian genre. When it came to John Osborne's double bill of *Plays for England* (1962), in which a married couple are revealed as sexually fetishistic, up to sexual games with knickers, Gwatkin reacted as if the stage was being immersed in new wave filthiness. 'I am sure that a lot of people will swoon with delight at this latest effluent. I should think that the morals of anyone who pretends to understand what the play is all about will already be beyond contamination and the remainder will ride the storm unsullied . . . I wonder what abnormality Osborne's bleary eye will light on next.'

From God to Sexual Satisfaction

Samuel Beckett's *Waiting for Godot* (1955) with its two tramps waiting in wasteland for relief from their bleak lives, confounded the prevailing belief that plays should proceed on orderly narrative lines, as clear-cut as the sequence of traffic lights. 'It shifted people's expectations of what a play was,' Peter Hall, who directed the first English production, wrote.[19] The fact that no theatre critic, save for the revelatory Harold Hobson, appreciated the shock of the new, has acquired a mythic status. Certainly the majority of critics were angry and bemused. 'This play comes to us with a great reputation among the intelligentsia of Paris. And so far as I am concerned [they] may have it back as soon as they wish,' wrote Cecil Wilson in the *Daily Mail* on 4 August 1955. But *The Times'* critic, despite wondering whether Godot was exactly a play, had no doubts about the way in which Peter Hall's 'brilliant' production helped *Waiting for Godot* shine a fresh kind of dramatic light. 'That Mr Beckett – an Irishman who lives in Paris and writes for preference in French – possesses the dramatic instinct in a most original sense one cannot doubt.[20]

The tramps' odd diction, with its oscillation between the learned and the crude and its conflation of both, posed censorship problems of a sort rarely encountered before. Beckett's play was a harbinger of the new outspokenness and demotic frankness that would challenge the Lord Chamberlain's idea of what constituted acceptable theatre language, long before the most outspoken new-wave playwrights. The problems posed by *Waiting for Godot* were not numerous, but they were significant. The final concession, wrung from Scarbrough after months of negotiation over such things as 'arses' and 'erections', serves as a suitable epitaph on what seems now like the grand preposterousness of post-war censorship. 'I write to inform you that the Lord Chamberlain agrees to the words "Who belched?" being substituted for "Who farted?" ', Brigadier Gwatkin wrote on 1 July 1954 to the play's producer, Donald Albery. All reference to farting, let alone a simulation of the sound, which would cause no end of problems in 1964 when a play about a chronic farter was presented by the Royal Shakespeare Company, was forbidden. Even Beckett's tasteful compromise suggestion of 'Who did that?' had failed to take the Chamberlain's fancy.

Albery received a letter from Brigadier Gwatkin on 31 March 1954 containing twelve objections. The censor drew the line at the action of fly-buttons being buttoned, let alone the pointing to an unbuttoned fly, and the use of the word 'pissing' was out of court. When it came to the incident of Estragon's trousers slipping down, the censor was one anxious step ahead. He wondered whether any male sexual organ might rear its shocking head. 'Estragon must be well covered when his trousers fall,' he insisted. 'You piss better when I'm not there,' may have been sexually innocent, but it had to go. Worse, a hand 'pressed to his pubis' was quite out of court, as were 'the privates'. Erections, of the male sexual sort, were similarly profane, so 'It'd give us an erection' had to go, as did 'arse'. Mysteriously the Lord Chamberlain even refused to allow the stage direction, 'he resumes his foetal posture', as if this stimulation was too nasty to be contemplated. Even 'Gonococcus! Spirochaete', a recondite reference to gonorrhoea and syphilis was censored.

In a letter to Beckett on All Fool's Day 1954, Gwatkin soothed, 'If you feel very strongly about any of these alterations it is always possible to discuss the matter with the Lord Chamberlain's department ... I have found that the most effective way is to produce alternative dialogue, if an omission matters to the play, and it is surprising how near and how strong you can make the alternative.' This assertion, as Beckett would discover, was fanciful. The playwright, replying from his Paris home on 14 April in a typed letter, surprisingly agreed to try to compromise. 'I am prepared to try and give satisfaction to the Lord Chamberlain's office on ten of the twelve points raised,' Beckett wrote. 'This is for me a big concession and I make it with the greatest of reluctance. Were it not for my desire to be agreed to [sic] Mr Glenville [Peter Glenville, the director whom Albery had chosen for the production] and yourself I should simply call the whole thing off without further discussion.' On two points, however, Beckett refused to compromise. These were, he insisted, 'vital to the play and can neither be suppressed nor changed. I cannot conceive in what [way] they give offence and I consider their interdiction wholly unreasonable. I am afraid this is quite final. Until these two passages are reinstated as they stand there is no point in my submitting amendments of the others.'

Albery then visited Beckett and came up with a series of compromises. The hand which touched the 'pubis' would go no further than the stomach. The British practice of hanging those found guilty of murder had also caused a problem in relation to a reference to involuntary erections, the suppression of which Beckett agreed to. 'You piss better' would become 'You piddle better' and for 'Gonococcus! Spirochaete' Beckett suggested the substitution of 'Lord Chamberlain! Civil Servant'. It was also agreed that Estragon would 'be well covered when his trousers fall' and that 'the privates' would become the 'guts'. After Charles Heriot had attended a reading of *Waiting for Godot*, Beckett's sticking points, which concerned 'religious blasphemy' no longer posed problems. Even the syphilitic allusion, with its nice reference to the Lord Chamberlain, was allowed. Beckett, in another letter to Albery on 23 June, confirmed that he agreed to almost all of Albery's original bowdlerising proposals. The fly-buttons, however, which the producer had removed altogether, became coat-buttons; 'piss' became 'do it'. But sadly the production never materialised.

Albery was looking for a star and Alec Guinness, h
choice, was eager to perform in it with Ralph Richardson, but
Richardson never seemed to be available, according to Guinness's recollection.[21] The lightly expurgated play was seen in its
original version the following year at the Arts Theatre under
Peter Hall's direction. 'Waves of hostility came whirling over
the footlights,' one of the actors, Peter Bull, recorded in his
autobiography. 'And the mass exodus, which was to form such a
feature of the piece, started quite soon after the curtain had
risen.' That hostility was tempered and transformed the
following Sunday when Harold Hobson wrote his paean to the
play. The new wave was rocking not just the Lord Chamberlain's boat.

John Osborne, that resentful lower-middle-class boy with a
remarkable talent for abuse, landed himself and his plays in
various seas of trouble. He seemed, to one critic looking back at
him thirty years later, 'to cultivate a freelance indignation which
was all the more lucrative for being unrestricted by any coherent
set of principles or beliefs.'[22] Not since Bernard Shaw had there
been such an agitating dramatist and agent provocateur.
Osborne was no intellectual. He did not oppose theatre
censorship with Shaw's unrelenting rigour and vigour in
newspapers and magazines, by lobbying his fellow writers and
speaking with the persuasioan of wit and eloquence before a
committee of MPs and peers as Shaw had done in 1909. But he
faced up to the Chamberlain's vetoes with determination and
fury. His directors and producers followed on.

Look Back in Anger surprisingly laid down no serious challenge
to the Lord Chamberlain to negotiate. Indeed reactions at St
James's Palace to the play and subsequent negotiations over six
short passages in it were remarkable for their friendliness. Chief
Examiner Heriot produced a more sympathetic and understanding review of the new work than some theatre critics. 'This [is
an] impressive and depressing play,' Heriot remarked in his
report on 1 March 1956, noting 'it's careful observation of an
anteroom to hell.'[23] There was none of the Chief Examiner's
familiar moralising, few signs of outrage that Osborne should
dare to challenge the tenets of the status quo. True to the

restrictions of the Lord Chamberlain's rules, he recommended the cutting of a 'lavatory' and a 'homosexual' reference and the alteration of a phrase that contained the words 'excessive love-making'. Lord Scarbrough and Brigadier Gwatkin both read Heriot's report and overruled these vetoes. There were six other problems which related to matters of taste and diction and they were minor. The play's director, Tony Richardson, endeavoured to solve these by the art of persuasion.

There was often a narrow line between the acceptable and the banned. The Lord Chamberlain was sometimes inconsistent. 'Short-arsed' had to be changed, because 'arse' was too impolite. Yet that same year *My Fair Lady* contained Eliza's challenge, 'Move your blooming arse,' which was allowed. Lieutenant Colonel St Vincent Troubridge had then written with soothing irrelevance, 'This is a homely word, well understood by everybody.'[24] Despite this concession Harold Pinter fell foul of the ban upon 'arse' when he resorted to the word in *The Caretaker* (1960). 'Ah,' said a disingenuous official in the Chamberlain's office when the example from the year before was produced. 'But in *My Fair Lady* there is a lot of noise on the stage at the same time.'[25] A couplet sung by Jimmy Porter, with the words, 'I could try inversion, but I'd yawn with aversion', was cut presumably on the grounds that homosexuality was frivolously treated. The amended and accepted lines, 'This perpetual whoring,/ Gets quite dull and boring,/ So avoid the python oil/ And pass me the celibate oil', at least boasted the virtue of a not quite penitent sinner. On the other hand, 'There's a smoke-screen in my pubic hair', which had to be cut, was replaced by Osborne's acceptable but far more salacious suggestion of 'You can quit waiting at my counter Mildred, 'cos you'll find my position closed.'

One lengthy speech caused exchanges of letters between the Royal Court and St James's Palace and would reveal how innocent the censors sometimes were. Jimmy Porter described his wife Alison in unusual terms. 'She just devours me whole every time, as if I were some over-large rabbit, and lies back afterwards like a puffed out python to sleep it off. That's me buried alive in there and going mad – in the peaceful coil of that

innocent-looking belly.' The reference to Jimmy being dev-
oured whole would today raise the suspicion that he was talking
about oral sex; the swallowing python could suggest this. Oral
sex would then have caused horror. The Lord Chamberlain's
men were so unsophisticated that you could have convinced
them that fellatio was an ailment affecting cats and cunnilingus a
variety of sore tongue. Osborne was saved by their ignorance.
The censor was concerned with the image of the sleeping,
puffed-out python rather than its efficient, swallowing activities
and the distinctly vulgar simile of the large rabbit swallowed
whole easily survived. Osborne had to remove the word 'belly'
so the phrase became 'in that peaceful looking coil'. By 28
March the tussling was over. *Look Back in Anger* was licensed to
make theatrical history.

Osborne's war with the Lord Chamberlain moved beyond
preliminary skirmishing when *The Entertainer* was submitted for
licensing. This time Assistant Examiner Troubridge read the
play and haughtily condemned it, not just for 'a good deal of
verbal dirt and smart Alec lines like 'The church-bell won't
ring tonight, as the Vicar's got the clappers', but for inducing a
mood of 'aversion and disgust' as well. He disparaged Osborne
for 'the vitriolic negativism' that Troubridge had already
discerned in *Look Back in Anger*. 'The whole play is impregnated
with sex, sexy references and half references, and general
lavatory dirt,' he reported.[26] What he meant by 'lavatory dirt' is
not clear, but Troubridge was probably referring to the vulgarity
of Archie Rice's turn of phrase. Osborne was offering vigorous
alternatives to the dull, doctored stage language of the time. A
compact inventory of profana was drawn up. In almost every
case the banned words, phrases or sentences had sex periphrasti-
cally in mind. 'Ass upwards', 'clappers', 'pouf', 'shagged',
'rogered', 'turds', 'camp', 'wet your pants', 'had Sylvia' and 'I
always needed a jump at the end of the day and at the beginning
as well' all had to be removed from the text. Phrases such as
'Poke the fire', 'pissed up', 'a couple of fried eggs', 'she needs
some beef putting into her' and 'Have you ever had it on the
table?' were, however, all permitted. It was hard to see any
consistency about the Chamberlain's rules.

Obviously such words as 'turds' and 'shagged' are vulgar but if 'had Sylvia' and 'wet your pants' were censored, how on earth could the blatant innuendo of 'she needs some beef putting into her' be permitted? Why was 'poke the fire' allowed when it was understood by the Examiner to be 'a double entendre on one of the words for having intercourse'? Why sanction 'a good blow through', 'pissed up' and 'a couple of fried eggs', when the eggs in question were 'the lowest words for breasts'? Buffeted by the waves of the new indecorousness, the Lord Chamberlain flailed in confusion. In reply to the Examiner's vetoes, Tony Richardson, directing *The Entertainer*, sent a pleading letter to Sir Norman on 21 March 1957, tactlessly signed for him by his secretary, Miriam Brickman. Richardson wanted to achieve the reinstatement of several of Osborne's phrases, but he appears to have been half-hearted in his efforts and gave up where even the most trivial infringements of verbal propriety were involved. 'We will omit "right up to the flies" . . . We will omit "wet your pants". We will omit "had Sylvia". We will omit "turds".' The letter was scrutinised by both Gwatkin and Heriot, whose negative comments decorate its pages. 'Ass-upwards' was changed to 'cock-eyed' without argument, but when it came to 'The church-bells won't ring tonight because the Vicar's got the clappers', Richardson's ingenuity failed to convince. 'Naturally as the play is in the music-hall convention, Mr Osborne wanted the pun on the word "clap" but thought that in doing this he was avoiding any possible offence to the majority of the audience and that the pun itself would only be appreciated by the sophisticated.' Gwatkin's marginal comment on this sugges-tion is a startling index of the Comptroller's loathing of the playwright. 'Good thing if J.O. had [the clap] he wouldn't pun so much then,' he wrote in school-boy tones.

So there could be no persuading them. The dull, euphemistic 'The Vicar's dropped a clanger', that Richardson had suggested, was of course approved. 'No. No,' Heriot wrote, when asked to approve the change of 'shagged' to 'screwed'. 'Yes, yes,' he approved, where Richardson agreed that the shocking, banned adjective 'camp' should be changed to 'weird'. When it came to 'balls', a word that would loom large and problematic in

Osborne's censorship battles over his play *Luther*, Richardson begged that the word should be given 'special consideration . . . The whole effect of this story depends upon its shock effect and we would suggest in this context that it is not in the least suggestive. This effect is meant to be a contemporary equivalent of the famous "not bloody likely" and there is simply no other equivalent we can possibly find.'

Richardson's reference to the sensational utterance of this adjectival expletive in the London première of Shaw's *Pygmalion* (1912) was to no avail. It must have been a rare blast of Edwardian libertarianism that overcame an earlier Lord Chamberlain when he permitted the word to be uttered upon the English stage. After all, Lord Chamberlain Sandhurst required the removal of the more innocuous 'damn' from Noël Coward's very early play *The Young Idea* (1920).[27] Peter Fryer in his *Mrs Grundy: Studies in English Prudery* found that 'bloody' was not spoken on stage again until Coward's *Red Peppers* in 1936, and even then a line was drawn at Coward's use of the word 'farting'. The popular scriptwriter Ted Willis was forbidden to use the expletive in one of his first plays in the late 1940s and it was not until *Billy Liar* (1960) that the word was freely voiced – some 249 times according to Willis's count.[28] In view of such an extreme tradition of prudishness it is no wonder that Heriot and Gwatkin reacted with contempt to this proposition.

'No. A thousand times No. Who does this Osborne think he is,' demanded Heriot irrelevantly in a scrawl in the margin of *The Entertainer*. 'Well, I'm really astonished,' Gwatkin wrote. After Gwatkin had seen the play he wrote a letter to Troubridge on 29 April in which he professed a surprising enthusiasm for it. 'It is a very good cast. You ought to see it if you can.' Troubridge replied the following day, 'It seems to me our venerable institution of the Revels is under stronger attack at the moment than at any time since Percy Smith's bill ten or twelve years ago.' Troubridge's allusion was to the Conservative MP E.P. Smith, also a minor dramatist, who had been one of the sponsors of Benn Levy's 1949 private members' bill. Levy, husband of the actress Constance Cummings and author of several, essentially light-hearted West End comedies, had been elected a Labour MP in 1945. Michael Foot, the most unswerving opponent of theatre censorship described Levy as 'a brilliant polemic writer' and Miss Cummings has recalled the intensity of his opposition to the Lord Chamberlain, even though his own plays did not suffer any major blue-pencilling emendations. But Levy could not attract sufficient support from MPs. His Censorship of Plays (Repeal) bill won a second reading by 76 votes to 37. But Mr Atlee's Labour government had insufficient parliamentary time to take the bill further.

With Osborne's musical *The World of Paul Slickey* and history play *Luther*, hostilities became more unpleasant. Not only words but whole sentences had to be excised from the scripts. The words 'crumpet' and 'crabs' were forbidden, and the words took on a grubbier complexion when in the context of Osborne's musical. 'They'll make it much too hot for us to tackle any crumpet' and 'stop fishing for trouble and catching any crabs',[29] were hot with innuendo. Oscar Beuselink, Osborne's lawyer wrote to Gwatkin on 28 March 1959, implying that the Lord Chamberlain was so far behind the times that he could not recognise what had become common parlance. 'With respect the expression crumpet is now fairly universal use and can be construed as referring to ladies or girl friends and not as appertaining to any part . . . of the physical anatomy . . . My client feels that "fairy" and "queer" have now become accepted expressions.' Gwatkin was not convinced. So Beuselink conceded to the changes on 9 April. 'My client is prepared to substitute for the word "fairy" the word "swishy" and for the word "queer" the word "queen".'

Once the show was out on tour problems began. Emile Littler, a West End producer of musicals, light comedies and pantomimes who was licensee of the Palace Theatre, where *Paul Slickey* was scheduled for London production, appeared bizarrely eager for the musical to be banned. An undated memorandum by Gwatkin to Lord Scarbrough reported on a visit to St James's Palace by an obviously disturbed Littler who had never seen 'anything so suggestive in the way of business on the stage before . . . Littler said that (at Leeds) whole blocks of seats got up and left and that there were boos and cat-calls at the end. He was very afraid that when the play came on in London [the following week] there might be a riot.' Gwatkin made a shrewd guess about Littler. 'I may be wrong, but I think he is backing a loser and would like the Lord Chamberlain to step in and relieve him of his trouble. He asks that someone from this office should go to Leeds and see the play in the hope, I believe, that it would be banned.' Scarbrough took the warning seriously and may have contemplated either banning the musical or making cuts in it before the production's arrival in the West End. 'If the first night is on Monday,' he wrote that same day, 'we may have to take quick action on Tuesday morning.'

The Chamberlain's resident master of bigotry, Ronald Hill, was despatched to see the potentially offending musical in Leeds. He was unable, however, to raise more than an odd quiver of irritation. As for walk-outs in the ranks of the disgusted, why there were only two people, he reported on 5 April, who left. He identified them as 'elderly and refined in appearance'. The cause for concern centred upon that flare-point for moral disruption, a bed. Osborne's stage direction had specified that a man should be seen respectably sitting on a large bed while beside him was a girl called Deirdre, wearing breeches and a slip.' But something had shockingly gone wrong on the journey from page to stage. 'The scene opens with Jack in his shirt and trousers lying on top of Deirdre on the bed, with Deirdre in the costume described. Since a good deal of the next part of the dialogue is punctuated by Jack stuffing his shirt back into his trousers and as the bed is disordered, it is plain that intercourse has just ceased,' Hill reported. What was even more telling: 'Deirdre doesn't trouble to stuff her slip back inside her trousers.' This is a useful example of Hill's sexually fixated mind at work. Why should the couple have not just been kissing and caressing? The scene would still have been illicit, since the Lord Chamberlain did not allow a man and a woman to be seen lying on a bed. Gwatkin stipulated in a letter to Littler on 4 May, 'I am directed by the Lord Chamberlain to inform you Jack and Deirdre must sit on the bed as allowed. They may not lie. Jack must be fully clothed, not *en deshabille* and Deirdre's slip must be in her breeches.' Furthermore the decency of the English civil service and aristocracy had to be protected from salacious mockery. 'No substitute referring to the Income Tax Inspector as a homosexual will be allowed.' The reference to the Honourable Penelope Cumming, 'Well I suppose she's always worth a few inches', had to be deleted as well, although Gwatkin creatively suggested, 'An acceptable substitute for "inches" would be lines.'

Osborne then lost patience and intervened, writing a fuming letter on 5 May, that revelled in Pooterish self-importance. 'The behaviour of your office has been determinedly frivolous and irresponsible, and because of my past public opposition to the function of your office it is difficult not to assume that the treatment I have received at your hands stems from a desire on your part to be wilfully obstructive,' he raged. On 7 May 1959, it is recorded in the *Paul Slickey* file that Gwatkin sent a memorandum to the Lord Chamberlain saying, 'I would like to reply as Lord Alfred Douglas to his father "You silly little man".' Of course he did not. Instead he politely turned the other cheek and wrote, 'The Lord Chamberlain wishes me to say there is no kind of prejudice against you in this office and to ask you to dismiss that from your mind.' Osborne would not have known what had been scribbled by someone in the Chamberlain's office, across his letter. Where Osborne had written, 'Your office seems intent upon treating me as if I were the producer of a third-rate nude revue', the words 'which he is' had been added.

Osborne was then at the height of his fame and reputation. He did not court publicity, but he attracted it as a dog does fleas. The Lord Chamberlain's censorship was for him like a chronic itching complaint. 'It's the sheer humiliation that's bad for the artist,' he told Kenneth Tynan in the early 1960s and gave a vivid impression of just what it felt like to be a forthright young dramatist at the time. 'I know playwrights who almost seem to be living with the Lord Chamberlain – it's like an affair. There's a virgin period when you aren't aware of him, but eventually you can't avoid thinking of him while you're writing. He sits on your shoulder like a terrible nanny.'[30] Osborne's refusal to treat the censor with traditional deference challenged the Lord Chamberlain in a way that may have given Scarbrough grounds for anxiety. First there was Osborne's attack upon the haphazard methodology of censorship, which, though it would have caused resentment, could be suffered. As Osborne wrote to Scarbrough:

> What I find most bewildering is the lack of moral consistency and objectivity which seems to characterise your recent decisions – decisions which seem to be reversed and changed because of the whim of any twisted neurotic who cares to write to you and exploit his own particular sexual frustration or moral oddity. In paying attention to what is without question an infinitesimal and lunatic minority you are doing a grave injustice not only to myself but to the general public and your own office. During the past three weeks something like 30,000 people have seen this play [*Slickey*].
>
> Do you honestly believe that the proportion of those who walked out (not one in Leeds) or who wrote to you – all of whom cannot number more than a few dozen – fairly represent decent and informed public opinion? In view of the recent relaxation of policy I can't believe that you wish to encourage this appalling situation at the expense of the serious writer and his public.

This charge was as nothing compared with the menace of his peroration. 'It is unquestionable,' he conceded in a sentence intended to placate, 'that public opinion is supportive of the liberality and enlightenment pursued by you on other occasions and public interest in the matter is tremendous.' On the other, more dangerous hand, Osborne revealed he had 'been approached by most of the national newspapers for the right to print the entire text of my correspondence with your office. This has seemed to me to be an invitation to sensationalism which could obscure a serious subject. Accordingly I have tried to behave responsibly in a difficult situation which is trying for all concerned.' This threat to publish must have tapped potentially raw nerves at St James's Palace. Scarbrough and his predecessors always wished to keep their censoring activities cloaked in confidentiality. The idea was to ensure that no one beyond those directly concerned knew the details of their censoring commands. Thus they could ensure there was no analysis of their actions or consistency. By the end of the 1950s, the Chamberlain and his staff knew that some of their decisions were vulnerable to derisive exposure in the press. Osborne would not play by their rules. Besides, Scarbrough had launched his investigations on the basis of two individual complainants – one of them a letter-writing member of the public.

Hill was sent to observe the West End first night and reported back on 5 May in voyeuristic tones reminiscent of those employed by the detectives watching *Fata Morgana* more than thirty years earlier. 'The Lord Chamberlain's requirements were ignored. The scene opened with Jack lying on top of Deirdre. There was no motion. On removing himself it was seen that his tunic shirt was unbuttoned all down the front.' But 'the shirt-stuffing back business' was much modified. 'Deirdre's slip was observed to be inside her breeches and she had an open jacket.' The significance of this alteration was that on the eve of the 1960s the Lord Chamberlain was still intent on banning not only what he regarded as lewd, but actions suggestive of lewdness having taken place already.

A year later, when Osborne's *Luther* was submitted to the Lord Chamberlain, Tynan recorded that the Chamberlain 'blue-pencilled eighteen passages – many of them entire speeches' and the playwright responded with a brave though supercilious ultimatum to his producers, George Devine at the Royal court and Oscar Lewenstein. 'I cannot agree to any of the cuts demanded under any circumstance. I don't write plays to have them written by someone else. Nor will I agree to any possible substitutes. I intend to make a clear unequivocal stand on this because (a) I think it is high time someone did so, and (b) the suggested cuts or alternatives would result in such damage to the psychological structure, meaning and depth of the play that the result would be a travesty.' All along the lines of protest he made it clear he would not yield an inch. 'I will not even contemplate any compromise . . . I am quite prepared to withdraw the play from production altogether and wait for the day when Lord Scarbrough is no more.'[31] For the first time that century the Lord Chamberlain bowed to a writer's complaint. After a meeting between Gwatkin and Devine and Lewenstein, Scarbrough sanctioned all but four of the sections which he had banned just two weeks earlier. The Chamberlain still drew the line at 'piss' or rather 'monk's piss and convent piss' and 'piss-scared', 'crap' and 'balls of the Medici'. But it was only the balls that caused the problem, since 'testicles of the Medici was allowed as an alternative'. In vain did Osborne plead that Shakespeare had made use of 'piss' in *The Tempest* ('Master I do smell all horse piss.') and that to make the change to 'testicles' would be simply absurd.[32] Some important victory had been won. Osborne had fought battles of attrition with the Lord Chamberlain and forced him to moderate his prudish grip upon the stage.

The Lord Chamberlain not only banished blasphemy from the stage he also showed his respect for the Almighty by ensuring that He could never appear on stage until 1966. *The Green Pastures* by the American dramatist Marc Connelly had been refused a licence in 1930 because God appeared on stage as a black man dressed in a white shirt and bow tie. The Archbishop of Canterbury and George V were consulted by the Lord Chamberlain about the idea and, whether or not they believed God was a white Englishman, they approved Lord Cromer's ban upon the play. In the 1950s and 1960s two archbishops, the conservative Fisher and the liberal Ramsey, continued to advise the Lord Chamberlain that God could not be seen or heard on stage.[33] Sir Alec Guinness, who recalls his generation of actors 'laughing in an outraged way' at the censoring of 'damns' and 'bloodys' from plays, went to a meeting with the Lord Chamberlain, accompanied by Arnold Wesker and Dame Sybil Thorndike. They had gone to plead for 'a play written by Wesker about Christ which required the personification of Christ on stage. I think we would have won if Wesker had not been so plain rude.'[34] You could not even speak the word 'Christ' or 'Jesus' as an expletive at the time.

Wesker had had three 'Jesus'es and 'Christ's removed from his *Chips with Everything* and four Christs from *The Kitchen*.[35] Such words, Cobbold said in his 1965 *Sunday Times* interview, 'still do give offence to a great number of people.'[36]

A typical example of the censor's attitude to irreligiousness is provided by the response at St James's Palace to Beckett's *Endgame* (1957 and 1962). The play was first presented in French at the Royal Court in 1957 under the title *Fin de Partie*. Problems over censorship began when an English translation was provided. On 25 January 1958 Lord Harewood, who was on the governing body of the Royal Court's English Stage Company, accompanied George Devine to St James's Palace to discuss the play's production in English. Brigadier Gwatkin commented, 'They came as far as I can see to try and blackmail us into passing the passage on page 28, because the press would make an uproar if this play could not be given in public for that reason.'[35] The offending blasphemous words about the Almighty – 'The bastard – he doesn't exist' – did duly cause problems of censorship. But the idea that the massed ranks of the press would fight for Samuel Beckett was wildly fanciful. The Lord Chamberlain drew the line at the blasphemous suggestion when it was printed in English. The Royal Court was informed that the sentence had to be removed. The Almighty was taken very seriously by the Lord Chamberlain. His name could not be taken in vain.

Gwatkin, in the weirdest of his effusions, wrote on 12 February 1958 to Troubridge, to explain his theory of how the process of corruption worked when you went to the theatre. 'I feel that the people erudite enough to go, understanding, to a French play, can take a great deal more dirt (I use the term broadly) than an average English audience seeing a direct translation in English. Quite apart from the fact that the French words sound more delicate than the English equivalent.' Here was an echo of the Victorian belief that the drama was often liable to provoke the working classes to insurrection. There was a trickle of publicity in the national newspapers when news seeped out that the Lord Chamberlain would not license the play in English without cuts. The *Evening Standard* asked, 'Does this mean that the Lord Chamberlain considers all people who understand French beyond hope – unredeemable atheists or agnostics who need not be protected from blasphemy? Or does he believe that knowledge of the French language bestows immunity from corruption?'[38] Negotiations between theatre and censor continued through the summer months. By 27 June 1958 a possible way of saving the atheistic sentiment on which Beckett insisted was contemplated. 'We shouldn't worry about "He doesn't exist"' the Lord Chamberlain's department conceded. But 'we do draw the line at calling the Almighty a bastard.' Or as Brigadier Gwatkin helpfully put it, 'Whether you refer to God as a dirty person or as a bastard it is blasphemy.'

Troubridge read the play on 5 July and reported, 'Though I still contend that the play is great nonsense and largely incomprehensible I saw nothing objectionable except "the bastard he doesn't exist".' Troubridge's bemused literalism was, of course, in line with generations of Examiners for whom modernism was anathema and a cause of bewilderment. Many theatre critics were of a similarly arthritic and reactionary cast of mind. But Harold Hobson often reacted imaginatively to the shock of the avant garde. In the case of Samuel Beckett it was Hobson not Tynan who first recognised and responded to the wealth of his bleak genius. '*Fin de Partie*,' he wrote, 'has outraged the philistines, earned the contempt of half-wits and filled those who are capable of telling the difference between a theatre and a bawdy house with a profound and sombre and paradoxical joy.'[39] The Lord Chamberlain and his censors did not, therefore, altogether speak for middle England when reacting with contempt to the puzzle of the new drama.

By 31 July Beckett had conceded the small but crucial alteration that God would be described as 'a swine' rather than a bastard. Similar euphemising stipulations meant that 'made a balls of' was changed to 'botch', while 'arses', 'balls' and 'pee' were all removed from the text. The Lord Chamberlain did, though, reluctantly acknowledge the mood of the times. Five years later the Royal Shakespeare Company presented a revival of the play. On 22 May 1964 Michael Hallifax and Donald McWhinnie, who was directing the play, went to St James's Palace to try to persuade the Lord Chamberlain to allow the return of the original offending words. The official memorandum dealing with the problems and the meeting was as po-faced and humourless as ever. 'They asked whether balls in the sense of having made a "muck-up" could be allowed. They particularly asked that they might be allowed the word "pee". The alternative is piss and also discussed piddle,' it was minuted. 'I am wondering just how offensive the word "pee" is now. They asked for arses. I said that in all probability this would be allowed.' It took several weeks for the censors to wrestle with these weighty matters of theatrical taste. On 30 June 1964 a decision was announced. 'The reinstatement of arses is allowed.' But 'balls', 'pee', 'piss', 'piddle' and 'bastard' remained outcast words, unspeakable on stage.

Hallifax did not remember this meeting but had vivid recollections of his frequent visits to St James's Palace. 'There was so much toing and froing and letter-writing. I used to take playwrights there as a last resort to see if they could sway the Lord Chamberlain's representative [Johnny Johnston, the Assistant Comptroller].'[40] RSC writers would regularly come at him complaining, 'Why the hell won't they allow that? It's just ordinary speech.' Hallifax would then suggest they should go and see Johnston and Mr Hill, 'to get a compromise. And when we were there they'd say you can't have "fuck" or "bugger" or some ludicrous word. I got on very well with Colonel Johnston. He was brilliantly cast. I liked him a lot. He looked perfect sitting there at his huge desk. He really did his best. I didn't like Mr Hill. He was a dreadful man. He was never particularly helpful.' It was a campaigning time, Halifax remembered, with Peter Hall and William Gaskill, from their firing-line positions at the RSC and the Royal Court, urging the end of theatre censorship. 'It was becoming stupid. The Second World War had changed so much. Theatre censorship really should have ended after the war – the whole world was different.'

Shock Troops from the Subsidised Theatre

In the 1960s state subsidy for the theatre, channelled through the Arts Council, and then with increasing lavishness when Jennie Lee was minister with responsibility for arts in Harold Wilson's 1964 and 1966 administrations, indirectly assisted in the campaign to terminate the Lord Chamberlain's control of the theatre. The new, large state-funded theatres – the Royal Court under George Devine, Peter Hall's Royal Shakespeare Company, the newly instituted National Theatre at the Old Vic and Joan Littlewood's Theatre Workshop at Stratford East – were all caught up in protracted censorship tussles with the Lord Chamberlain. The artistic directors of all these theatres, supported by the liberal ethos of the Arts Council, were relatively free from the imperative of profit-making. Their bold choice of plays by avant-garde dramatists meant they were forever negotiating and haggling with the Chamberlain's staff over scenes and words. Most of the commercial producers, though Michael Codron and Donald Albery ranked as admirable exceptions, were primarily concerned to achieve profit with honour, that honour being a knighthood. This meant they did not risk annoying the Lord Chamberlain.

Peter Hall's decision in December 1961 to give the newly incorporated Royal Shakespeare Theatre Company a year-round presence in London remorsely stiffened opposition to the Lord Chamberlain's censorship. Ever since he had run the Arts Theatre Club in the 1950s Hall had been set upon directing work by playwrights new and old that offended the censors' notion of theatrical propriety. He remembered that he and the other subsidised theatre directors saw it as their duty to fight the censorship war. 'We had a sense of taking on the Lord Chamberlain. We derided him and his office and it made copy for the newspapers. We said the Chamberlain can't survive. We've got to go on pushing. One of the reasons the Lord Chamberlain caused controversy and embarrassment was that he was part of the royal household,' Hall told me.[41] 'My main memory of the Lord Chamberlain's censorship was of a conspiracy to maintain a totally fictional idea of society, with a patriotic, prep-school attitude to life. All the censors were retired military men with the most appalling sense of humour. When it came to RSC production of *US* they could not find a way of banning it. Censorship was such a live issue that if they had declined a licence there would have been uproar.'

'We were always straying into that dangerous area where sex becomes violence. In David Rudkin's *Afore Night Come* [a key new play at the RSC in the 1960s] there was homosexual attraction and a beheading. I have this memory of being alternately guffawed at and patronised by the Lord Chamberlain.'[42] The Arts Council sympathised with Hall's feelings. In 1965 it formed a committee to consider the subject of censorship and listened to evidence from interested parties for a month. It also drafted a private member's bill to submit to the Commons which, in the enthusiastic analysis of Tynan, 'provides for the abolition of the Chamberlain's theatre censorship, [and] the abolition of the powers of local authorities to impose censorship.'[43]

Hall disputed the notion that all playwrights, producers, actors and directors were set upon being rid of the Chamberlain. Impresarios, and the most influential of them all, Binkie Beaumont, who ran H.M. Tennent, were particularly reluctant to give up the royal imprimatur. 'There was an enormous fear in certain sections of the theatre about the abolition of the Lord Chamberlain. They were worried about what would happen. They thought the floodgates would open,' he recalled.[44] On the other hand, 'It began to look more and more absurd that the theatre was gagged by an official of the court . . . and our theatre did not have the same freedom as novelists, journalists, or broadcasters whose only curb was rightly the law of the land.'[45]

A fear of being deluged by forces beyond the control of mere politicians was a characterising anxiety of Establishment England in the 1960s. Margaret Thatcher wrote off the entire decade as one swamped by 'permissive clap-trap', the old virtues of 'discipline and self-restraint put in abeyance by the youth generation'.[46] If the 1960s were swinging, then in her view they swung to the immoral beat of people who had nothing more than sex, drugs and rock'n'roll on one-track, pleasure-oriented minds. From a countervailing perspective, the young

American theatre director, Charles Marowitz, who reached London in 1956 and stayed for twenty years, recollected the period in terms that would have confirmed all Lady Thatcher's misgivings. 'Between 1960 and say 1973 to be English was to be thought of as being swinging, loose, innovative, experimental, freaky, transcendental, off-beat and trendy,' he wrote. In his crazed retrospective he discerned the forces of 'dissent, anti-establishment fervour, the underground press, mini-skirts and pot all swirled together in a bubbling stew.'[47] In fact the flower-powered hippie seasons of love, peace and acid were a brief late 1960s phenomenon.

The seeds of dissent had been sown in the 1950s. By the early 1960s the social climate was subject to the stealth of change and some of the young revelled in this new dispensation. Norms of behaviour were being challenged and rejected by a gallery of seductive role-models and influential soothsayers. Acts of parliament in the 1960s began to enlarge the scope of personal freedom and opportunity. The Labour administrations of 1964 and 1966 reflected the new mood, with liberalising legislation on abortion, homosexuality, Sunday entertainment and the abolition of capital punishment. The more liberal and radical playwrights and directors reflected this move towards a more tolerant and civilised, though consumer-led society. Theatre audiences may have continued to be principally middle-class in this new circumstance, though there were no polls taken to test whether such a governing conviction was true. But within a few years theatre-goers would be younger and more adventurous in their tastes.

'Permissiveness' was the word which the liberal Home secretary, Roy Jenkins, chose to describe the more tolerant sexually liberated spirit affecting some of the young and the youthful. You could trace sensational lines of defiance, candour and vulgarity in key plays of the 1960s. The new school of playwrights and artistic directors rebelled against the traditional notions of propriety and reticence demanded by the Lord Chamberlain. Joe Orton's *Loot* (1964), with its jovial mockery of a corpse, Catholic ritual and the gravity of funeral ceremonies, and Wedekind's *Spring Awakening* (1963), that showed what grief and catastrophe could be engendered where sex education was proscribed, were typical protest-plays of the decade. They provoked the censor to much cutting and carping. Not only playwrights, but film directors and television producers and executives refused to accept the rigid policing of the boundaries of good taste. So, as John Sutherland noted, 'There was a new charter for the BBC in 1964 and liberal direction under Hugh Carleton Greene. At the British Board of Film Censors, John Trevelyan liberated film licensing.'[48] The late-night BBC TV programme of the early 1960s, *That Was the Week That Was*, had introduced the idea of mocking and ridiculing politicians and went so enjoyably far that Carleton Green actually apologised to the Prime Minister, Harold Macmillan, for a sketch which he said 'went beyond reasonable limits'.[49] The release in 1959 of Jack Clayton's film of *Room at the Top* was reckoned to herald the British cinema's engagement with working-class realism, the equivalent of the theatre's kitchen-sink school of drama. The film, taken from John Braine's novel of the same name, belonged with the Movement novels of Amis, Wain and the drama of Osborne and Wesker, in a school of protest and anger against the dominance of upper-crust, old-school-tie England. So Lords Scarbrough and Cobbold must have appreciated that they were practising a form of rear-guard censorship, to preserve the standards and values of a world that was passing. Harold Macmillan's government, fortified by a majority of more than a hundred, but consisting mostly of elderly or middle-aged, upper-middle-class gentlemen, was quite out of touch with the disrespectful cut and thrust of these new young writers. For such Conservatives stage censorship was suitably left to the Lord Chamberlain.

When Michael Foot's older brother, Dingle, tried to pass a bill abolishing stage censorship in 1962, it was rejected by 134 votes to 77. As late in January 1963, when Scarbrough was about to be succeeded by Cobbold as Lord Chamberlain, the much reviled, reactionary Home Secretary, Henry Brooke, expressed his 'keenness' for the censorship to continue.[50] Five years earlier Rab Butler and the Cabinet's Home Affairs Committee had opposed any change in the system, even though

Scarbrough was anxious to be relieved of press criticism. Butler appended 'in his own hand' the unctuous words, 'My colleagues marvel at your success and say in fact "leave it to the Lord Chamberlain and he will tighten up where he thinks fit".'[51] The Chamberlain's tightness served as one of the incentives for his undoing, as his prudish cuts and excisions increasingly attracted adverse press comment as well as aggressive attacks from within the field of censorship. But not many parliamentarians, even in the Labour Party, were much concerned about the unduly repressive nature of the Chamberlain's censorship.

Good taste, that supposed gentleman's agreement by which the Lord Chamberlain had been able to find common cause with producers and directors, was not what it used to be. Where there were disputes in the 1960s between theatres and the Lord Chamberlain they turned upon opposing ideas of whether drama required rules of decorum. The nude tableau, featuring a voluptuous young Britannia, flaunting a sceptre and sitting atop a small bulldog in Osborne's *The Entertainer* was scrutinised for fear of the sight of a pudendum. In Lionel Bart's *Fings Ain't Wot They Used T'Be*, 'The builder's labourer is not to carry the plank of wood in the erotic place and at the erotic angle that he does and the Lord Chamberlain wishes to be informed of the manner in which the plank is in the future to be carried.'[52]

Such fatuous remarks give the impression of an absurdly old-fashioned censor, hopelessly swimming against the tide, but concerned to maintain polite relations with the theatre. Cobbold always tried to foster this view of his censorship. 'Most of the managements have been in touch with the people in my office for years, and are on very good terms with them,' he said in his *Sunday Times* interview.[53] 'They write in and they come in and explain and ask for reconsideration.' Such comfortable arrangements clearly refer to the old-school, conservative producers who wished to keep on good terms with the censor. To the new generation of producers, however, Cobbold's 'people' presented the ugly face of authoritarianism and the threat of criminal prosecution whenever they stepped well out of line. Michael White produced the *Star-spangled Jack* show in July 1965. This revue, according to a letter from the Lord

Chamberlain's Comptroller, Eric Penn, to White on 24 August, had been the subject of a complaint made by a member of the public. After the play had been inspected in performance the Chamberlain's Examiner had discovered that between a half and two thirds of the entertainment, including 'a playlet mocking revivalist meetings' and 'a playlet referring to a clothing store managed by a homosexual' had not been submitted for the Lord Chamberlain's scrutiny.

The licensee of the Comedy Theatre, where the revue was being performed, took what was described as 'remedial action' at once. But on 22 October Penn's deputy, Johnston, wrote another threatening letter. If evidence laid before the Lord Chamberlain had been accepted in court, thirty offences against the Theatres Act of 1843 would have been committed, and a fine of up to £50 could have made 'for each particular offence'. Johnston wanted White to know that if the licensee had not taken any action, papers would have been sent to the Director of Public Prosecutions. This was the Lord Chamberlain's way of dealing with offenders against the censorship. It was hardly an example of being on gentlemanly good terms with producers.

It was Hall's seasons of plays at the Royal Shakespeare Company's new home at the Aldwych & Arts Theatre that dramatically polarised the gulf between the avant garde and the old order. In August 1964 Emile Littler, the President of the Society of West End Producers, made newspaper headlines when he accused the RSC of running seasons of 'dirty plays', of sustaining a 'theatre of cruelty and bestiality'.[54] Peter Weiss's *Marat/Sade*, with its asylum of the mentally disturbed and physically violent, David Rudkin's *Afore Night Come*, with its homosexuality and ritual killing, Beckett's *Endgame*, and Roger Vitrac's *Victor* whose flatulent heroine's anal discomfort was represented by the sound of a tuba, was a repertoire to make the Lord Chamberlain blanch. Littler spoke for the *derrière garde* who wanted a bland and emasculated form of boulevard theatre, but there was little support for him and he resigned his governorship. Actors, directors, producers, theatre critics and newspapers rallied to Hall's support. Cobbold was served public notice that play-goers no longer wished to be shielded from playwrights' darkest imaginings.

The Lord Chamberlain's reaction to the Royal Shakespeare Company's production of Genet's *The Screens* (1963) gives an acute sense of how angered his censors were by sexual plain-speaking. Genet's script was submitted for licensing while a club performance was scheduled. By then the Lord Chamberlain's department had become glumly accustomed to the new candour, as staff excised the rawest, rudest devisings of the dramatists. In this instance, when that indefatigable scrutineer of theatrical improprieties, Ronald Hill, read the play and saw the club performance, he came up with a wild scheme to do down the RSC.

At first the reaction from within St James's Palace was restrained. 'The author seems preoccupied with anal eroticism,' Heriot wrote wonderingly about *The Screens*, before banning the play's roll-call of profana: 'fucking, pissing, farting, screwing, crap, shit, b'Jesus, unbutton my fly, bugger off, bullshit'. 'Forbid all farting,' he then instructed, as well as 'up my arse . . . a spot of sperm . . . it was my pair of balls. Otherwise recommended for licence.' Hill was sent to see a rehearsal of this cleaned-up, censored play and wrote, 'The only objectionable business was the old woman going off to relieve herself in Scene 6. For all that was left to the imagination she might as well have squatted on the stage.'[55] He was pleased to see that where the buttoning of fly-buttons occurred, this potentially unseemly business was conducted with relative decorum. It was the two top buttons that you saw buttoned up 'not the more suggestive ones in the middle'. Anyone who considers the 'middle-fly' buttons 'suggestive' when compared with those further up surely boasts a mind of more than low-level prurience. Hill, unlike Heriot, recognised the play as a defining point in the battle over theatre censorship. *The Screens* was notorious, he believed, for its 'open and sadistic enjoyment of filth and cruelty'; it dealt with reports and descriptions of atrocity and cruelty. There were similar incidents in Greek drama but perhaps Hill was unaware. 'The play is not a trumpet call for justice and freedom. It seems to me rather to be an attempt by the author to relegate all the nobler aspirations of men to the stage-farm which apparently bounds his horizons.'

Hill rose to the challenge with an improper suggestion. 'I would feel that the Lord Chamberlain would be justified in meeting the usual campaign of calumny that would result (if the play were banned) by sending a list of the cuts without comment to some popular paper such as the *Daily Mail* which used to have the public weal as one of its motives.' Johnston referred to Hill's visit and Genet's script, but omitted all mention of the plan to incite the *Mail* to an outburst of moral outrage. 'While commending the play's technical excellence,' Johnston wrote of Hill in his book, 'he nevertheless did not feel it merited any specially sympathetic treatment.'[56] This is not an accurate precis of what Hill said. Hill justified his proposal by citing *The Screens* as 'one more example of the pressure being brought on the Lord Chamberlain to abandon all the conventions of decency in favour of dramatic needs.' Hill's call to arms and action was ignored by the Lord Chamberlain. Cobbold was far too grand to stoop to the business of currying support from newspapers. He would surely have considered such proselytising behaviour beneath him.

Joe Orton was one of the slyest and sharpest saboteurs of the old theatrical school of gentility. His play *Loot* threatened taboos involving all manner of unquestioning reverences, for the Catholic faith, for its apparatus of consolation to help the bereaved, for the police force, for family life. Orton, who loved writing letters to the *Daily Telegraph* under an assumed name, and expressing outraged opinions about his plays, may have been directly involved in writing mock protest letters to the Chamberlain. In the Chamberlain's files on *Loot* there is a letter from one 'Howard Godfrey' of the suspiciously named 'Utopia Court, Sandbanks' in Poole, saying, 'I do not think I have ever witnessed such an unpleasant and wickedly filthily-worded play in my life. We left before the end of the first act, completely disgusted, and I can only say I was thankful that our women-folk and young people were not present.' The Lord Chamberlain's Assistant Examiner, Kyrle Fletcher, felt very much the same as this apparent protester. 'The play is unpleasant in many of its details,' he wrote in his report, itemising, 'blasphemy . . . an offensive reference to homosexuality . . . filthy dialogue . . . a mixture of filth and blasphemy . . . a reference to flagellation . . . to a voyeur watching homosexuals.' This roll-call of profana is predictable, save for Fletcher's objection to 'an offensive reference to homosexuals', since the Lord Chamberlain had long approved the practice of being offensive to gay men. But even this list was insufficient to give vent to Fletcher's distaste. 'I find the whole atmosphere of the play repellent. Typical is the scene from 2.4 to 2.6 in which Fay undresses the corpse and describes it in callous and indecent language to Hal the son.'

These censors were unable to contemplate the idea that 'bad taste' as they termed any incident or expression which departed from the realm of civilised decorum, might serve a valuable function. When Johnston came to read the play on 17 December he was just as appalled. 'I have now finished [*Loot*] and I agree with the reader's view that it should be banned,' he wrote in his own hand to Cobbold. When he came to write *The Lord Chamberlain's Blue Pencil*, Johnston strangely overlooked his original reaction. 'I did not much care for the play,' he wrote in his account of a visit to a performance at Wimbledon Theatre in 1965, 'but it confirmed my view that it would have been wrong to withhold a licence.'[57] It was the corpse, of course, that constituted the prime problem. The thought of an actor playing a dead person was beyond the pale; it would have smacked of irreverence. 'Even if a dummy is used for the corpse I am not happy at the thought of it.' After all, as Johnston pointed out to Cobbold, the dead woman had to be removed from a coffin, placed in a cupboard, and seen naked while having a false eye restored to its socket. No audience ought to be allowed to witness such stage goings-on. But Heriot on this occasion succumbed to liberalism and exploited his knowledge of theatre history to plead against censorship. 'Black comedy indeed,' he reported on 23 December, defying Johnston and recommending a licence. 'The point seems to me that the macabre element isn't all that important. The Grand Guignol season at the Little Theatre during the 1914–18 war went much further in horrific action.' The Lord Chamberlain and his Comptrollers, who would have passed no examination in theatre history, probably thought that black comedy was some importation from Africa. The problem posed by *Loot*, Heriot judged, was 'the shocking bad taste', which ought to have instigated the Chamberlain's veto.[58]

The play had to be cleansed and made decent. 'Such vulgar expressions as 'shag their birds' and 'catch a dose' were not acceptable. But 'ever since we reached puberty together' may have been exised because of a faint innuendo of adolescent male homosexuality. But what agitated everyone most was that corpse. 'We would like to assume that it is possible to retain some of the undressing, though we would like to explain to you in person . . . how this can be decorously affected,' Michael Codron, the producer, wrote in suave tones to Eric Penn, the Comptroller. 'We would also be most anxious to retain the false eye business as we feel that with all possible source of offence removed, the business of the false eye must surely strike audiences as a reductio ad absurdum of all police enquiry.' Accordingly a meeting was set for Codron, his director Peter Wood, Johnston and Ronald Hill to meet and discuss the corpse. Wood recalled that his meeting with Johnston began with a question and answer session. 'Are you going to direct this play?' 'Yes I hope so.' 'And the writer, do you know him? Is he a friend?' 'I have a working relationship.' 'What's he like?' The next sentence was 'only just audible . . . Is he a bugger?'[59]

Wood at once gave three undertakings. The corpse would not be played by an actor, it would never be seen by the audience, and no one would ever speak disrespectfully about it. In the first scene, when the body was clad in the dignity of WVS uniform there would be no spoken reference to bondage, nor would any of the uniform be removed. In view of the respect with which the corpse was now to be treated, Wood hoped the Lord Chamberlain would allow the glass eye to be retained. This plea did not fall on unsympathetic ears. Johnston was entrusted with ensuring that stage directions made clear how the corpse would be manoeuvred from the coffin on stage to the cupboard without the offending dummy being seen by the audience. 'Much as I expected, this is pretty dreary entertainment,' Johnston reported when he went to see the original, ill-fated production on 15 March 1965 at Wimbledon. 'It is a brand of sick humour which probably goes down well with certain sections of the public, particularly those people who like to be shocked at the outset in some unusual way.'

The extent to which tastes changed in the decade after the Lord Chamberlain ceased to censor the theatre can be gauged by Irving Wardle's notice of the play's revival in a production by Lindsay Anderson. 'Ten years ago when *Loot* first appeared, Orton was giving plenty of offence; since then his work and this play in particular has been taken into the standard modern repertory and one hears no more complaints about bad taste and brutality.'[60] And this review was not untypical.

The Lord Chamberlain's concept of good taste lagged so far behind that of the theatre-goers he aspired to protect, that several banned *causes célèbres* became part of the British theatrical repertoire, without anyone turning a protesting hair when presented after the end of censorship. As late as 1965 the slightest intimation of sexual activity was still being outlawed on stage. Edward Bond's *Saved*, scheduled for production at the Royal Court that year, caused Johnston to send out a three-page list of erotic actions, raw words, plain-speaking and expletives which the Lord Chamberlain would not permit. 'The couple must not lie down on the couch so that one is on top of the other,' he stipulated[61]. Even the first, small hints of sexuality were forbidden. 'Pam must not undo Len's belt,' the censor warned. 'Pam must not have unbuttoned too far.' When Orton's *Entertaining Mr Sloane* was submitted for a licence, an appendix of disallowances from the Lord Chamberlain's office referred to a stage direction where the libidinous, middle-aged Kath 'rolls' on top of young Mr Sloane, remarking as she does, 'You should wear more clothes . . . I believe you're as naked as me'. The appendix note says, 'Kath's action with Sloane is not to exceed that given in the stage directions. You are particularly warned that any movements implying or simulating copulation have not been allowed, and furthermore, that such actions in such a context have been described in judge's obiter dictum given in the High Court of Justice as "obscene".' The irrelevant reference to the High Court, which had no jurisdiction over plays performed on stage, must have been intended to intimidate.

A far more disturbing and dramatic example of this censoring process is provided by the reaction to *Spring Awakening*, the 1891 play by the German dramatist Frank Wedekind, which the Royal Court tried to stage in 1963. The company decided to make do with a production for members of its private club, the English Stage Society, after cuts had been required by the Lord Chamberlain. The play questioned a prevailing belief that sex education was akin to corruption of the innocent. Cobbold was alarmed by the idea that adolescents should be shown confused and consumed by the first, significant prickings of sexual desire. Two years later, in a virtually unique example of interventionist censorship, the board of the National Theatre, led by its prudish chairman, Lord Chandos, prevented its director, Laurence Olivier, from staging a version of the play that had already been censored to the point of acceptability by the Lord Chamberlain when the play had been submitted by the Royal Court. Frank Wedekind, Germany's prime example of modern consciousness in late-nineteenth-century theatre, possessed a pre-Freudian idea of sex as an elemental drive that man had both to control and channel. Even after the 1961 spurt of liberality, signalled by the Old Bailey jury's decision to acquit D.H. Lawrence's *Lady Chatterley's Lover* of obscenity charges, there was no great change in the governing British conviction that sexual desire and its consummation was a matter best left to two consenting heterosexuals, over 18 and married, in the privacy of their own home. The sexuality of adolescents was problematic and provocative for adults.

Even in Germany Wedekind's play had initially been condemned as a pornographic text and could not be produced on the German stage until 1906 when Max Reinhardt staged a diplomatically cut version. Six years later Berlin audiences were allowed to see the play in its full form. The *Berlin Post* commented in explanation, 'The ban imposed by the Prussian Administrative Court has been revoked on the ground of the general seriousness of the piece as a whole. The offensive passages are not presented in such a way as to arouse or gratify the prurience of the audience. Nor is it possible to see how the onlooker could receive from it any impulse to conduct offensive to the police or public morals.' Such a pragmatic and mature attitude would not be achieved for many years in England. There were, however, no objections to an uncut production given in 1910 by the Stage Society and when the play was given a private performance in 1931 by the Sunday Theatre Club, the *Daily Telegraph* reviewer jingoistically celebrated a British form of sexless infantilism that preserved the country from premature interest in the erotic. 'Thank heaven that we in England have always grown up too slowly and set too much store by childish pursuits and games.'[63] If adults were not permitted to behave erotically on stage how much worse to portray adolescents in the first grip of desire. Of the three youngsters in *Spring Awakening* who discover sex just one lives to survive the ordeal. One dies from an abortion. The second kills herself. Far worse than death, though, was a scene in which youths masturbate in unison, though not mutually, and another where two kiss.

'This is one of the most loathesome and depraved plays I have ever read,' snarled the Assistant Examiner, Maurice Coles, on 21 May 1963. The adolescents, in *Spring Awakening*, were 'repressed by parents who themselves take a sadistic delight in punishing the children for a variety of minor misdeeds.' This was and is a perverse misreading. The youth and his girlfriend who come to such wretched ends in *Spring Awakening* are victims of parental cruelties. They are adolescent casualties in a prudish society that seeks to rear its children in sexual ignorance, fear and anxiety. Eric Penn ordered that the harmless words 'penis' and 'vagina' should be excised. He required that a vaguely homosexual scene in which a tentative, tender kiss is exchanged between two youths should be excised, as well as the masturbation game in a male reformatory. Two English films of the early 1960s, *Victim* and *The Leather Boys*, had introduced the innocent to homosexuality and Shelagh Delaney in *A Taste of Honey* (1958) depicted a camp gay youth. But simulated masturbation was an affront to the censor.

The artistic directors of the Royal Court staged a single

Sunday night performance of the full text for the members of its English Stage Society in May 1963. Both Sir Eric Penn, then Comptroller, and a retired predecessor, Lieutenant-Colonel Tim Nugent, attended the production, perhaps because they were curious to see just what the actors would make of masturbation and they reported back in a shocked memorandum on 11 May. The incident was delicately managed, with the actors keeping their backs to the audience, but the Chamberlain's lieutenants were not appeased. 'This action is accompanied by the most unattractive moves . . . also their individual actions, seen from the back, are entirely unacceptable,' Penn wrote. When a full-scale production, with the cuts required by the Lord Chamberlain, was presented in April 1965, 'There will be no kissing, embracing or caressing between the two boys allowed,' the Lord Chamberlain's office warned nervously. For Ronald Hill, the Lord Chamberlain's most disturbed watchdog, had barked most anxiously. '[Masturbating] is unequivocally an indecent action,' he wrote and put the offensive activity in its outlawed place. 'In the past we refused to allow a man to sit on the lavatory [on stage, that is] and having prosecuted in another case have a precedent that the simulation of copulation on the stage is indecent.' The Royal Court directorate, informally allied with the National Theatre and the RSC in the battle to be rid of the censor, included a cheeky note in the programme, specifying those actions in *Spring Awakening* that the Lord Chamberlain had banned and to what extent he had relented after the Royal Court had challenged his decision. 'Lord Cobbold demanded the omission of the scene in the reformatory where adolescents play a game which leads to mutual masturbation and the love scene in the vineyard between Hans and Ernest.'

After representations had been made by the author's agents, the Lord Chamberlain decided to allow the scene in the vineyard providing there was 'no kissing, embracing or caressing'. An alternative to the masturbation scene was submitted and allowed. 'It will be for a future audience in England to see the play as the author wrote it.' This note highlighted in vivid fashion the anomaly of theatre censorship. A play-text might be truncated before it could be performed. 'This play has a stormy history,' Bernard Levin wrote in his *Daily Mail* review on 20 April. His approving notice was one more symptom of the gulf between proponents of censorship and liberal opponents of the system. Conservative moralists did not wish the growing sexual doubts of disturbed adolescents to be discussed in plays. Their liberal opponents advocated a new climate of freedom in which sex education was not denied. 'Being pure and true and warm, it has naturally attracted the hatred of the prurient, the fearful, the cold throughout the 60-odd years since its first rapidly banned production. The agonies of adolescence are set down at white-heat; the boy to whom the onset of puberty comes "like a thunder-bolt"; his serious-minded friend for whom it is a time of abandoned faith,' Levin judged. Philip Hope-Wallace the critic for the *Guardian* was as enthusiastic: 'No one with any sense of theatre could fail to see the power of this tremulously true and touching play of the agonies of adolescence.'[64] Such reviews helped to cast this example of censorship as reactionary.

Some months previously, on 29 October 1964, Kenneth Tynan, who by then was literary manager of the National Theatre, wrote to Lord Cobbold about *Spring Awakening*. Both he and Laurence Olivier wanted to include the play in the National's repertoire, but they did not wish to lose the three banned scenes. Tynan's analysis of the play and its offending portions might have served as a comment on the censorship's stultifying impact upon the English stage. 'Its general theme,' he wrote, 'is the danger of employing Victorian severity to prevent adolescents from discovering the facts of normal sexual life. It contains two short scenes which illustrate the damage that can be done when brutal repression forces healthy instincts into unhealthy channels.'[65] Tynan's widow Kathleen recorded that, on 5 November, Olivier sent a letter to Lord Chandos, in which he made a 'strong plea for *Spring Awakening*. He submitted that with *Hay Fever*, *The Crucible* and *Much Ado About Nothing* in the repertory, the theatre needed something provocative.'[66] But within days Tynan was telegramming in anger to John Dexter, Olivier's associate director, 'By unanimous decision of Board and without consultation with Larry production of *Spring Awakening* has been banned outright. Board further said it intended henceforth to supervise all repertoire decisions. Larry, Bill [Gaskill] and I feel that as long as [National] Theatre has confidence of public we must insist on artistic control as minimum requirement for self-respect. Please cable reactions and suggestions.'

Tynan's melodrama of a telegram, with its fatuous assertion that Olivier's 'artistic control' of the National depended upon public confidence and was the minimum requirement that 'self-respect' demanded, obscures the significance of this revelation. Chandos had refused to allow the play to be presented with the cuts that the Lord Chamberlain had required. He had usurped Olivier's power to function as an independent artistic director. Tynan's subsequent telegram to Dexter on 12 November alluded to an abject surrender: 'Dear John. Larry says keep situation quite dark. All hope lost if facts divulged at this moment.' The facts were, therefore, concealed. 'Tynan wanted the National to stage it, with the cuts demanded by the Lord Chamberlain, which meant the omission of one scene; but the board took the view that the standards of the National should be "above" those of the censor. Tynan accepted that decision,' according to the National Theatre's biographer.[67] The evidence provided by Tynan's letters proved Elsom wrong: Tynan wanted to battle. So too did Dexter who replied combatively to the telegram, 'Board censorship intolerable and insulting. My resignation is for Larry to use as and when he sees fit.'[68]

The governors of the National Theatre were appointed by the Prime Minister. In the words of Hugh Willatt in 1967, who would soon become the secretary-general of the Arts Council, they were 'trustees of the public interest'. Chandos, whose appointment as chairman was surprisingly extended that year, had interfered with Olivier's artistic policies. 'The Board should give the artistic director the greatest independence possible – and I repeat possible – in a modern society,' he told the *Sunday Times* in 1967 when the debate over *Soldiers* was in full, agitated flow. 'Now suppose you had a satire of the present [Labour] government – well only a board can decide if it's harmlessly amusing . . . or concerted propaganda to win a few Conservative votes.'[69] This crude hypothesis is interesting. Here was a retired Cabinet minister who argued for censorship by a theatre's board of directors, claiming that the stage remained a potent forum for political persuasion. In some sense, though, Chandos was accurate and the theory still holds good. Indirect censorship of state-funded theatres remains a potential menace to the artistic licence of a director who seeks to bring theatre into direct and critical contact with contemporary politics.

Spring Awakening was, however, a play whose ability to offend dwindled and died in the post-censorship years. Nine years later the play was presented under Peter Hall's directorship of the National Theatre and in a new translation by that bane of the censor's last years, Edward Bond. It raised not a whimper of protest. No one expressed the sense of revulsion that had been sparked less than a decade earlier. Britain had not become a less prudish nation, but the theatre was no longer muzzled and subject to the Lord Chamberlain's severe priggishness.

Notes

1. Quoted in Findlater, op. cit., p. 169.
2. Kenneth Tynan, *Tynan on Theatre* (1964), pp. 30–1.
3. Ibid., p. 31.
4. Peter Vansittart, *In the Fifties* (1995), p. 64.
5. Dominic Shellard, *Harold Hobson, Witness and Judge* (1995), p. 150.
6. Harry Ritchie, *Success Stories* (1988), p. 1.
7. LC file on *Desire Under the Elms*, Eugene O'Neill
8. LC file on *Saved*, Edward Bond.
9. LC file on *Oscar Wilde*, Leslie and Sewell Stokes.
10. LC file on *The Connection*, Jack Gelber.
11. LC file on *A View From the Bridge*, Arthur Miller.
12. LC file on *Tomorrow – With Pictures*, Anthony Creighton & Bernard Miller.
13. LC file on *The Connection*, Jack Gelber.

14. LC file on *Entertaining Mr Sloane*, Joe Orton.
15. Tynan, *A View of the English Stage*, p. 42.
16. Ibid., p. 84.
17. LC file on *Look Back in Anger*, and Anthony Aldgate, *Censorship and the Permissive Society* (1995), pp. 66–7.
18. John Johnston, *The Lord Chamberlain's Blue Pencil* (1990), p. 217.
19. Peter Hall, *Making an Exhibition of Myself* (1993), p. 106.
20. *The Times*, 4 August 1955.
21. Alec Guinness, interview with author, February 1999.
22. Ritchie, op. cit., p. 130.
23. LC file on *Look Back in Anger*, John Osborne.
24. LC file on *My Fair Lady*, Alan J. Lerner
25. Richard Findlater, *Banned* (1967), pp. 170–1.
26. LC file on *The Entertainer*, John Osborne.
27. Philip Hoare, *Noel Coward, A Biography* (1997), p. 84.
28. Findlater, op. cit., p. 170.
29. LC file on *The World of Paul Slickey*.
30. Kenneth Tynan, *A View of the English Stage* (1975), p. 362.
31. Ibid., p. 363.
32. Findlater, op. cit., p. 187.
33. Ibid.
34. Alec Guinness, op. cit.
35. Findlater, op. cit., p. 152.
36. *Sunday Times*, 11 April 1965.
37. LC file on *Endgame*, Samuel Beckett.
38. Findlater, op. cit., p. 153.
39. *Sunday Times*, 7 April 1957.
40. Michael Hallifax, interview with author, 13 December 1998.
41. Peter Hall, interview with author, April 1994.
42. Ibid.
43. Kenneth Tynan, *Letters*, ed. Kathleen Tynan (1995), p. 332.
44. Ibid.
45. Hall, op. cit., p. 195.
46. *Guardian*, 28 March 1982.
47. Charles Marowitz, *Burnt Bridges, A Souvenir of the Swinging Sixties and Beyond* (1990), p. 2.

48. John Sutherland, *Offensive Literature: Decensorship in Britain 1960–1982*, (1982) p. 2.

49. Aldgate, op. cit., pp. 4–5.

50. Johnston, op. cit., p. 166.

51. Ibid., pp. 156–66.

52. David Roper, *Bart* (1994), p. 32.

53. *Sunday Times*, 11 April 1965.

54. *Daily Telegraph*, 25 August 1964.

55. LC file on *The Screens*.

56. Johnston, op. cit., p. 191.

57. Ibid., p. 195.

58. LC file on *Loot*.

59. Peter Wood, interview with author, 14 September 1998.

60. *The Times*, 4 June 1975

61. LC file on *Loot*, Joe Orton.

62. *Berlin Post*, 5 April 1912, quoted in the programme for the 1965 Royal Court production.

63. Ibid.

64. *Guardian*, 20 April 1965.

65. Kenneth Tynan, *Letters*, ed. Kathleen Tynan (1995), p. 310.

66. Ibid..

67. John Elsom and Nicholas Tomalin, *The History of the National Theatre*, (1978), p. 198.

68. Tynan, *Letters*, p. 311.

69. *Sunday Times*, 30 April 1967.

6

THE IMPORTANCE OF
BEING SAVED

The outrage sparked by *Spring Awakening* was as nothing compared with the political furore that erupted over the Royal Court's production in November 1965 of Edward Bond's *Saved*. No other play this century posed such pressing, practical problems for a government. The Home Secretary, Lord Chancellor, the Attorney-General, Director of Public Prosecutions and various law officers were all involved in deciding whether to take the Royal Court's artistic director to court and test the extent of his powers under the 1843 Theatres Act. For *Saved* was given as a performance for members of the Court's private club, circumventing the Lord Chamberlain's demands for a host of cuts and omissions. Cobbold was appalled by a scene in which a sleeping, silent baby is stoned to death by a gang of alienated south London youths. *Saved* became a *cause célèbre*, and it inspired a sequence of events that would lead to the downfall of the Lord Chamberlain.

Cobbold refused to grant the play a licence without substantial cuts; Bond would not allow *Saved* to be done in censored form. When Gaskill presented the members-only performance, Cobbold hustled and bustled to prosecute the Royal Court for failing adequately to make certain that only bona fide members saw the play. He pressured the Home Secretary, Roy Jenkins, to ensure that the prosecution was allowed. Jenkins' artful *quid pro quo* turned out to be an inquiry into theatre censorship, for which he arranged that a joint parliamentary committee be appointed. Cobbold's predecessor, Lord Scarbrough, had felt that that the New Watergate club challenged the authority of his censorship. Although he overstated the point, there were glimmers of truth in the assertion. But the Home Office doubted a law officers' opinion that the Lord Chamberlain could 'prevent theatre clubs putting on unlicensed plays'.[1]

Saved was a bother and a bugbear for Cobbold from the moment Heriot produced his report on it at the end of June 1965. 'A revolting amateur play . . . The writing is vile and the conception worse,' he wrote in familiar denunciatory style. Yet he recommended 'reluctantly' that it be licensed. It is one of the rare cases I have discovered where Heriot took a more permissive line than the Comptrollers or the Lord Chamberlain. In this instance, though, Heriot's recommendation was cast aside, if not at once. The play was passed up the ladder of the command. 'The death of the baby is very unpleasant and in my opinion you may like to consider modifying the stone throwing,' Johnston, the Assistant Comptroller, wrote to Cobbold. Eric Penn, the Comptroller, then called upon the advice of Tim Nugent, his elderly predecessor.

'I've read this revolting play which certainly ought not be shown on any stage,' Nugent wrote back on 25 July. 'The scene of the killing of the baby is the most revolting I have ever read.'[2] He gave a warning about the threat to the Lord Chamberlain posed by his wily theatrical opponents. 'I suppose the Lord Chamberlain is not the arbiter of taste and taste seems to be sadly low today. If the play is banned could not Devine tone it down considerably and then put it on at his threatre club as an example of the Lord Chamberlain's prudishness, whereas if the play is not banned, but merely cut to ribbons he couldn't bring off this childish score off [sic] the Lord Chamberlain.' This suggestion was ignored. 'I am not disposed to compromise very much on this play,' Cobbold wrote on 5 August. A letter had been sent to Doreen Dixon, the Court's general manager on 29 July, with four whole pages of disallowances. Most of the cuts required had to do with vulgarity. To read these pages of disallowances is to appreciate the unnatural wholesomeness of stage diction that the censors required. 'Arse', 'bugger', 'get stuffed', 'crap', 'piss off', and 'shag' all had to be removed. But even crudely imaginative insults had to go as well. 'Ye're as tight as a flea's arsehole' and 'You must be the only stiff outside the churchyard she ain't knocked off' were to be removed as well.

Standards of propriety had to be scrupulously maintained. 'The couple must not lie down on the couch so that one is on top of the other,' it was decreed, and with straight-faced gravity, 'There must be no indecent business with the balloon.' The Examiners were not always so successful in weeding out filth. The actor Bernard Gallagher recalled that in John Arden's *Sergeant Musgrave's Dance*, one of the great post-war English plays on a political theme, premièred at the Court in 1959, there was reference to a welcoming landlady whose open arms 'let 'em all come in'. This was felt to be too suggestive, so the Examiner advised that the words 'let 'em all come' would be allowed, a phrase spoken with gleeful relish by Sebastian Shaw.[3] William Gaskill, the Royal Court's new artistic director, may have been aloof, and without charisma when facing up to public scrutiny or attention, but he was a dogged fighter, indefatigable and brave in the struggle against the Lord Chamberlain. He determined to resist the censor and the form of his resistance incited Cobbold into action that helped hasten the end of the censorship. 'He was limiting not just the scope of what could be shown on the stage, but the strength and vitality of the language,' Gaskill wrote later.[4] Gaskill laid his plans for *Saved* astutely.

First he consulted his predecessor George Devine, who read the play and proposed a series of tactical deletions to help the chances of securing a licence. Devine's recommendations provide a vivid illustration of how the playwright had to stoop to conquer the censor's objections. 'I suggest that Charles Wood's technique is a good one,' Devine wrote, referring to another Court playwright often troubled by the censor's injunctions. 'Swallow pride and reinvent, even one's own swear-words and phrases. Rewrite scenes, if necessary, to retain intrinsic rhythms rather than arguing over words and phrases he will never yield on.'[5] Because Bond was obstinate and refused to compromise, Gaskill determined to repeat the procedure used in the case of *A Patriot for Me* to evade the censor's control.

The Court's governing council, Gaskill recalled in his memoirs, 'had read the play and were completely behind it and me.' Gaskill did go to see Johnston and the two men discussed the scene of the stoning of the baby, an incident which could not be staged with any great degree of realism. The director later acutely described the impact of this murder upon the audience as a form of ritual. 'The killing of a child in a pram when it doesn't cry – it can make no statement about the pain it feels – has already a kind of abstract symbolic quality about it although one tries to do it as naturalistically as possible. But there is something very strange about it because you know there is only a dummy. You are watching a kind of ritualised action. What you're really watching is the boys.'[6]

At the meeting Gaskill also told Johnston of the Court's intentions to present the play for members of the English Stage Society. Cobbold was quick to take the challenge. The Director of Public Prosecutions was informed of the Court's intention by the Lord Chamberlain's office on 8 September. On 6 October Cobbold himself wrote to the DPP Norman Skelhorn to ask what action he would take. Judging by Skelhorn's letter of reply to Cobbold six days later, the Lord Chamberlain believed the Court could be persuaded not to proceed with the members-only production if Skelhorn threatened court proceedings. But the DPP, whose sympathies were with Cobbold, disagreed. 'I have again considered your suggestion whether some form of warning might suitably be given,' he wrote on 12 October 1965.[7] 'I feel, however, that it is undesirable to do so where those responsible are plainly contending that the prosecution of the play in the way in which they are proposing does not constitute any offence under the [Theatres] Act.' He believed the Royal Court would reply 'that they do not agree that they are committing any offence and in effect to challenge us to prosecute.' Sir Norman was willing and probably eager to take the case of *Saved* to the magistrates' court and have the 1843 act elucidated. He and Cobbold wished to discover whether an unlicensed play could be presented for an entire season to audiences who were members of a theatre club or society rather than the usual, single performance. In the past, Lords Chamberlain had generally been prepared to accept single club or society performances of plays that they had banned. If, however, a theatre management, such as that at the Royal Court, was legally entitled to present an unlicensed play to members of the public who joined a mythical Royal Court club or society, then the Lord Chamberlain's censorial powers were useless.

Less than a week after the production had opened, with reviews which ranged from the delighted to the outraged, Cobbold had a fateful lunch with Dingle Foot, the Solicitor-General. They had met two or three weeks earlier when Foot had dined with the Lord Chamberlain and deferentially suggested another meeting. Cobbold wrote a memorandum on their meeting that is included in the *Saved* file. Foot, a leading opponent of stage censorship, seems to have been oddly discursive when the two men met. According to Cobbold, Foot had said, 'he would be glad of an informal word about *Saved* and about censorship problems generally.' But why? The Solicitor-General and his senior government colleague, the Attorney-General Elwyn Jones, had to make a decision as to whether to prosecute the Royal Court. It was a delicate matter, yet here was Sir Dingle discussing a quasi-legal matter with a senior member of the Queen's household, who was urging the prosecution. The Solicitor-General also disclosed that the government had problems about censorship. Foot was unwisely candid and did not trouble to conceal the government's embarrassment. 'He said that the law officers were in something of a dilemma about *Saved* and had not yet reached any decision,' Cobbold reported. 'They had little doubt that the production was illegal and that a prosecution would be successful, but they thought this would bring up the whole question of stage censorship and were not sure whether or not this would be desirable.'

So much for the government's reformist eagerness to strip the Lord Chamberlain of his role as theatre censor, its critics would have argued. But with a precarious majority of just four, there could be no question of the Labour government using valuable parliamentary time for a reform that was of minimal electoral appeal or of any significance for the voting majority. Besides there was no indication that such a reform would win the support of the Conservatives. As recently as May 1964 Lord Derwent, a Home Office minister of state, had replied in negative terms to a question from a television playwright about the abolition of stage censorship. 'The government considers that [the Chamberlain's censorship] has worked well in practice and that no alternative system is likely to be found which would command general support.'[8] On matters of theatrical freedom the Conservatives then favoured the status quo.

Foot apparently believed there would be no need to prosecute if *Saved* was presented only for a short time. Cobbold disagreed, urging that if theatres went on 'breaking the law' by presenting these members-only performances, the Lord Chamberlain would be put 'in an impossible position which sooner or later he would have to try to clarify in public.' Foot tried to placate Cobbold, who threatened to speak in public about his sense of being let down by the government. Foot told him that the government was contemplating setting up an inquiry into theatre censorship. Cobbold replied that he welcomed the idea, though his manner was typically high handed. 'I said that I should personally welcome this . . . provided that it was done on a sensible and realistic basis.' The two men then discussed whether the inquiry should be a Royal Commission or a select committee of the Houses of Parliament or a committee of enquiry appointed by either the Home Secretary, Roy Jenkins, or Gerald Gardiner as Lord Chancellor. It was remarkable that Foot even asked Cobbold if he had any ideas about what course of action to adopt and who should serve on the committee. For a Labour minister to have asked a High Tory, who administered an illiberal, autocratic, anomalous form of censorship, to recommend people to serve on such a committee was bizarre.

Rumour and alarm engulfed the Royal Court during rehearsals. Richard Butler, who was in the cast, recalled the first night, on 3 November 1965, as fraught with offstage dramatics. 'Bill [Gaskill] was white at the gills and we were all a bit edgy, more so than at an ordinary first night and I remember him saying to us "Look, don't get upset if people protest from the front. If people walk out, be prepared for that" . . . [he was] almost visibly shaking and in the event nothing like that happened. The audience were a very civilised lot . . . there was one walk-out and that was a critic's wife. It was a nail-biting time.' Memory, though, is a great self-deceiver: another first-nighter recalled a far more fraught première. 'I've always felt the stories of the opening of *Ghosts* and the first performance of Stravinsky's *Rite of Spring* to be exaggerated romance . . . That night at the Royal Court I came to believe in their veracity. There was verbal interruption and abuse in the course of the play and there was the odd physical punch-up in the foyers at the interval and afterwards. The cause was in particular the scene in which the baby was stoned to death.'[9] This is not a reliable recollection. Helen Montagu, the Court's general manager, does not recall any such fisticuffs or vocal outbursts of fury. There were, she recalled, a few murmurs of outrage during the baby-stoning scene.[10] Peter Lewis, theatre critic for the *Daily Mail*, confirmed Montagu's estimates though in more dramatic terms. 'It is not often in that hardened audience that you hear the cry "Revolting" and "Dreadful" and the smack of seats vacated, but you did last night,' he wrote.[11] You would think that this was an ideal occasion for a *Daily Mail* campaign against depravity in the theatre. Lewis, however, did not follow the main line of outraged critics at all. 'It is a muddled and a muddling play. But it is certainly a moral one,' he concluded.

In reviewing *Saved* many, though certainly not all, of the daily and weekly theatre critics succumbed to the moral outrage that had afflicted their Victorian counterparts when reviewing Ibsen's *Ghosts* at its London premiere in 1891. Their responses indicate the power of the theatre to disturb many English hearts and minds, unused to violent speech and incident in contemporary contexts. The theatre censorship had protected them from life. 'Nothing is quite like the critics when they are morally outraged . . . I think I was still naive enough to think that quality would surely be recognised,' Gaskill recorded. 'The accumulated bile of the critics was vented on the play.'[12] This is an inaccurate judgement which surrenders to an understandable exaggeration. Ronald Bryden in the *New Statesman* and

Penelope Gilliatt in the *Observer* were forceful admirers and interpreters of the play. Gilliatt wrote in her review on 7 November that *Saved* was not a 'brutish play, it is about brutishness'; the review by Philip Hope-Wallace, the *Guardian*'s theatre critic, disproves the idea that every reviewer charged against Bond on a moral high-horse. The fairly enthusiastic notice, displaying Hope-Wallace's familiar sophistication and unshockable urbanity, served as an antidote to his colleagues' fury. 'No more horrible than some episodes in *Titus Andronicus*,' he noted. 'The squeamish are duly warned.'[13]

The most damning reviewers sought dishonestly to characterise Bond as a morally delinquent purveyor of thrills which only the perverted would enjoy. J.W. Lambert, the *Sunday Times*' self-important arts and literary editor, deputising for Harold Hobson who was in Paris, provided a factually dishonest account of the baby-stoning scene. Lambert's review misled readers into believing that the scene of infanticide was far more disgusting in its realism and explicitness than was actually the case. 'Past the Limits of Brutality' read the headline to his lengthy review.[14] It is a disgraceful piece of writing because it perverts the truth to lend credence to the idea that Bond sought to brutalise the stage and its audiences. The review read like a vindication of Cobbold's decision to withhold a licence. Lambert argued that *Saved* was a play of dangerous significance; the boundaries of permissiveness had been rudely breached by its performance. He diagnosed the writer as a man whose motives were far from respectable. 'Cruelty and viciousness on stage are no strangers to the theatre. But was there ever a psychopathic exercise so lovingly dwelt on as this, spun out with such relish and refinement of detail?' Lambert claimed that he described the atrocity as 'impassively as possible because it and the play which frames it represent something of a crux in modern drama: a clear demonstration of what is permissible, what is not and why.' He tried to explain what he meant. 'The psychopath says you can put a baby to sleep by pulling its hair – and pulls it quite gently at first. The others join in; one of them punches it, also quite gently at first. But soon they are pummelling it, fists and faces working. They tear off its drawers and nappies – are disgusted to see that it is dirty. They roll it over and rub its face in its own excrement, dancing madly around the pram. They pick up *handfuls of sharp stones* and bombard *the tiny, filthy, bleeding body*' (my italics).

This account was as gross as it was mendacious. There was no baby, no filth, no bleeding body. There were no stones, sharp or blunt. 'I knew there was no baby in the pram, just as I could see there were no stones in the actors' hands, wrote W.A. Darlington, the *Daily Telegraph*'s *derrière garde*, septuagenarian theatre critic, who was half-blind and hard of hearing. He detested the play and ranked it with Orton's *Entertaining Mr Sloane*, but did not seek to exaggerate its shock effects.[15] Even Lambert conceded that no sounds of an infant's distress were heard, but perversely complained that 'a perfunctory reference to [the baby] having been dosed with aspirin' sounded contrived. Irving Wardle, *The Times*' level-headed theatre critic, usually to be relied on as a coherent, astute, highly eloquent advocate of the new drama, sensationally accused Bond of writing what amounted 'to a systematic degradation of the human animal'.[16] He argued that the most 'charitable interpretation of the play would be as a counter-blast to the theatrical fashion, stripping off the glamour to show that cruelty is disgusting . . . but the writing itself, with its self-admiring jokes and gloating approach to the moments of brutality and erotic humiliation does not support this view.' Lambert, and to a far lesser extent Wardle, were so revolted by *Saved* that they seem, in this retrospect, to have scaled heights of sensationalism. Their revulsion may have to do with the draconian success of the censorship for whose demise Wardle at least longed. Having been accustomed throughout their lives to a censored theatre in which no contemporary dramatist was permitted to outrage the Chamberlain's concept of good taste, they were emotionally unprepared for the violence of Bond's imagining or the habitual language of its perpetrators.

Wardle conceded the point when he gave a lecture at Banf the following year. 'This was the biggest mistake of my reviewing career,' he said. 'If I hadn't indulged in the sense of outrage, I might have remembered there were plenty of plays –

from *King Lear* onwards – that match or outclass *Saved* in violence, and that what really got to me was that these people spoke like urban cavemen. In other words – in spite of the prevailing taboo on "literary theatre" – what reconciled, me, us, to the enactment of atrocities was a nice turn of phrase, such as you find in Pinter and Joe Orton. The other factor was social ignorance. People like Bond's stunted characters didn't live down my street, so I leapt to the conclusion that they didn't exist at all outside the playwright's sordid imagination.'[17] John Peter, later the *Sunday Times* theatre critic, then on the staff of the *Times Educational Supplement* went to see the play. 'I found it extremely shocking. The fact that the stoning was formalised made no difference. It made it both less revolting and more shocking. The aesthetic difference is vital. If you are shocked you are in a position to make moral judgements on the contents of the scene. If you are revolted then you are making a judgement on the person committing the revolting act.'[18] Hobson, it later transpired, would not have adopted Lambert's dishonourable stance. 'It is the first both in time and merit of those plays which have exposed the facts of irrational violence in our society, and the cowardice even of good men in the face of it,' he wrote approvingly when the play was revived four years later.[19]

Bond stood accused of being in bondage to sadistic impulses gratified by performances of lingering cruelty. He expressed his credo years later. 'The idea that human beings are necessarily violent is a political device, the modern equivalent of the doctrine of original sin . . . [violence] occurs in situations of injustice. It is caused not only by physical threats, but even more significantly by threats to human dignity.'[20] The murderers in *Saved*, with their dead-end, aimless lives could be categorised as violent 'because of an unconscious motive, an unidentified discontent'. Yet theatre audiences had witnessed incidents far more graphic and appalling than those in *Saved*. For Lambert, however, a defining point of vital significance had been reached. '[The baby-stoning scene] is becoming more sharply and urgently associated with contemporary life than it has been for centuries, as ever things as horrible as this baby-killing happen every day; but it is not enough merely to enact them. Without the shaping hand of art in the writing the result is only reporting. And when to reporting is added the intensification of stage-craft and powerful acting, and the prolongation of sadistic antics far beyond the time to make a valid point, in circumstances carelessly rigged, the conclusion is inescapable: that we are being offered ... a concocted opportunity for vicarious beastliness.' Lambert's contention was not persuasive. His idea that audiences were being offered the chance to indulge sadistic appetites passes no muster and, his review serves as an indictment of the narrowness of his imagination and the dishonesty of his argument. For the brutal murder in *Saved* is implied rather than acted. Acts of stage violence, he argued, required 'the shaping hand of art,' though what this creative limb would or does achieve is left shrouded in doubt. Perhaps Lambert meant that violence should be artistically wrought, in the sense of being committed by people who speak their intentions and feelings in fine language.

Whatever Lambert's point, the critics' abuse was countered by theatre-leaders rallying to the Royal Court's playwright. Laurence Olivier wrote a convincing apology for *Saved* in a letter to *The Times*. That typically 1960s concept, 'a teach-in', was held on 14 November, under the chairmanship of Kenneth Tynan, so that opinions about freedom of theatrical speech and action could be vented. Wardle, who attended the event, reiterated his attack in *The Times* the next day, casting aspersions at Bond's motives and accusing the playwright, in terms familiar from Lambert's diatribe, of pandering to those who wished to see acts of sexual cruelty. 'Neither [Bond] nor his director can be accused of exploiting violence for its own sake. But the fact remains that the production is as much an invitation to share erotic and sadistic fantasy as to understand it.'[21] This allusion to perverse complicity was strange, since it rendered the author's intention as malign and disturbed for no reason that the critic renders coherent.

By this point the die was cast. Having drawn the DPP into his battle with the Royal Court before the production had opened, Cobbold now had to face the consequences of his lofty pique.

The DPP, Sir Norman Skelhorn, was obliged to consult the government's law officers, the Attorney-General, Sir Elwyn Jones, and the Solicitor-General, Sir Dingle Foot, who were both strong opponents of theatre censorship, to see whether they would authorise prosecution of the Royal Court. Sir Dingle informed Cobbold that the government was undecided about what action to take. The dilemma was understandable, since if the case was taken to court the problems posed by the Lord Chamberlain's system of theatre censorship, on which the government had shown no eagerness to legislate, would be highlighted.

A man with more developed political antennae than Cobbold would not have attempted to force the government's hand on censorship. Although he professed a wish to see the Lord Chamberlain divested of his duties as theatre censor he wanted to do so on his terms, and a Labour government was unlikely to share his views. He argued, however, that the Royal Court threatened to make a mockery of his powers by presenting *Saved* to members of the theatre's own club, the English Stage Society. In a sense he was right, though it would have been wiser to regard the Royal Court as simply widening the loophole afforded by a members-only performance. But Cobbold, instead of allowing any furore to die down, as it would have done, sought to exacerbate the furore. If the Court had simply been warned by the Lord Chamberlain that it had strictly to ensure that tickets for *Saved* were sold only to those people who provided proof that they were already bona fide members of the English Stage Society, the confrontation and the prosecution could have been avoided.

A few months later, in March 1966, the Theatre Royal Stratford East decided to present Barbara Garson's *Macbird* and turned itself into a theatre club to do so. Cobbold, who took advice from Paul Gore-Booth, the permanent secretary at the Foreign Office and David Bruce, the American ambassador, had already refused to give the play a licence. Yet in this instance when the play was presented, Cobbold wrote to the Director of Public Prosecutions, 'not requesting him to take any action *provided the performances were genuine club performances* [my italics].'[22] It was the Royal Court, after his defeat over *A Patriot for Me* and pyrrhic victory over *Saved*, that Cobbold hated. In October 1967, when it looked as if the government was poised to repeal the Chamberlain's powers, Helen Montagu wrote to Cobbold saying that the theatre intended to present a three-week members-only performance of Charles Wood's *Dingo*. Assistant Examiner Harward had described the play as 'a bitter, pungent attack on war and heroism' when the National wished to stage it three years earlier.[23] Johnston had thought it 'perfectly dreadful' and wanted to advise Cobbold not to license it. Hill, the Lord Chamberlain's in-house adviser on legal matters, pointed out that the chief magistrate had ruled that a play 'could not be legally presented without the Lord Chamberlain's permission if actors were remunerated or if the audience paid'. When the Court had presented *America Hurrah* for members-only performances, the Lord Chamberlain 'in view of the censorship committee' had taken no action. But in this instance Hill recommended that the Court should be refused an interview to discuss the matter. 'Sooner or later unless legislation is not too long delayed, we must again come into conflict with the Royal Court,' he concluded. The final, unfriendly decision on the part of the Comptroller, Eric Penn, was to pass the Royal Court's letter to the DPP. No action was taken. The censors tried to frustrate the Court to the bitter end.

Roy Jenkins, who told me he was 'very keen' to see the Lord Chamberlain's control of the theatre terminated, seized the chance offered by Cobbold's strident blundering.[24] The Home Secretary's artful process, which James Callaghan would deftly complete on becoming Home Secretary in 1967, would overcome attempts by the Prime Minister and Cobbold to keep the Walpole censorship principle alive. At a meeting on 22 November 1965 Cobbold gave Roy Jenkins a veiled ultimatum. If *Saved* was not prosecuted, the Lord Chamberlain told Jenkins he would declare publicly that his position as theatre censor had been irreparably undermined. He failed to appreciate however that the Labour government was reluctant to be seen giving any public support to a system of censorship which was increasingly regarded as anachronistic, repressive and unfair.

R.M. Morris, the Home Office official who wrote the minute of the meeting, explained the message Jenkins was trying to convey with all due deference to Cobbold. 'The law officers and the Lord Chancellor had felt particularly strongly that some public enquiry should be set up, since there would probably be a considerable furore over any prosecution of *Saved* and the law officers would feel much fortified in taking any steps if, in doing so, they could announce the institution of an enquiry.' Jenkins, at his most emollient, conceded that he was 'not entirely convinced that any prosecution [of the Royal Court] would necessarily provoke the public outcry his colleagues thought.' But he had agreed to an inquiry, 'on condition that it would be limited to theatre censorship alone.' As far as the exhibition of films was concerned, he felt voluntary censorship by the British Board of Film Censors worked satisfactorily and television had statutory duties to maintain 'acceptable standards'. Jenkins may have opened the way for prosecution of *Saved*, but he was cleverly exploiting the situation to launch that inquiry into stage censorship. When I put this interpretation of events to Lord Jenkins he said that he could not remember the details, but it was likely that he would have played the situation in such a way.[25]

Morris's memorandum may have been written in the neutral diction of the civil servant but it revealed Jenkins' artful suavity in dealing with Cobbold. The fact that Jenkins was supported by the permanent secretary to the Home Office, Sir Charles Cunningham, and two civil servants and that Cobbold brought Johnston with him underlined the seriousness of the encounter. Cobbold replied to Jenkins saying that for some time he believed 'his office as theatre censor could not be maintained indefinitely. That much was sensible and indisputable.' But then he went on to the attack. Ever since taking office, he said, he had anticipated his 'authority' under the 1843 Act would be challenged. After the refusal of the law officers to prosecute the Royal Court over *A Patriot for Me*, he had not been 'reluctant to meet the challenge *Saved* represented to his position.' If once more the law officers decided not to prosecute on the grounds that it was not in the public interest, 'then he could not say too strongly that he would feel it his duty somehow to represent to parliament that it was impossible for him to carry out his duties as theatre censor under the Theatres Act of 1843.' These were not the words of a compromiser. Cobbold was threatening to inflict maximum embarrassment upon the government if it did not support his strenuous interpretation of his duties. He was understandably fearful of a refusal to prosecute being declared at the same time as the announcement of an inquiry into theatre censorship.

His pressurising did not work. 'It was agreed that the Lord Chamberlain's proper course, if he felt his position undermined, would be to make representations to the Home Secretary as responsible minister,' the memorandum recorded. Cobbold was being warned, with all due politeness by Jenkins personally, that it would be constitutionally improper for him to make a public fuss. This, though, was not all. The Lord Chamberlain sought to intervene in the process of government. The memorandum recorded that Cobbold welcomed the idea of an inquiry, his main reason for enthusiasm being his conviction that the Theatres Act of 1843 was out of date. But he 'felt that the government would find it impossible to restrict an inquiry to plays' and that films and television should come within its purview as well. Jenkins disagreed. Besides it was not for Cobbold to give his unsolicited advice in matters quite beyond his stewardship. The moment when the Lord Chamberlain's fate as theatre censor was sealed, therefore, arrived at a moment when it looked as if he was about to be vindicated.

While *Saved* was running at the Court, Gaskill was approached in the foyer. 'Mr Gaskill?' 'Yes.' 'We are police officers. Could we have a word with you? Are you responsible for putting on this play?' 'Yes I did direct it and I am the artistic director of the company.'[26] With Greville Poke, the English Stage Company's secretary and Alfred Esdaile, the licensee of the theatre, Gaskill was charged with presenting a new play 'for hire' under Section 15 of the Theatres Act of 1843 before it had been licensed by the Lord Chamberlain. The Royal Court's counsel was certain what had caused the prosecution. 'I think the censor is gunning for the Royal Court as an avant-garde theatre. There are pressure groups watching the plays and presenting complaints in a concrete form and forcing him to take action. It is an attack on the Royal Court and not on club theatres in general.'[27] Cobbold's subsequent treatment of *Macbird* suggested that the counsel's contention was accurate. Findlater suggested unconvincingly that Cobbold was upset because the Royal Court was presenting *Saved* for club members in repertoire with plays that were open to the public. 'It was the mixture of public and private that upset the [Lord Chamberlain's] office.'[28] Cobbold, however, made no such written complaint nor did he make any protest along these lines to Jenkins or Dingle Foot.

William Gaskill was hauled up before a stipendiary magistrate on 14 February 1966, charged with offences against the Theatres Act of 1843, 'The whole atmosphere of everybody fighting together for what they believed in, cemented friendships, cemented beliefs,' Greville Poke recalled.[29] 'Theatre Defies the Censor. "Take this play off"' Court plea rejected', read the front-page lead of that day's London *Evening Standard*. Laurence Olivier and Lord Harewood attended court to give their influential evidence for the theatre. It was in vain: Leo Gradwell, the magistrate, ruled on 1 April that any performance 'for hire' under the 1843 Act had to be licensed by the Lord Chamberlain. The effect of this judgment was devastating. In theory it made it illegal for a theatre to present an unlicensed play to paying customers. Mr Gradwell, however, gave a bold hint that he was unhappy to have to make his ruling. 'I am tied to the rock of the law waiting for some Perseus to rescue me.'[30]

That Perseus had already arrived. For two days after *Saved* came to the magistrate's court, Lord Annan, Provost of University College London, initiated a debate in the House of Lords on theatre censorship. His proposal that a joint committee of both Houses be appointed 'to review the law and practice relating to the censorship of stage plays' was not his own innocent idea. For Annan was acting on the instructions of the Home Secretary, Roy Jenkins, as part of his stratagem to ease the Lord Chamberlain's depature from his theatrical office. 'Roy asked me to do this. It was the first thing I ever did for the

Labour government,' Annan told me. 'I was originally simply going to have a debate, but Roy changed this and said that the thing he would like me to do was to put a motion that a select committee of both Houses be appointed. It was Jenkins who got things going. Stowhill [his predecessor as Home Secretary] was a stick-in-the mud.'[31] Annan, who remembered the London stage before the war and the limitations placed upon it, thought theatre censorship absurd. 'You could refer to the dangers of syphilis provided you didn't refer to people's cocks. I remember the play *When Parents Sleep*, which was thought to be tremendously risky, frightfully daring because someone said, "Don't knock that thing arse over tip." ' The debate was stage-managed to ensure that the Lord Chamberlain was not ridiculed. 'I was frightfully careful not to mock the Lord Chamberlain and his officers. I thought that would be counterproductive,' Annan explained, 'though it was terribly difficult to praise the Lord Chamberlain. Cobbold was really an awfully stupid man. Governor of the Bank of England. But the old greybeards were clearly in the majority in the Lords.'

The antique greybeards, reactionaries and enemies of liberalism were reluctant to support the idea of a select committee. Lord Carrington, Conservative opposition leader in the Lords and Lord Dilhorne, an unadmired Lord Chancellor, favoured a Royal Commission. How strange it was that Lord Goodman, the Arts Council chairman who was Harold Wilson's solicitor, confidant and devout supporter, argued against a select committee. Goodman even ridiculously suggested that the Lord Chamberlain 'had in some ways been responsible for a more liberal theatre in recent years and that he had licensed a number of plays for the London theatre which, without the Lord Chamberlain, might not have seen the light of day.'[32] Perhaps Conservative speakers realised a select committee – its composition reflecting Labour's large majority in the House of Commons gained at the 1966 election – would recommend the institution of a far more liberal system.

The two independents on the committee were Annan himself and Goodman, who despite his tribute to the Lord

Chamberlain opposed theatre censorship. The Earl of Scarbrough, the former Lord Chamberlain, Lord Kilmuir, a far-right Lord Chancellor loathed and despised by all liberals, and Sir David Renton were the only Conservatives liable to oppose the dissolution of the ties between the Lord Chamberlain and the stage. Kilmuir died and was replaced by Lord Dilhorne, who had succeeded him as Lord Chancellor and shared many of his views, but was regarded as stupid. The evidence Cobbold gave to the committee, his speeches in the House of Lords while the Theatres Bill to abolish stage censorship was being considered, and his 1965 interview with the *Sunday Times*, are all indicative of his authoritarian cast of mind. Until the end he struggled to persuade the Prime Minister and Home Secretary to ensure that playwrights could not represent living people on stage. 'I believe there must be somebody with general supervisory powers over the theatre,' he told the select committee. When the committee's report was published in autumn 1967 it unanimously recommended the termination of pre-censorship of the theatre. Cobbold reacted by suggesting that there should be 'some more reserve censorship powers to cover all the art forms, theatre censorship and the media.'[33]

A mere month after Home Office lawyers had begun drafting the bill to remove theatres from the Lord Chamberlain's control, a play was submitted for licensing that played into the hands of those believing a liberated theatre would give licence to scandalously offensive drama. If some satirist had been asked to dream up a theatrical scenario designed to outrage the Lord Chamberlain he would not have done better than Edward Bond. Bond's *Early Morning*, a surreal and farcical melodrama, created a mad wonderland, inspired by the politics of Victorian England. The play discovered Queen Victoria in the grip of a lesbian love affair with Florence Nightingale. This epitome of Victorian self-sacrifice was, more shockingly still, discovered in the arms of one of her Prime Ministers. The royal family, Gladstone and Disraeli were depicted as internecine gangsters plotting to do away with each other and ended up in a heaven which was not so much beatific as bestial, a hell where people ate each other for pleasure. What situation could have been better calculated to enrage the Chamberlain than a scene in heaven where Victoria herself is seen happily munching a bloody, human hand? What lines could have better inflamed Cobbold than Nightingale's 'The Queen has raped me. Her legs are covered in shiny black hair.' Heriot was comparatively restrained in his report. 'The play appears to this reader to be the product of a diseased imagination. Cannibalism and lesbianism may be legitimate themes for a dramatist, but not in this context.' Indeed, not when it was such distinguished people eating each other. 'I think the author must have a very sick mind,' Johnston said in a note on 5 November 1967. 'And I cannot conceive that anyone would want to see the play. To me the cannibalism in the third act is disgusting.'[34] There was no question of disgust being an emotion that any self-respecting playwright should be allowed to stir in other people's minds. The play was banned outright. As far as the Lord Chamberlain was concerned, *Early Morning* ranked as the apotheosis of impertinence. Cobbold wrote on 9 February 1968 that he would not license a play in which the Queen's ancestors were mixed up with 'various unsavoury practices.' A line of strict precedence was being followed. The Lord Chamberlain traditionally refused to allow plays about royalty to be staged until the monarch concerned was long since dead. A play about George IV's consort, Queen Caroline, took twelve years of intermittent pleading to achieve a licence. Lord Spencer, Chamberlain in 1910, refused to allow the play, *Pains and Penalties*, to be staged, commenting, 'It dealt with a sad episode of comparatively recent date in the life of a lady of Royal rank.'[35] When it came to royalty playwrights were obliged to descend to a level of hagiography at which even the most devoted royal historian would balk. The sovereign was after all the final arbiter of which plays about royalty could be staged. George V vetoed Louis Parker's *Queen Victoria*, due for production in 1924. He found it 'vulgar and in many ways historically incorrect.' Not until George VI's accession were plays about Victoria even considered for licensing.

When William Gaskill asked why *Early Morning* had been refused a licence, Johnston replied in a letter reminiscent of Joe

Orton's style when pastiching the tone of indignant middle-England in one of his mock letters to the *Daily Telegraph*. '[It] comprises mainly historical characters who are subjected throughout to highly offensive and untrue accusations of gross indecency,' Sir John wrote on 18 January 1968, as though anyone could imagine Victoria was either a cannibal or a feaster on the flesh of Nightingale. 'They are selected for insult apparently as being nationally respected figures with long records of devoted service to their country and fellow citizens.' Gaskill paid a visit to Sir John at St James's Palace in a vain attempt to achieve a change of heart and mind. Johnston spoke again in that prim, pompous Chamberlain diction, like one of those Orton characters only able to speak in the jargon of bureaucratic formality. The trouble, Sir John explained, was the 'linking of historical personages with various unsavoury practices including cannibalism.'

Instead of conforming to practice and tradition, and allowing a club performance, Cobbold wrote to the Director of Public Prosecutions about the proposed Sunday night performance of *Early Morning*. As Johnston revealingly put it, 'We told them that the Lord Chamberlain felt strongly about the play and suggested the Director might wish to consult the Attorney-General which he did.'[36] Cobbold was adhering to the strict letter of the 1843 Act, section 15 of which had been recently elucidated in the *Saved* court case and made it an offence either to present a play before it had been licensed or if it were refused a licence. He was attempting for the first and only time this century to make use of his power to ban the performance of a stage play, even when it was a private members-only performance. But the approval of the Attorney-General, Elwyn Jones, was required after the DPP had decided there was a case to answer. Given the earlier refusal of Elwyn-Jones to prosecute in the case of *A Patriot for Me* and given the way Roy Jenkins had exploited Cobbold's anxieties about *Saved* to initiate an inquiry into stage censorship, Cobbold's aggressive tactics appear rash. The two performances would have passed with little notice, had not Cobbold, with his blunderbuss approach, threatened the panoply of the law and the 1843 Act.

In fairness to the Lord Chamberlain, however, he may well have felt that *Early Morning* constituted an almost personal affront to the sovereign. It is also possible that the Queen, when she was given the horrid details, was offended by the play's surreal mockery of Victoria. I referred in the first chapter to Cobbold's note in the *Early Morning* file, that said, 'I mentioned last night to the Queen the present position about *Early Morning*. Her Majesty agreed that *this should be put firmly in the Attorney's lap* [my italics].' The use of the word 'firmly' suggests that the Queen may herself have supported the pugnaciousness of Cobbold's tactics. The Lord Chamberlain recorded that he told the Queen he would be grateful if she would mention the censorship bill to the Prime Minister. For a month earlier, according to Johnston, Cobbold had been informed in a letter from the Prime Minister that he was 'not too hopeful of the bill completing all the stages during the session'. The Lord Chamberlain was anxious about continuing to administer an act of parliament which was scheduled to be repealed, but had yet to be put out of existence. The Queen duly raised the matter with Harold Wilson in her weekly audience with him. 'Perhaps as a result,' Johnston dryly writes, 'the Prime Minister was able to give the Lord Chamberlain on 11 April rather more encouraging news about the passage of the Bill.'[37]

The first performance of *Early Morning*, for members of the English Stage Society, took place on the evening of Sunday 31 March. John Calder, publisher of the American novel *Last Exit to Brooklyn* by Hubert Selby, that had been prosecuted under the Obscene Publications Act, was in the audience. He noticed the presence in the audience of the 'same police officer who had served the notice of prosecution on Calder for his publishing Selby's novel.'[38] Two days later Gaskill and Alfred Esdaile, the theatre's licensee who was at odds with his artistic director over choice of plays, were questioned by two police officers. They were told that an enquiry had been launched which might end in a report to the DPP. Johnston noted that 'a Vice Squad inspector became a club member without any difficulty and attended the performance'. But Mary Fisher, a junior member of the Chamberlain's staff, was unsuccessful in so doing. The membership rules were being slackly observed.

At this point of crisis for the Royal Court, Alfred Esdaile, vice-chairman of the management committee, turned against Gaskill. Although the committee, after taking legal advice, decided to continue with the second performance, Esdaile exploited his rights as licensee and banned any further showing of the play. Helen Montagu vividly recollected the sense of furtive excitement with which Gaskill and the theatre staff retaliated and decided that the show would still go on. Club members were ushered to a dress rehearsal of *Early Morning* the following Sunday afternoon, escorted into the theatre by way of a side-door.[39] This was a device to keep within the ambit of the law. If the production was not 'for hire,' with admission charges, the play did not have to be licensed. News of the Lord Chamberlain's activity had, of course, reached the national press. A trenchant Gaskill was quoted in *The Times* observing, 'The Lord Chamberlain is a member of the Queen's household as well as a censor of plays. Here the two functions have come into conflict. He obviously felt that the play would be distasteful to members of the Royal family.'[40] The day of the special dress rehearsal, to which an audience was to be admitted, the *Sunday Times* reported how two police officers had quoted the 1843 Theatres Act when interviewing Gaskill. A Scotland Yard spokesman agreed that an investigation 'had been launched which might ultimately lead to consultations with the Director of Public Prosecutions.'[41]

The theatre critics did not wave flags of royalist outrage in support of Cobbold when reviewing the special dress-rehearsal performance. It has been wrongly claimed that the reviews were loud in their condemnation. Many reviews were disparaging, but not all of them. No critic suggested that royalty had been wounded let alone insulted by the play. Irving Wardle wrote, referring to the Victoria–Nightingale connection, 'It no fault of Mr Bond's that this stray detail should have been inflated out of proportion to its significance. Heaven knows he makes little enough of the lesbian attachment once he has established it.' What Wardle regretted was that 'the Royal Court's just and necessary fight for theatrical free speech should be conducted on behalf of a piece as muddled and untalented as this.' In a faint but distinct echo of Johnston's objection to the play he asked, 'What on earth is being proved by taking a group of well-known historical figures and inventing an action fantastically at variance with their lives.'[42]

It is a question which goes to the heart of the debate about censorship and the reluctance of some English politicians to allow themselves to be impersonated on stage. For if you outlaw that element of creative fantasy that allows writers to create fictional existences for historical figures then you fetter and confine the free play of the playwright's invention and imagination. In *Early Morning* Bond had dared write openly what Fielding had done by parody when satirising Walpole, and what Elizabethan writers had achieved in a similar vein. The English law, both before the 1968 Theatres Act and after it, would prosecute where there was a case to be answered against the charge of defamation of a living, identifiable individual. After death, the lives of the famous and infamous alike may be subject to any creative act of defamation. The performance of Bond's play caused anxiety among senior officials at the Arts Council because there was a residual fear that an amendment to the Theatres Act might be tabled and passed by which no reference to living persons, the sovereign or her predecessors would be allowed. In the end, though, no such restriction was made. The theatre was sensibly subject to the laws of libel and slander.

Most reviews were more enthusiastic than Wardle's. Hobson suggested that the play was the negation of drama. But the *Daily Mail*'s Peter Lewis, who disliked the play, nevertheless reacted with a sophisticated realism that Cobbold never mastered. 'For the Lord Chamberlain so near to the end of his censorship function to ban it as the offensive representation of historic and royal persons is solemn to the point of idiocy,' he judged. 'But it would be equally idiotic to make a great issue of principle and liberty out of the play, which seemed to me obscure, inconsistent, pointless and boring and greatly inferior to Mr Bond's previously banned play *Saved*.'[43] Lewis's stance was one with which the government seemed to find sympathy. On 1 April 1968 Sir John had minuted, 'The Director of Public Prosecutions tells me that having talked again with the Attorney-General their present plans are if these two Sunday night performances pass off quietly to take no action. The DPP will then write to the Royal Court and and warn them that if there are any further performances they may be prosecuted.' The memorandum does not explain why or how it came to pass that Gaskill was interviewed by Scotland Yard officers before the two Sunday performances, which passed off without any demonstrations or expressions of outrage from the audience.

In 1969, by which time the Lord Chamberlain no longer served as the worm in any theatrical bud, *Early Morning* was given a full, free public performance. No breasts were beaten, no peace was disturbed, no royalists revolted. The play passed by with all the decorum of the Queen's own motorcade. Philip Hope-Wallace, the *Guardian*'s critic, interestingly commented on 'the really succulent, chewy, lip-licking cannibal feast [in heaven], prolonged for something like forty minutes.' It left him untouched and unshocked, though he had admired much of the play as 'quite original and strange in a way that Strindberg, author of the Dream Play, would have endorsed or anticipated if he could.'[44]

Bond's precipitatory role in accelerating the Lord Chamberlain's demise has been overlooked or unappreciated. One commentator on Bond reduced the censorship furore over *Saved* to a single sentence. He made passing reference to 'the moral indignation of the Lord Chamberlain who insisted on cuts which would have made a performance of the play impossible.'[45] Why were the Lord Chamberlain and many critics so revolted by a scene in which a dummy is stoned to death by a small gang of yobs. The blinding of Gloucester in *King Lear*, the ghastliness of *Titus Andronicus* in which Lavinia's tongue and arms are torn away and human flesh consumed, the strangling of the Duchess of Malfi and the killing of her children and the refined atrocities of Tourneur's *The Revenger's Tragedy* may still disturb audiences, especially as the simulation of extreme violence on stage can look all too life-like. But in a stage performance it is very difficult to make violence horrifically realistic. Irving Wardle's original response and his subsequent retraction says much about the sensibilities and sensitivities of audiences so long protected from the smack and crackle of real-life, demotic speech whose vulgarities had been exiled from the theatre. If Bond's louts had spoken in Shakespearean syntax the play would probably have been received in respectful horror.

The select committee's report had been received on all sides, even that of the Lord Chamberlain, with approval. Yet the legislative procedures by which the Lord Chamberlain's regime was phased out were tenative and anxious. On 1 November 1967 *The Times* reported that Jenkins' theatre censorship bill had been dropped because of lack of parliamentary time. Jenkins assigns the blame clearly. 'It was Crossman [as leader of the House of Commons] who succeeded in blocking me, though he may have been acting on this issue as an agent for the Prime Minister. He recorded me at the time as "getting more imperious" about the bill.'[46] Callaghan's success in coaxing the bill through parliament brought him no fanfares of thanks. There was no public rejoicing or glee on the part of dramatists whose work had been so long suppressed, stifled and interfered with by successive Lords Chamberlain. Nor were there any serious attempts by theatre critics and commentators to pass condemnatory verdicts on a system that had ensured that contemporary classics were banned from the stage. Cobbold, having been instructed by Roy Jenkins on 25 July 1967 that theatre censorship would have to continue until new legislation had reached the statute book, carried on with unbalanced conservatism. He was going to end his regime with the flags of reaction still boldly flying.

Cobbold's personal reaction to the script of the musical *Hair* was characteristic. The musical's Vietnam war-dodgers, its flower-power, hirsute hippies revelling in a joyful clutch of sexual freedoms, whether straight, gay or both, and joyfully succumbing to whatever drugs came to mouth or mind, sang anthems of permissiveness and dissent. The musical celebrated everything the Lord Chamberlain's censorship abhorred. The

American crusade against communists, the hippies of *Hair* believed, had to be resisted.

T.B. Harward, the Assistant Examiner, reported that if those forbidden words 'piss, balls, fart, shit and cock' were removed, together with a stage direction, 'Berger puts his hand on Claud's crotch', a licence could be given. But by 5 April 1968 Ronald Hill had scrutinised the musical and caught more than a whiff of its liberated essence. 'This is a demoralising play,' he wrote, apparently unaware that it was a musical. 'It extolls dirt, anti-establishment views, homosexuality and free love and drug-taking and it inveighs against patriotism.' To suggest at the closing-point of the Lord Chamberlain's regime that a script should be banned because of its anti-establishment convictions reveals how close to totalitarianism the Chamberlain's censorship could sway. Heriot, having read the text, supported Hill. 'This piece is dangerously permissive. Not recommended for licensing,' he wrote on 6 June. The old Chief Examiner was not prepared to let the new world speak or sing its new lines in the theatre. There is also a charmingly old fashioned note in his report where Heriot mentions the words 'freaked them out' and writes, 'I don't understand this.'[47] However, Johnston as Comptroller, recommended that the musical be licensed. Lord Cobbold thought otherwise: he was disturbed by the problems of male and female nudity. Cobbold banned three different versions of the musical in the last few months of the Lord Chamberlain's power, *Hair* triumphantly took the stage weeks after he lost control of the theatre that September.

Only three years earlier Cobbold, in his *Sunday Times* interview, had claimed 'My personal objective is to try to assess the norm of educated adult opinion and if possible to keep just ahead of it.' But he would have not recognised a norm even if it had goosed him.

The Society of West End Theatre Producers was the only theatrical constituency to oppose the repeal of the Lord Chamberlain's powers. These impresarios, however, were motivated by short-sighted self-interest. They believed that the Lord Chamberlain's imprimatur gave them an imposing seal of approval, a protection from lawsuits. Cobbold vainly protested against the idea of a theatre that would be allowed to stage plays in which the monarch and her family were characters. He unsuccessfully tabled amendments to the Theatres Act designed to protect the royal family and practising politicians from being criticised, mocked or ridiculed upon the stage. He even wanted a clause to 'prevent reference on the stage to living persons in a way calculated to offend public feeling'.[48]

The absence of jubilation when the Theatres Act became law was remarkable. So too was the refusal to blame Lords Chamberlain for the extent of their repressiveness and arrogant philistinism. The damage done by these men was enormous and enduring. They forced the English theatre to cut itself off from depicting and discussing crucial aspects of life with such thoroughness that generations of play-goers came to forget that the theatre could be a forum for expressing political or social protest. Anyone scrutinising the twentieth-century English theatre canon, up to 1968, will be struck by its parochialism, its apparent refusal to concern itself with the greatest issues and anguishes of this violent century, as England, Europe and the world beyond experienced them. *The Times*, in a mendacious leading article, 'Last of the Blue Pencils', that debated the conclusions of the select committee's recommendations, closed its eyes to that library of classic plays banned or butchered by the Lord Chamberlain. It suggested the Chamberlain's censorial powers had exerted no adverse effect on modern drama. '[The censor] cannot convincingly be represented as a stifling influence on English drama,' it claimed. 'Most of the excisions and changes he demands concern the trivia of indecency, which are not the stuff of intellectual and artistic freedom.'[49]

In a narrow sense the leader-writer was accurate. Many twentieth-century disallowances, especially those in the last decade, had to do with vulgarities of language. But the rules by which English playwrights, producers and directors had to live ensured that certain subjects were regarded as off limits and could not be brought to theatrical life. The Lord Chamberlain did not rank as a serial-killer of plays, but he ensured that the theatre was prevented from dealing with substantial areas of life and behaviour. A theatre censor who banned work by Ibsen,

Strindberg, Pirandello, Arthur Miller, Shaw, Bruckner, Brieux, Osborne, Bond, Granville-Barker and Rattigan cannot be said to have been concerned with mere vulgarities. To compare, as *The Times* did, the stage with cinema and television censorship, was not apposite. For the objections to theatre censorship had always to do with its autocratic nature, its administration by a senior official of the monarch's court and the sweeping rules of oppression by which it operated under acts of parliament.

At least *The Times* conceded that the Chamberlain's 'political censorship, his interpretation of a duty to prevent anything "calculated to impair relations with a friendly power" is more objectionable and here the case against has more weight.' Indeed. But not just plays about foreign leaders fell victim to the Lord Chamberlain. All political plays were liable to turn the Chamberlain's pencil blue. The veto on plays which impugned the leadership of a so-called friendly power worked with deadly effect. No English dramatist apparently was driven to deal with the fascist regimes of the 1930s, the process that led to the atomic bombing of Hiroshima and Nagasaki, the ghastliness perpetrated by Hitler and Stalin, or the tyrannies experienced in China and under other totalitarian leaderships. No wonder. Their plays would have been disallowed. In the 1930s you could not win licences for plays that might offend Hitler or Mussolini or Stalin. In a few other countries some rare playwrights, whether writing directly or under cover of allegory, managed to speak out on forbidden themes. At the close of one of the great British plays of the century, Shaw's *Heartbreak House*, the sound of some seismic disturbance sounds to us like the intimation of catastrophe. But for the chattering, well-heeled eccentrics of the Heartbreak House that serves as Shaw's microcosm of Britain, the noise is greeted with excitement. In just such an atmosphere of misguided frivolity the English theatre was forced to bask, prevented by authority from facing up to life.

Yet to damn the institution of theatre censorship in Britain, as opposed to indicting the values and beliefs that guided its application to specific plays, is crapulous and unfair. The Lord Chamberlain's role was a relic of a time and a state of mind understandably convinced that the stage could and might become an agent of social disruption and subversion. Victorians clung, with some justice, to that belief and in the twentieth century, at periods of social unease, it is possible to understand why governments were sometimes fearful of what impact a play might have. In the same century other countries banned plays and witnessed riotous first nights. Tolstoy's *Power of Darkness* was banned in Russia until 1902. It was not possible to première Strindberg's *The Father* in Sweden and *Miss Julie* was not produced on stage there for sixteen years after it had been written and even then it was censored. Gerhart Hauptmann's *The Weavers* (1892) was initially banned 'for police reasons connected with public order'.[50] There were riots in 1907 at the Irish first night of Synge's *The Playboy of the Western World*. Sean O'Casey's *The Plough and the Stars* was greeted in 1922 with a rain of vegetables, shoes, chairs and stink bombs. Ernst Toller's *Masses and Man*, dedicated to world revolution, caused riots in Nuremberg in the 1920s. Leonid Andreyev's *The Life of Man* (1907) was banned in Odessa 'and other places where the authorities feared a civil disturbance'.[51]

Britain, where the Lord Chamberlain could not empathise with the radical, modernist sense of an absurd world from whose stage God had departed, suffered no riots, no stink bombs, no uproar. Its theatre was tamed into a habit of deference and even thirty-one years after the Lord Chamberlain ceased to censor and confine and insist upon conformity, it has not fully re-established its traditional eagerness to question, dissent and provoke.

Notes

1. John Johnston, *The Lord Chamberlain's Blue Pencil* (1990), p. 112.
2. LC file on *Saved*, Edward Bond
3. Philip Roberts, *The Royal Court Theatre* (1986), p. 161.
4. William Gaskill, *A Sense of Direction* (1988), p. 68.
5. Roberts, op. cit., p. 162.
6. Ibid., p. 36.

7. LC file on *Saved*, Edward Bond.
8. Johnston, op. cit., p. 184.
9. Both accounts came from Roberts, op. cit., p. 40.
10. Helen Montagu, interview with author, 21 June 1966.
11. *Daily Mail*, 4 November 1965.
12. Gaskill, op. cit., p. 67.
13. *Guardian*, 4 November 1965.
14. *Sunday Times*, 7 November 1965.
15. *Daily Telegraph*, 4 November 1965.
16. *The Times*, 4 November 1965.
17. Text of Wardle's lecture (undated, summer 1966); supplied by Irving Wardle.
18. John Peter, interview with author, 8 May 1999.
19. *Sunday Times*, 9 February 1969.
20. Edward Bond, *Plays One* (1994), pp. 12–13.
21. *The Times*, 15 November 1965.
22. Johnston, op. cit., p. 113.
23. LC file on *Dingo*, Charles Wood.
24. Roy Jenkins, interview with author, 20 July 1999.
25. Ibid.
26. Gaskill, op. cit., p. 69.
27. Roberts, op. cit., p. 41.
28. Findlater, op. cit., p. 173.
29. Roberts, op. cit., p. 42.
30. Gaskill, op. cit., p. 69.
31. Lord Annan, interview with author, September 1994.
32. Johnston, op. cit., p. 221.
33. Ibid., pp. 235 and 239.
34. LC file on *Early Morning*, Edward Bond.
35. The details of bans on plays about royalty are found in Johnson op. cit., pp. 103–104.
36. Ibid., p. 107.
37. Ibid., p. 240.
38. Roberts, op. cit., p. 83.
39. Helen Montagu, interview with author, 8 July 1999.
40. *The Times*, 8 April 1968.
41. *Sunday Times*, 7 April 1968.
42. *The Times*, 8 April 1968.

43. *Daily Mail*, 8 April 1968.
44. *Guardian*, 4 March 1969.
45. David L. Hirst, *Edward Bond* (1985), p. 45.
46. Roy Jenkins, interview with author, 20 July 1999.
47. LC file on *Hair*.
48. Johnston, op. cit., p. 241.
49. *The Times*, 22 June 1967.
50. Styan, *Modern drama in Theory and Practice* (1981), vol. 1, p. 50.
51. Styan, op. cit., vol. 2, p. 90.

Epilogue

THE LIMITS OF FREEDOM

The freeing of the theatre from the Lord Chamberlain's suppressing vigour and his Victorian values did not mean that playwrights at once took advantage of his departure by composing scenes of lurid sexual debauchery or by seeking to break those taboos that the Lord Chamberlain maintained. Producers and directors proceeded with caution. The Theatres Act of 1968 was a liberalising measure. In harmony with other such legislation it was guided by the conviction that the law of the land was intended to suppress forms of conduct or behaviour that could be identified as harmful to the moral well-being of a significant number of individuals. Lord Devlin had argued in *The Enforcement of Morals* (1959) that where legislation was concerned with matters of morality the state should not only protect society from harm, but should also be designed to affirm a moral consensus. That moral consensus did not hold good in an increasingly secular world where the doctrines of the Church of England or Catholicism no longer commanded general acceptance. Pluralistic values had come to take the place of Christian absolutes. John Stuart Mill in *On Liberty* (1859) argued that freedom of expression was a defining aspect of liberty. His notion of a market-place in the trading of ideas remains valuable. For, as he suggested, we cannot know what 'social, moral or intellectual developments will turn out to be possible, necessary or desirable for human beings and for their future, and free expression, intellectual and artistic . . . is essential to human development.'[1]

The changes permitted by the dismantling of the 1737 and 1843 acts restored an important element of this theatrical trade in relatively free ideas. Playwrights were allowed the right to create characters whose speech seemed natural, not rigorously bowdlerised. Indeed, dramatis personae could say more than human beings in real life. People speaking in public could still be arrested for threatening to disturb the peace with the vulgar or abusive nature of their speech. Those on stage were far less likely to be prosecuted. Yet the theatre retained its capacity to disturb and provoke the censorious, particularly in relation to homosexual behaviour. The depiction of such activity became an index of the new liberality. In the three decades since the Lord Chamberlain ceased to act as the arbiter of what could be shown on stage, opponents of theatre freedom initially concentrated their energies upon discouraging the graphic depiction of homosexual behaviour.

It has taken more than twenty years for it to become acceptable to stage scenes of gay intimacy with elements of the candour allowed for heterosexual modes. In 1982 the director Michael Bogdanov appeared at the Old Bailey charged with attempting to procure an act of gross indecency between two males in defiance of the Sexual Offences Act of 1956. Mrs Mary Whitehouse had brought a private prosecution against Bogdanov on the basis of a scene in the National Theatre production of *The Romans in Britain*, where an act of male rape was simulated. The case was withdrawn on the intervention of the Attorney-General and did not go to trial. Yet a ruling by Mr Justice Staughton that the Sexual Offences Act could, in theory, be applied to performances on stage and that the simulation of buggery on stage might constitute gross indecency, bequeathed a potentially dangerous legacy. For in refusing to distinguish between the simulated and the actual Staughton implied that in cases of gross indecency an aspect of the offence might lie in the spectacle of the offence. The *Guardian* commented in a leading article that this ruling had driven 'a coach and horses through the Theatres Act of 1968 . . . The draftsmen . . . forgot to ensure that statutory as well as common law could not be invoked against the theatre.'[2]

Perhaps it was because of the fracas over *The Romans in Britain* that for the next decade there was no attempt to challenge the limits of theatrical decorum in relation to gay sexual activity. It was not until the National Theatre's 1992 production of Tony Kushner's *Angels in America* that a scene of homosexual buggery was again simulated on stage. On this occasion, however, the dramatic technique was non-representational. The two actors stood at a distance from each other and did not even mime the action. Even so there were audible first-night gasps of shock when the act took place, a faint murmuring of unease. It may well be, however, that the audience reaction was inspired by the thought of an unsafe sex act about to be simulated with one of the perpetrators, a desperately unhappy young man, who when a condom breaks expresses his wish to be infected with the HIV virus.

The theatre critic of the *Daily Telegraph*, Charles Spencer, was horrified. This was the newspaper which had railed against *Ghosts* at its 1891 première. Its septuagenarian critic, W.A. Darlington, had on 5 May 1964 likened the effects of Joe Orton's *Entertaining Mr Sloane* to 'snakes writhing about my feet'. Spencer lived up to *Telegraph* tradition and the newspaper's headline, describing him as both 'appalled and exhilarated', conveys the reviewer's emotional turbulence. He gave the impression that he had been shocked to the core, or so close to it that he departed from his usual standards of accuracy, rather as J.W. Lambert had when reviewing *Saved*. Spencer may not have been so much disturbed by the unprotected nature of the act as the simple fact of its representation, however decorous in its stylised form. He and others of his ilk would watch scenes of extreme cruelty with few qualms, if perpetrated in Shakespeare or Webster, but for Spencer two actors simulating consensual homosexual intercourse was brutal and almost unwatchable. 'In the second interval, several hardened theatre critics were looking distinctly green about the gills,' he wrote sensationally. 'Its author spares his audience nothing. The language would make a swearing squaddie blush, while the depiction of the messy misery of full-blown AIDS and of a brutal homosexual encounter in New York's Central Park are almost unbearable to watch, even though the latter scene is mimed, with the two actors standing several yards apart.[3]

I was there and saw not a sign of green-complexioned critics. Spencer's extravagant imaginings harked back to the 1891 Ibsen première. On that occasion a reviewer from the *Licensed Victuallers' Mirror* condemned the audience for having in its midst 'sickly-looking socialists' and 'green-complexioned, oddly dressed females of unhealthy aspect, their bodies seemingly as diseased as their minds.'[4] In the case of both *Ghosts* and *Angels in America* a taboo is broken. Ibsen dealt with syphilis as the secret saboteur and destroyer of family life. Kushner suggested what self-destructive urges existed in people whose sexuality exiles them from the support and mutuality of close, family relations. Mill's apology for the value of the free trade in new ideas is affirmed. The erosion of the taboo upon the representation of gay sexual activity occurred spasmodically, rather as societal attitudes shifted. In *Poor Superman* by Brad Fraser, at the Hampstead Theatre in 1994, an act of buggery was graphically mimed. Spencer confessed himself worried about 'the present triumphal progress of gay theatre'. Why, he wondered did 'many gay writers assume sexuality was "the be-all and end-all" of individual existence.' Worse, 'some new dramas seem intent on making any heterosexual in the audience feel uncomfortable if not unwelcome.'[5] Homosexual characters and situations having been exiled from the stage for decades, the heterosexual Spencer was experiencing that sense of exclusion that homosexuals knew from bitter experience. But there was otherwise no outburst of complaint.

Mark Ravenhill's *Shopping and Fucking* at the New Ambassadors Theatre in 1996 then took sexual candour to what seemed to be the limits of propriety and acceptability. Here was a twilight world of homosexuality no 1950s high court judge would have even dared imagine. The simulation of the buggery of a fourteen-year-old masochistic rent boy, who wished to be violated with a knife, and a bloody example of analingus, was depicted with a harsh, dispassionate candour. These shocking scenes, the director Max Stafford-Clark explained, were not inspired by a wish to sensationalise. They were based upon experiences retailed by rent boys interviewed in the course of research for the play. The scenes of queer sexual congress opened doors upon a world of adolescent male prostitution, drug-taking and sexual exploitation. It was actually the title rather than the contents that caused problems of censorship. In the summer of 1998 a series of neon askerisks appeared on the façade of the Gielgud Theatre when the play transferred to Shaftesbury Avenue: 'Shopping and F★★★★g by Mark Raven-hill'.

A stranger to Britain, reading this neon sign, might have concluded that the use of the asterisks was to poke fun at old-fashioned notions of decorum and restraint. Both the author and the producer had been eager to emblazon the word in full upon the neon-lit frontage of the Gielgud. But a robustly surviving Victorian statute, which belongs to that volume of English law designed to protect an easily offended public from awareness, discussion or depiction of sexual desire or activity, forbade any such display. In just such a minor incident can be detected the residue of that largely defunct twentieth-century system of controlling and censoring the stage. The Indecent Advertisements Act of 1889 had not only outlawed advertisements 'relating to syphilis, gonorrhoea . . . or other infirmity arising from or relating to sexual intercourse.' It also forbade the exhibiting in public view of 'any written matter which is of an indecent or obscene nature'. Underlying this legislation is an implicit taboo relating to all public discussion of sexual matters. That taboo still flourishes and exerts an influence on the nature, subject-matter and scope of English drama.

A governing concern about the morality of depicting violence resurfaced in 1995 when *Blasted*, by the then unknown Sarah Kane, was performed at that old hot-house of controversy, the Royal Court. James Macdonald's production infuriated the enemies of relatively unfettered freedom on stage by depicting acts of brute force, goaded by sexual and violent impulses. Kane's Grand Guignol, nightmare fantasy, devised to suggest what thin, frail lines of civilisation and social mores separate men from their atavistic and violent selves, was set in a Leeds hotel which surrealistically transformed into a battlefield.

Here a mentally retarded girl and a dying tabloid journalist were abruptly removed from the real world when civil war broke out in their room and civilised standards were abruptly discarded. The morning after the première the *Daily Mail* broke out in a display of outrage which set in train a rash of media reports, articles and discussions. It was a useful reminder that the urge to censor rather than just to deplore specific stage plays may have been sleeping but had not died.

'Finally I have been driven into the arms of Disgusted of Tunbridge Wells,' wrote the *Daily Mail's* Jack Tinker, who a year later hailed *Shopping and Fucking*.[6] 'For utterly and entirely disgusted I was by a play which appears to know no bounds of decency yet has no message to convey by way of excuse.' In a peroration, that drew attention to the ever-watchful armies of the moral Right, and their belief in renewed censorship, he wrote, 'but with the hounds of repression snapping at the heels of sex and violence, the Royal Court have surely fed them a feast with this.' The *Daily Telegraph's* Charles Spencer sounded a note of relative moderation in merely condemning the experience as a 'nauseating dog's breakfast of a play'. What with male rape, the eating of eyeballs gouged from the journalist's sockets and a bite taken from the corpse of a baby (not well played by a less than life-size doll) there was something for most critics to condemn. The *Sunday Times* even sent its media correspondent, Jonathan Miller, to give a blow-by-blow account of the play. 'Judging by the warm applause, the audience were pleased with all this,' he wrote. 'But then many of them were carrying copies of the *Guardian* and were presumably intellectuals for whom this masterwork was replete with significance.'[7]

Reviewers suggested that Kane had transgressed unwritten rules of taste and decorum as they applied to the stage, although there was no suggestion that the Theatres Act had been defied. The old desire to censor had been reawakened. Kane's depiction of violence, her use of shock tactics, was in a historic tradition, but there was no recognition of that crucial fact in the notices of reviewers who impugned Kane's methods or her purposes. The Elizabethan fear of the theatre's potency to stir dissident behaviour had returned with the vengeance of the morally fervent.

The critical and public response to Ravenhill's play suggested that the English theatre had at last achieved an unfettered freedom to show and do what it liked. This supposition was wrong. If theatre reviewers had condemned *Shopping and Fucking* as obscene, if national newspapers and a significant number of MPs had taken the line that the play constituted a theatrical obscenity, the Attorney-General could have authorised a prosecution. Section 2 of the Theatres Act rules that a play shall be judged obscene if, 'taken as a whole', the effect of a play is 'such as to tend to deprave and corrupt persons who were likely, having regard to all relevant circumstances, to attend it.' This section of the act, the 'Prohibition of Presentation of Obscene Performances', was designed to subject stage plays to the same tests of obscenity as those set for books, magazines and periodicals, and itemised in the Obscene Publications Acts of 1959 and 1964. The Theatres Act, however, afforded stage performance one specific protection not permitted to publications.

In 1971 Lord Widgery, an irascible and reactionary Lord Chief Justice, heard an appeal by the three editors of the hippy magazine *Oz*, whose special 'School Kids' issue was judged to be obscene. He ruled in an explication of the 1959 and 1964 acts that a magazine could be judged obscene if just one item within it was liable to have a corrupting effect upon the minds of likely readers. But the Theatres Act, as if wishing to give particular protection to theatrical revues with numerous individual sketches, ruled that such a production would not 'infringe the law by reason only of one salacious scene, unless it is sufficiently dominant or memorable to colour the entire presentation.' This equivocal form of protection may have saved one or two early 1970s West End revues, like *Oh Calcutta!*, *Let My People Come* and *The Dirtiest Show in Town*, in which individual items might have been considered obscene. The sixth section of the act, 'Provocation of Breach of the Peace', does, however, pose a potentially serious threat to the stage because of the vagueness of its terms:

If there is given a public performance of a play involving the use of threatening, abusive or insulting words or behaviour, any person, who whether for gain or not, presented or directed that performance shall be guilty of an offence if

a) he did so with intent to provoke a breach of the peace;
b) the performance, taken as a whole, was likely to occasion a breach of the peace.

In 1989 Jim Allen's play, *Perdition*, directed by Ken Loach, went into rehearsal at the Royal Court Theatre and raised almost immediate problems for the artistic director, Max Stafford-Clark. For *Perdition* charged Zionist leaders of the Jewish community in Hungary with colluding with Nazis by agreeing to conceal the fact that Jews were being sent to extermination camps in exchange for the saving of the lives of selected Jews. Such outrage and anger was expressed by some influential Jews that the board of the Royal Court met to consider whether *Perdition*'s production should be cancelled. Subsequently Max Stafford-Clark decided to withdraw the play. Ten years later it was staged at the Gate Theatre without a squeak of protest.

It is perfectly possible to envisage a situation today in which a contemporary play could be threatened with prosecution under section 6 of the 1968 act. If some new play, presented at a theatre of high reputation, impugned the government's good faith and honest practice on a matter of public concern, it might face section 6 charges. Besides, the directors of government-subsidised theatres have become well versed in the arts of self-censorship to ensure that they do not offend the politicians who provide them with the financial means to survive and flourish. They would recoil from the idea of presenting any play that offered a serious critique of government policies or those of an individual minister, or of any businessman whose support was crucial to the administration. The Theatres Act is a slumbering giant. It is entrenched with safeguards that would allow the government to prosecute and thereby to censor in extreme case. The British theatre has been liberated; the chains and handcuffs have been put away; but the power and the temptation to bring them out again remain.

Notes

1. Bernard Williams, *Report of Committee on Obscenity and Film Censorship* (1979), p. 55.
2. *Guardian*, 19 March 1982.
3. *Daily Telegraph*, 27 January 1992.
4. Michael Egan, *Ibsen, The Critical Heritage* (1985), p. 202.
5. *Daily Telegraph*, 21 September 1994.
6. *Daily Mail*, 19 January 1995.
6. *Sunday Times*, 22 January 1995.

INDEX

abortion 42, 43, 48, 49, 165, 166
Absolute Hell 110
Ackerley, J.R. 95, 96–98
Ackland, Rodney 87–88, 109–110
Act, 1968 *see* Theatres Act (1968)
Acton, William 38
actor-managers 40, 50, 93
actors
  attitude to censorship 46, 50
  Equity 91
  public attitudes to
    16th century 18, 19–20
    Roman 17–18
adultery 26, 28, 29, 43, 48, 62, 63
Advisory Board *see* Lord
    Chamberlain's Office
Afore Night Come 196, 200
Agate, James 65, 97, 145
AIDS 247
Albery, Donald 112, 114, 179–181,
  195
Aldwych Theatre 146, 200
Alexander, Sir George 60
Alfie 177
Alice, Princess 108
Allen, Jim 252
Alliance of Honour 70–71
Ambassador's Theatre 70, 71
America Hurrah 226

American ambassador 148, 151, 225
Amis, Kingsley 170, 198
Anatomy of Abuses, The 19
Anderson, Lindsay 205
Andreyev, Leonid 242
Angels in America 132, 247, 248
angry young men xv
Ann Veronica 40
Annan, Lord 123, 229–231
anti-Semitism xi, 11, 138, 144, 147,
  148, 252
Antrobus, John 8
appeasement and censorship 138–145
appointment, Lord Chamberlain xi
appointment, Comptrollers xi
Archbishops 191
Archer, William 27, 28, 50
Arden, John 171, 216
Ardrey, Robert 146
Aristotle 17, 161
Arlen, Michael 97
Arlen, Stephen 112
armed forces 87, 157
Arnold, Matthew 28
Arnold, Tom 104
art
  function of 17
  modern 39, 46–47
Artaud, Antonin 177–178
Arts Council 121, 150, 172, 195, 196,
  210, 236

Arts Theatre Club 69, 74, 82, 112,
    168, 181, 195, 200
Ashcroft, Dame Peggy 146
Ashwell, Lena 46
Asquith, Herbert Henry xii, 39, 43,
    50
L' Assommoir 38
Athanaeum, The 68
Atholl, Duke of 51
Attlee, Clement 186
atomic bomb 241
Attorney-General 4, 126, 127, 132,
    214, 218, 225, 233–234,236,
    246, 251
Auden, W.H. 138
audiences 18–19, 23, 26, 27, 40–41,
    151–152, 176, 220, 237,238,
    242, 247, 248, 251
Austria, annexation 139
Ayliff, H.K. 141

Baldwin, Stanley 77
Ballad of the False Barman, The 131
Banbury, Frith 88, 101, 145
Bancroft, Sir Squire xii, 51, 61, 68,
    129
Bannerman, Campbell 43
Barrie, J.M. 43, 46, 50
Bart, Lionel 199
Baxter, Beverley 104
BBC 13–14, 114, 120, 198
BBC Radio *Children's Hour* xiii
Beaumont, 'Binkie' 88, 94, 103, 105,
    106, 112, 113, 114, 115,196
Beckett, Samuel 123, 167, 177,
    178–180, 192–194, 200
Bedsitting Room, The 8
Bendall, Ernest 53
Bennett, Alan 12, 118
Bennett, Arnold 40, 50
Benson, A.C. 86

Benson, Sir Frank 50
Berlin, Sir Isaiah 160
Berlin Post 206
Beuselink, Oscar 186
Beyond the Fringe 12, 15, 118
bi-sexuality 64, 93, 101
Bill abolishing stage censorship
    (1962) 198
Billy Liar 185
Biloni, Herbert 144
Binder, Pearl 17
Bird, John 13
birth-control 40, 48
Bishop of London 36, 65, 70
Bitter Sweet 99–101
Blackfriars 19
blasphemy 191–192
Blasted 249
Bloomsbury Group 87
Board of Education 75
Boer War 39
Boeuf sur le Toit 88
Bogdanov, Michael 132, 246
Bond, Edward 3, 121, 167, 171–172,
    205, 211, 214, 216,221–224,
    231, 236, 237–238, 241
Braine, John 170, 198
Bray, Alan 83
'Breach of Peace' 251–252
Breaking Point, The x, 43
Brenton, Howard 132
Brickman, Miriam 184
Brieux, Eugene 53, 241
Bright Young Things 56
British Board of Film Censors 198,
    227
British Medical Association Report
    on homosexuality 129
Brook, Peter 148, 152
Brook, Clive 94
Brook, Faith 94
Brooke, Henry 147, 148, 198

Brooke, P.L. 16

Brookfield, Charles 46, 52–53

brothels 86

Brown, George 5, 7, 9, 10, 11, 149, 152

Brown, Ivor 102

Bruce, David 151, 225

Bruckner 241

Bryden, Ronald 220

Buckmaster, Lord xii, 51, 54, 58, 59, 60, 67, 75, 170

buggery 132, 247, 248

Bull, Peter 181

Burgess, Guy 89

Butler, R.A. 115, 116, 170, 176, 198–199

Butler, Richard 219–220

Bystander, The 71

Cabinet Home Affairs Committee 198–199

Cabinet meeting, July 1967 1–3

Cabinet ministers, and scripts 10

Caccia, Harold 148

Calder, John 234

Call it a Day 101

Callaghan, Audrey 10, 11

Callaghan, James 2, 5, 15–16, 226

Campbell, Lord 38

Campbell, Mrs Patrick 46

Cannan, Dennis 148

cannibalism 4, 82, 232, 233, 237

Canterbury, Archbishop and censorship 45, 54

Caretaker, The 174

Caroline, Queen 232

Carriages at Eleven 41

Carrington, Lord 230

Carson, Edward 52

Case of Robert Oppenheimer, The 159

Casson, Sir Lewis 68

Cat on a Hot Tin Roof 111–112, 115, 119

Catholic Church 18, 22, 23, 146–148, 245

Catholic Federation 55, 73

Cave of Harmony, The 87

Cenci, The 28, 30, 67, 167

censorship

criticism of x, xv, 27, 43, 46, 104, 127, 136ff 229–231

defence of 46

history of

15th century 138

16th century 18–21

17th century 21–23, 138

18th century 24–25

19th century 25–31

20th century ix, xiv, xv, 1–16, 43–46

classical 17

pre-censorship 1, 231

reform 1–16

stage

removal of 1ff, 229–231, *see also* Theatres Act 1968

secrecy of ix–x, xi

trials 120, 206

Censorship of Plays (Repeal) Bill (1949) 113, 185–186

Chandos, Lord 155, 156, 157, 159, 162, 206, 210

Charles I xv, 22

Charles II 23

Chartism 26

Chekhov, Anton 47

Cherwell, Lord 155, 156, 157, 159

Chesterfield, Lord 24

Chesterton, G.K. 50

Children's Hour, The xiii, 103, 105, 111

Chips with Everything 192

Christie, Agatha 108, 115

Church of England 18, 43, 48, 54, 68, 245

Churchill, Sir Winston 6, 86, 146, 155, 156, 157, 159, 162,177

cinema 198, 227, 241

City of Westminster 24

Clarendon, Lord 4, 35, 36, 64, 71, 104, 105, 144–145, 166

class censorship xiii

Claxton, Ernest 129–130

Clayton, Jack 121, 198

Clerkenwell 19

Cleveland Street, brothel 86

Cobbold, Lord xv, 1, 4, 6, 8–9, 10, 11, 12, 14–16, 120–122,124–130, 136–138, 147–148, 150–154, 159, 167, 175, 192, 198, 199–200, 206, 209, 214–219, 225–234, 238–240

Codron, Michael 195, 204

Coles, Maurice 207

Collier, Rev. Jeremy 23

Colman, George 26

comedy, Restoration 23

Comedy Theatre, The 112, 200

Common Council of London 18, 19, 21

communism 146, 147, 239

Comptrollers *see* Lord Chamberlain's Office

confidentiality of censorship process ix–x, xi

Connection, The 158, 174, 177

Connelly, Marc 191

Conrad, Joseph 43

conscription 87

Conservative Party 39, 43

Contagious Diseases Act, (1864), (1866), (1869) 37

Conway, Sir Edward 22

Conway, William 106, 107

Cook, Peter 12, 118

Cookman, A.V. 97

Coronation, The 52

Cotes, Peter 103, 105, 165, 166

court proceedings, Joan Littlewood 6, *Saved* 229

courtier plays 22

Covent Garden 24, 25

Coward, Noël 56, 61, 62, 63, 64, 65, 66, 88, 93–94, 99, 101,119, 171, 185

Creighton, Anthony 173

Crichton, G.A. 73

Crime and Punishment 170

Crisp, Quentin 87

critics 65, 97, 104, 107–108, 113–114, 168, 220–224, 235–236

Cromer, Lord xiii, 51, 58–59, 61–62, 66, 67, 68–69, 73–74,75, 191

Crossman, Richard 2, 14, 238

Crucible, The 209

Cuckoo in the Nest 76

Cudlipp, Hugh 90

Cummings, Constance 185–186

Cunningham, Sir Charles 227

Cupid and Mars 88

Czechoslovakia 139, 142

Daily Express 56

Daily Gazeteer 5

Daily Graphic 58

Daily Herald 55

Daily Mail 89, 104, 111, 178, 202, 209, 220, 236, 250

Daily Telegraph 28, 30, 75, 97, 202, 207, 222, 233, 247, 250

Damaged Goods 53–55

La Dame aux camélias 27, 38

Darlington, W.A. 97, 222, 247

Dawson, Sir Douglas 60–61, 63, 66

Dean, Basil 75

Dear Old Charlie 53

Dearmer, Geoffrey xiii, 96, 140, 142–143

Delaney, Shelagh 116–117, 207–208

Delysia, Alicia 70–71

Derwent, Lord 219

Design for Living 63–66, 93

Desire Under the Elms 77, 170

Devils, The 45

Devine, George 125, 172, 190, 192,
    195, 215, 216

Devlin, Lord 245

Dexter, John 209–210

Dilhorne, Lord 230, 231

Dingo 226

Director of Public Prosecutions 6, 89,
    125–128, 167, 200, 214, 217,
    224–226, 233, 234, 235, 236

Dirtiest Show in Town, The 251

Disraeli, Benjamin 3, 231

dissent and censorship xiv, 17–27, 52,
    55, 251

divorce 37, 50, 57, 63, 76

    Divorce Law (1857) 37

    Royal Commission on Divorce
       (1913) 40

Doll's House, A 41

Donmar Warehouse 64

Donne, William 26, 27

Dostoevsky, Alexander 38

Douglas, Lord Alfred 188

Douglas-Home, William 107

drag 109

Dream Play 237

Dresden 155

dress 69, 70, 71–72, 77, 108, 109,
    124–125, 187–188

drug-taking 56, 158, 238

drunken behaviour 7

Drury Lane 24, 25

Druten, John van 74, 101

du Maurier, Gerald 93

du Maurier, Guy 39, 46

Dubliners 39

Duchess of Malfi, The 171, 237

Dumas, Alexander 26, 27

Early Morning 3–4, 167, 177, 231–237

Ede, Chuter 165

Eden, Anthony 146, 153–154

Edinburgh, Duke of 8

Edinburgh Festival 129

Education Act (1944) 170

Edward II 21

Edward VII 41, 42

Edwardian
    anti-censorship campaign 27
    society 40–41

effeminacy 55, 56, 84–85, 93,
    99–101, 118–119

eighteenth century, theatre
    censorship ix, 4–5

election, (1966) 230

Elizabeth I xv, 17, 18, 21

Elizabeth II 1, 2, 4, 12, 14, 15, 232,
    234

Ellis, Arthur 36

Elsom, John 210

Elwyn-Jones, Lord (formerly Sir
    Elwyn Jones) 17, 127, 218,
    225, 233

Encore 152

Endgame 177, 192–194, 200

English Stage Company 125, 192,
    206, 228

English Stage Society 217, 225,
    234–235

Englishman's Home, An 39

Entertainer, The 184, 185, 199

Entertaining Mr Sloane 48, 119–120,
    175, 205, 222, 247

Equity 91

Ervine, St John xiii

Esdaile, Alfred 228, 234–235

Essays on the Principles of Population 37

Essex, Earl of 20–21

Esslin, Martin 177
Evening Standard 63, 104, 113, 193, 229
Examiner of Plays *see* Lord Chamberlain's Office, Examiner

Fabian Society 50, 141
family life 40
Farmer, George 152–154
fascism 140, 141, 142, 241
Fata Morgana 72–74, 190
Festival Theatre, Cambridge 66
Fielding, Henry 4–5, 23–24, 236
files, Lord Chamberlain's ix–x, xiv–xv, 3, 50, 112, 188, 202
films 198, 227, 241
Fin de Partie 192–194
Findlater, Richard 113, 229
Fings Ain't Wot They Used T'Be 118, 199
Fisher, Archbishop Geoffrey 191
Fisher, Mary 234–235
Flaubert, Gustave 38
Flemyng, Robert 93
Fletcher, Kyrle 130, 157, 202–203
Flower, Sir Fordham 153–154
Follow My Leader 138–145, 168
Foot, Sir Dingle 121, 198, 218–219, 225, 229
Foot, Michael 124, 186, 198
Foot, M.R.D. 160
Foreign Office 139–142, 143–145, 147–151, 225
Foreign Secretary 5, 7, 146, 149
foreign politics and censorship 138–155, 241
Fortune and Men's Eyes 131, 158
Fortune Theatre 12
Foucault, Michel 94, 99
Fox, Robert 117
Frank, Mrs Mary 112

Fraser, Brad 248
French plays 26–27, 28, 46, 53
French Without Tears 138
Fry, Roger 46
Fryer, Peter 185
Functions and Disorders 38
Fussell, Paul 95
Fyffe, Sir David Maxwell 91

Gaitskell, Hugh 3
Gallagher, Bernard 216
Galsworthy, John 40, 43, 46, 50, 53
Game, Henry 64, 78, 88, 139–140, 143–144, 165–166
Game at Chess, A 22
Gardiner, Gerald 219
Garnett, Edward x, 43, 48
Garson, Barbara 225
Gaskill, William 125, 137, 167, 194, 210, 214, 216–217, 219–220, 228–229, 232–233, 234–235
Gate Theatre 103, 252
Gelber, Jack 158, 177
General Strike 63
Genet, Jean xii, 111, 174, 201–202
Geneva 140–141, 142, 143, 144
George III 24
George IV 232
George V 46, 54, 55, 58–59, 61–62, 191, 232
George VI 90, 232
Gelber, Jack 174
Germany 39, 139–145, 147–148, 206, 242
Getting Married 42, 50
Ghosts xii, xv, 29–30, 31, 41, 55, 107, 220, 247, 248
Gide, André 115, 168
Gielgud, Sir John 88, 90, 91, 99
Gielgud Theatre 249
Gilbert, W.S. 44
Gilliatt, Penelope 221

Gladstone, Herbert 43
Gladstone, William Ewart 3, 231
GLC 162
Glenville, Peter 180
Godfrey, Howard 202
Goebbels, Joseph 139
Goering, Hermann 139
Goldschmidt, Anthony 142
Goodman, Lord 124, 129, 230–231
Gordon
  John 91
  Major C. L. 76, 77, 78
Gore-Booth, Sir Paul 149–151, 225
Gradwell, Leo 229
Grand Theatre, Islington 28, 29
Granville-Barker, Harley xv, 40, 42,
  43, 48–49, 52–53, 168, 241
Graves, Robert 95
Greece, Ancient 17, 84, 201
Green Bay Tree, The 101–102, 103
Green Hat, The 97
Greene, Hugh 13
Green, Julian 115, 168
Green Pastures, The 191
Greene, Graham 106
Greene, Sir Hugh Carleton 198
Grein, J.T. 27, 49
Grundy, Sydney 28
Guardian, The 209, 237, 246, 250
Guilpin, Edward 84
Guinness, Sir Alec 181, 191
Gurney, Ivor 95
Gwatkin, Norman 64–65, 103, 104,
  105, 106, 113, 117, 121, 142,
  144–145, 166, 173, 176,
  178–180, 182, 184, 185,
  186–188, 192–193

Hailsham, Lord 82–83
Hair 238–239
Haldane, Lord 50–51
Hall, Sir Peter 115, 137, 146, 148,
  152–154, 158, 162, 167, 172,
  178, 181, 194, 195–196,
  200–201, 211
Hallifax, Michael 194
Halls, A.N.M. 9, 10
Hampstead Theatre 131, 132, 158,
  248
Hankin, St. John 40, 42
Hardy, Thomas 43
Hare, Sir John xii, 46, 50
Hare, Robertson 142
Harewood, Lord 124, 129, 192, 229
Harris, Sir Arthur 159, 160, 162
Harris, Robert 98–99
Harrison, Frederick x
Harvey, Sir John Martin 50
Harward, T.B. 226, 239
Hauptmann, Gerhart 242
Hawtrey, Sir Charles 46
Hay Fever 209
Haymarket 30, 90
Heartbreak House 241
Hellman, Lillian 103–104
Henry, Joan 119
Henry VIII 18, 19
Herbert, John 131
Heriot, Charles xii, 6–8, 9, 109,
  110–111, 117, 123, 130, 140,
  148, 151, 172, 173–174, 180,
  184, 185, 203–204, 215, 232,
  239
Hiawatha 13
Hicks, Sir William Joyson 77
Hidden Years, The 107
Higgins, H.H. 61
Hill, Ronald 12, 13, 109, 123–124,
  129, 157, 158, 161, 187,194,
  201–202, 204, 208, 226, 239
Himmler, Heinrich 91
His Chinese Bride 107
Historical Register for the Year 1736 5
Hitler, Adolf 138–145, 147, 148, 241

HIV virus 247
Hobson, Harold 107–108, 113–114, 127, 131, 178, 181, 193, 221, 223, 236
Hochuth, Ralph 146–147, 155, 157, 159–161
Home, Lord 8, 147
Home Office 14, 15, 30, 71, 215, 219, 227, 231
Home Secretary 1, 3, 15, 43, 91, 115, 126, 147, 148, 165, 176, 197, 198, 214, 219, 226, 228, 231
Homecoming, The 48
homosexuality 48, 62, (82–135)
homosexuality
  16th century 83–84
  19th century 83, 86
  20th century
    1910s 95
    1920s 87, 92–94, 95, 99–101
    1930s 87, 101–103
    1940s 87–88, 95, 103–105–8
    1950s 82–83, 85–92, 94, 108–121
    1960s 118–131, 158, 203
    1970s 131–132
    1980s 246
    1990s 98, 246–249
  Ancient Greece & Rome 84
  armed forces 87
  ban, stage 82–83
  blackmail 87, 109, 115
  BMA Report 129
  legalisation 14
  Lord Chamberlain's rules 118, 119
  poetry 95–96
  trials 84, 85, 86, 87, 89, 90, 91, 108
  USA 88–89
Hope-Wallace, Philip 90, 209, 221, 237
Hopkins, Gerard Manley 96
House of Commons x, 25, 107, 146, 219

vote on Lord Chamberlain's role 1, 238
House of Lords x, 24, 25, 38, 39, 90, 114, 123, 136, 137–138, 229–231
Housman, A.E. 96
Higgins, Patrick 85
Hugo, Victor 26
Huis Clos 94, 168
Hume, Kenneth 89
Hunter, Ian 112
Hunter, N.C. 90
Hynes, Samuel 39

'I Just Can't Say No' 108
Ibsen, Henrik xii, xv, 27, 28, 29–31, 42, 47, 168, 220, 241, 248
Immoralist, The 115, 168
In the Days of the Comet 50
incest 28
Indecent Advertisements Act, (1889) 249
Independent Television Authority 13
Ingrams, Richard 6, 17
inquiries 27
Ireland 242
Irish issues 26, 38, 39
Irving, David 160
Isherwood, Christopher 95
Isle of Dogs, The 20

Jackson, Barry 69
James, Henry 43, 44, 46
James I xv, 21, 22
Jarry, Alfred 168
Jenkins, Roy 1, 2, 3, 4, 5, 7, 14, 15, 122, 126, 197, 214, 219, 226–228, 229–230, 233, 238
Johnson, President Lyndon 11, 13, 148, 153
Johnston, Sir John 9, 12, 14, 17, 36,

45, 61, 120, 123–125, 126,
128, 130, 137, 157, 159, 160,
177–178, 194, 200, 201–203,
204, 215, 217, 226, 227,
232–233, 234, 236, 237, 239
Jones, H.A. 28
Jonson, Ben 20
Joyce, James 39
Judgement Day 140, 144–145

Kane, Sarah 249
Keynes, Maynard 87
Killick, Charles 115
Killing of Sister George, The 94, 130
Kilmuir, Lord (formerly Sir David
Maxwell Fyffe) 91, 231
King, Philip 109
King Lear 24, 223, 237
Kingston, Jeremy 117
Kingsway Theatre 55, 67
Kinsey Report 88–89, 105
Kithchen, The 192
Kushner, Tony 132, 247, 248
Kustow, Michael 148

Labour government 51, 63, 186, 195,
197, 225
relations with Lord Chamberlain
8–9, 121, 126–127, 150,
218–219, 225, 226–228
Labour Party 55, 138
Lady Chatterley's Lover 108, 120, 121,
206
Lambert, J.W. 128, 221–224, 247
Lanchester, Elsa 87
language, censorship of 11, 21, 125,
131, 139–140, 147, 148,
154–155, 173–175, 179,
180–211, 201, 203–204, 207,
215–216, 238, 239, 240, 246
'Last of the Blue Pencils' 240
Last of the de Mullins 42

Last Exit to Brooklyn 234
Laughton, Charles 87
lavatories 106–107
Lawrence, D.H. 39, 120, 206
Leather Boys, The 207
Lee, Jennie 195
Leeds 186–187, 250
'legitimate' drama 24, 25
Leigh, Vivien 105
lesbianism 94, 103, 104, 111, 130,
231–232, 235
Let My People Come 251
Letters to *The Times*
1907, Oct 43
1912, Feb 46
Levin, Bernard 209
Levy, Benn 185–186
Lewenstein, Oscar 190
Lewes, George Henry 26
Lewis, Peter 220, 236
libel 156–157
Liberal Party 38, 51
Licensed Victualler's Mirror 248
Licensing Act, (1921) 56
licensing of plays ix, 18, 24, 25, 45,
49, 50*ff*, 83, 104
Life of Man, The 242
Light Fantastic 146
Lindemann, Charles 162
Linnit, Bill 78
Little Theatre 203
Littler, Sir Emile 115, 186–187, 200
Littlewood, Joan 6, 7, 195
living persons, stage portrayal 15–16,
236
Living Room, The 106–107
Loach, Ken 252
London
16th century xiv, 18*ff*
17th century 19
19th century 41–42
20th century

1920s 56
1940s 88
London Council for Promotion of
Public Morality 65, 72, 73
London Mercury 95
Longfellow, Henry 13
Lonsdale, Frederick 93, 103, 119
Look Back in Anger 48, 166, 167, 170,
175–176, 181–184
Look on Tempests 119
Loot xi, 197, 202–205
Lord Chamberlain
appointment process xi
criticism of xv, 50–51, 119, 196,
226, 240
files ix–x, xiv–xv, 50, 112, 188,
202
political bias 8–9
role xiv, 24–25, 27, 44–45, 121,
136–137, 241–242
termination of 1, 122, 136,
137–138, 196, 225, 226,
227–229, 237, 238, 239–241
Lord Chamberlain's Blue Pencil, The
125, 203
Lord Chamberlain's Office ix–xvi
Advisory Board, licensing xii, 45,
51, 52, 66, 75
Comptrollers
appointment of xi
function of 45
Examiner ix–x, xii, 45, 52
Lord Chancellor 214, 219, 230
Lord Mayor of London 18, 19–20
Luther 185, 186, 190
Lyall, Beatrix Hudson 73
Lyric Theatre, Hammersmith 68, 146
Lyttleton, Oliver *see* Chandos, Lord
Lytton, Bulwer 25

Macbeth 171
Macbird 225, 229

Macdonald, James 249
MacDonald, Ramsay 51
Maclean, Donald 89
Macmillan, Harold 8, 12, 15, 147,
198
Madras House, The 42
magistrates 229
Maids, The 111
Malthus, Thomas 37
Malvern Festival 141
Manchester Guardian 97
Marat/Sade 200
Marcus, Frank 130
Marlowe, Christopher 21
Marowitz, Charles 152, 197
marriage 40, 50
Married Women's Property Act 37
Mary, Queen 165
Mary Queen of Scots 156
Mask Theatre, London 66
Masses and Men 242
Masters of the Revels 20, 21, 23
masturbation 166, 203, 207–208
Mathew, Sir Theobald 89
Mathias, Sean 64
Maugham, Somerset 57–58
Maupassant, Guy de 38
McCarthy, Desmond 141
McCarthy, Joseph 88–89
McWhinnie Donald 194
memoranda, internal xiv, xv
Mercer, David 171
Merry Widow, The 58
Middleton, Thomas 22
Mill, John Stuart 245, 248
Miller, Arthur 112, 113, 241
Miller, Bernard 173
Miller, Gilbert 141–142
Miller, Jonathan 12, 118, 250
Milligan, Spike 7
Ministry of Health 85–86
Ministry of Information 85–86
Miss Julie xiii, 66–67, 140, 242

Mitchell, Adrian 148
modern movement 46–47, 168
monarch, role as censor 45, 58–59
Montagu, Helen 220, 226
Montagu, Lord 89, 90
Moore, Dudley 12, 118
morality
    and censorship 19, 21–22, 26–31,
        48*ff*, 57
marriage, unmarried pregnancy x
National Council of Public Morals 47
Morley, Robert 117
Morley, Sheridan 63
Morning Post 47
Morris, R.M. 227
Mousetrap, The 115
Mowat, A. 74
Mrs Grundy 185
Mrs Warren's Profession xi, xv, 49–51,
    168
Mrs Wilson's Diary 5–16
Much Ado about Nothing 209
Muller, Robert 111
musicals 238–239
Mussolini, Benito 141, 241
My Fair Lady 182
My Lady's Undress 70
Myers, J.B.B. 35, 36
Mystery plays 18

Nashe, Thomas 20
National Campaign for Venereal
    Diseases 53
National Council of Public Morals
    47, 50
National Service 87
National Theatre 129, 131–132,
    155–157, 161–162, 195,
    206, 208, 210, 211, 226, 246,
    247
National Viewers and Listeners
    Association 129, 131–132

National Vigilance Association 38
Naughton, Bill 177
Nazi party *see* Germany
Neglected Child, The 26
New Ambassadors Theatre 248
Now Barabbas 107
New Boltons Theatre Club 103–104
New End Theatre 98
New Lindsey Theatre Club 165, 166
New Statesman 14, 97, 220
New Theatre 162
New Watergate Club 112–113, 114,
    115, 214
New Wave 152, 169
New York Times 62
'Newgate dramas' 26
News Chronicle 97
News of the World 85, 114
Newspaper Proprietors' Association
    85–86
Nicols, Robert 95
Nightingale, Florence 3, 177,
    231–233, 235
No Concern of Mine 117, 118
Norwich, Lord 136
Novello, Ivor 88
nudity, censorship of 11, 48, 69, 70,
    71, 78, 166, 199
Nugent, Sir Terence 104, 106, 107,
    112, 114, 126, 145, 151–152,
    171–172, 208, 215

Obscene Publications Act, (1959) 3,
    120, 234, 251
Obscene Publications Act, (1857) 38
obscenity 7
Obscenity Act 38
Observer, The 97, 102, 107, 176, 221
O'Casey, Sean 242
Oedipus Rex xii, 52, 104, 129
Offenbach, Jacques 69
Oh! Calcutta! 251

O'Hara, Gerald 147

Oklahoma 108

Old Vic 195

Olivier, Sir Laurence 90, 105, 124, 129–130, 155, 156, 160–162, 206, 209–210, 224, 229

On Liberty 245

O'Neill, Eugene 77, 170

Open Space 131

opening nights 219–220, 242, 247, 250

Ordinance, Common Council, (1574) 19

Orton, Joe xi, 48, 119–120, 174, 175, 197, 202, 205, 222, 223, 233, 247

Osborne, John 48, 121, 122–123, 129, 166, 167, 170, 171,173, 174, 176, 177, 178, 181–191, 198, 199, 205, 241

Otway, Travers 107

Our Betters 57, 59

Owen, Wilfred 95

Oxbridge
   homosexuality 86–87, 93
   satirists 12–13

Oz 251

pacifism 155

Page, Anthony 124, 125, 128, 137

Pains and Penalties 232

Palace Theatre 186

Palliser, Sir Michael 12

Parker, Louis 232

parliamentary inquiries, stage censorship xi

Patriot For Me, A 121, 122–124, 128–131, 137, 175, 216, 226, 227, 233

Penn, Sir Eric xi, 171, 175, 200, 204, 207, 208, 215, 226

Percy, Lord 75

Perdition 252

Peter, John 223

Peters, A.D. 145

petition against censorship, 1910 46

Philanderer, The 42

Phillpotts, Eden 46

Pick-Up Girl 165–166

Piffard, Frederick 166

Pigott, E. F. Smyth 29, 30

Pinero, Arthur 28, 35–36, 43, 47

Pink Dominoes, The 27–28

Pink Room, The 109–110

Pinter, Harold 48, 171, 174, 182, 223

Pirandello, Luigi xii, xv, 47, 67–68, 168, 241

Plato 17

Playboy of the Western World, The 242

Playfair, Nigel 68

plays
   banned x, xv, 25, 43, 48–49, 50–52
   licensing ix, 25

Plays for England 174, 178

Plough and the Stars, The 242

Plowright, Joan 161

Poetics, Aristotle's 17, 161

poetry 96
   classical 96
   war 95

Poke, Greville 228, 229

police 228, 234, 235, 236

political censorship xiv, 137*ff*, 241

political stability and censorship
   16th century xiv
   17th century 21–22
   19th century 26–27
   20th century, (1967) 2

politicians
   sexuality 48–49
   see also satire, political

Poor Superman 132, 248

Pope, W. Macqueen 41

Pope Pius XII 146–147

Popham, Lord Chief Justice 21

Index

Portsmouth 74, 87
Post Impressionists 46–47
Pound, Ezra 39
Power of Darkness xv, 242
pre-censorship 1, 231
pregnancy, extra-marital x
prejudice *see* anti-homosexuality, anti-Semitism
Priestley, J.B. 66
Prime Minister
    criticism of censorship 127
    mockery of 4–5, 8, 11, 226
    scripts referred to 45
    and sexuality 86
Prince of Wales Theatre 165
prison drama 158
Prisoners of War 95, 96–99
Private Eye xv, 5–6
Private Lives 63
private members bill, (1965) 196
private performances 10, 28–29, 30, 95, 103, 112, 122,214*ff*, 233
Privy Council 18, 19, 22
producers x, 114–115, 245
'Prohibition of Presentation of Obscene Performances' 251
prosecutions 6, 227, 228–229, 234, 236, 246
prostitution 37, 48–50, 165, 249
    Royal Commission on 91
protests against censorship x–xi
public figures, stage representation of 1–16
Public Morality Council 36, 65–66, 72, 107, 108
Public Record Office xiv
publishing, censorship x, 1, 3, 38, 47, 85–86, 170
Puritanism 22
Pygmalion 185

Quayle, Sir Anthony 113

Queen Victoria 232
Queensberry, Marquis of 101

Raffles, Gerry 11, 17
Raleigh, Sir Walter xii, 54
Ramsey, Archbishop Arthur 191
Rankin, Peter 7, 17
Rattigan, Sir Terence 88, 117, 119, 138–139, 142–145, 168, 171,241
Ravenhill, Mark 248, 249, 250
Ravensdale, Baroness 108
Raymond, Harry 87
Read, Herbert 95
realistic drama 28
Red Peppers 185
Redford
    Alexander 31, 42–43, 44, 45
    George x
reform of censorship 1–16
Reformation xiv
Reinhardt, Max 206
religious censorship xiii, 18, 23, 191–193
Renton, Sir David 231
repeal of Lord Chamberlain's powers 1*ff*
Representative, The 146–148
Republic 17
Restoration drama 22–23
Reugen Island 95
Revenger's Tragedy, The 237
revolution 146, 242
Ribblesdale, Lord 46
Rice, Elmer 140, 141
Richard II 20–21
Richard II 20–21
Richardson, Sir Ralph 90, 115, 181
Richardson, Tony 182, 184–185
Richmond, Sir William 47
'Right Hand Man' 146
riots 242
    (1592) 20

Rite of Spring 220
Robertson, Johnston Forbes xii, 67
Robins, Elizabeth 42
Rockingham club 88
Romans in Britain, The 132, 246
Rome, Ancient 17, 84
La Ronde 64
Room at the Top 121, 198
Rosmer, Milton 66
Rotherham 85
Royal Commission on Prostitution 91
Royal Commission on Venereal Diseases 37, 53
Royal Court 10, 122–128, 132, 137, 166, 167, 172, 190, 192, 194, 195, 205, 206, 208–229, 232–237, 249–250, 252
Royal family 145, 231, 232, 235, 240
Royal Proclamation, (1549) 18
Royal Shakespeare Company 129, 146, 148, 150–155, 162, 195, 200, 208
'The Royal Smut Hound' 119
Ruddock, E.K. 64
Rudkin, David 196, 200
Ruffian on the Stair, The 174
Russia 157, 242
    revolution 146

saloons 26
Sandhurst, Lord 50, 51, 53, 54, 71, 185
Sartre, Jean-Paul 94, 168
Sassoon, Siegfried 99
satire, political 2, 4–16, 21, 23–24, 118, 120–121, 138, 198, 236
Saunders, Peter 115
Saved 121, 171, 177, 205, 214–229, 233, 247
Scarbrough, Lord 12, 45, 83, 105,

109, 111, 112, 115–116, 117, 118, 119, 146, 173, 182, 186–190, 191, 198, 214, 231
Scarbrough Rules, (1958) 118, 119, 122, 127
Schiller, Friedrich 156
Schnitzler, Arthur 64
'School Kids Oz' 251
Scotland Yard 237
Scott, Clement 30, 107
Screens, The 201–202
secrecy ix–x, xi
Secret Service 155, 157, 160
Secret Woman, The 46
Selby, Hubert 234
Select Committee on Theatre Censorship
    1832 25
    1892 31
    1909 xi, 43–45, 46, 53
    1967 1, 3, 15, 24, 215, 219, 229–231, 238, 240
Semi-Monde 93
Senior Examiner xii
Sergeant Musgrave's Dance 216
Serious Charge 109
sex
    extra-marital 50
    under-aged 165
    sexual intercourse, stage portrayal 35–36
    sexuality
        female 37
        male 37
    see also adultery, homosexuality, morality, venereal disease
Sexual Offences Act, (1967) 14, 246
Shadow of Heroes 146
Shairp, Mordaunt 101–102
Shakespeare, William 20, 84, 191
Shaw, Bernard xiii, 28, 36, 40, 42, 48, 49–51, 52, 67, 140–141,

143, 146, 181, 185
and stage censorship xi, xv, 27, 30, 31, 43, 46, 168, 241
Shaw, Sebastian 216
She Follows Me About 78
Shelley, Elsa 165, 166
Shelley, Percy Bysshe 28, 67, 167
Shelley Society 28
Sherek, Henry 121
Sherrin, Ned 13
Shopping and Fucking 132, 248–249, 250, 251
Short View of the Immorality and Profaneness of the English Stage 23
Sikorski, General 155, 157, 160
Sillitoe, Alan 170
Sinfield, Alan 102
Six Characters in Search of an Author xii, xv, 67
sixteenth century xiv, 83–84
Skelhorn, Sir Norman 6, 125, 125–126, 127, 167, 217, 225
Skialetheia 84
Smith, Dodie 101
Smith, Percy 113, 185
social dissent 39 censorship xiii–xiv, 20, 44, 242
socialism 39–40, 44, 52
Society of West End Theatre Producers 115, 200, 239
sodomy 83–84, 101, 157
Soho 56, 118
Soldiers 155–162, 177, 210
Solicitor-General 121, 218, 225
Sophocles xii, 52, 104
Soskice, Sir Frank 16, 126
South 112, 115, 168
Southey, Thomas 26
Southwark 19
Spain 22
Spectator, The 40

Spencer, Charles 247–248, 250
Spencer, Colin 131
Spencer, Lord 232
Spender, Sir Stephen 95
Spring Awakening 156, 177, 197–198, 206–211, 214
Spring Cleaning 93, 103, 119
Squire, Jack 95
St. John, Christopher 52
Stable, Mr. Justice 91
Stafford-Clark, Max 248, 252
Stage Licensing Act (1737) ix, 1, 4–5, 24, 245
Stage Society xiii, 207
Stalin, Joseph 147, 241
Stamfordham, Lord 58–59
Star, The 166, 167
Star-spangled Jack 199
Staughton, Mr. Justice 246
St. Martin's Theatre 109
Stowhill (formerly Sir Frank Soskice) 230
Strachey, Lytton 87
Stratford East *see* Theatre Royal
Strauss, George 15, 16
Stravinsky, Igor 220
Street, George 55, 57–58, 59–60, 62, 67–68, 76, 95, 96, 97, 101, 102, 170
Streetcar Named Desire, A 105–108, 167
strikes 39, 63
Strindberg, August xiii, 47, 66, 67, 168, 237, 241, 242
Stubbes
  John 83–84
  Philip 19
subsidies 150, 152, 195, 211
subversion, political 20
Suddenly Last Summer 82
Suez 148
suffrage 26, 57

suffragettes 39
suicide x
Sunday Express 71, 91
Sunday Pictorial 90, 106
Sunday Referee 35
Sunday Theatre Club 207
Sunday Times 65, 107, 108, 127, 128, 145, 192, 210–211, 221, 223, 231, 235, 239, 250
Sutherland, John 198
swearing *see* language
Sweden 242
Synge, J.M. 242
syphilis *see* venereal disease

Taste of Honey, A 116–117, 119, 207–208
Tea and Sympathy 111, 112, 114
teach-in 224
television 13, 227, 241, *see also* BBC
Tempest, The 191
Tennent, H.M. 115, 196
Terry, Ellen 50
That Was the Week that Was 12–13, 120–121, 198
Thatcher, Margaret 196, 197
'The Enforcement of Morals' 245
Lancet, The 86
theatre
    16th century 18–21, 83–84
    17th century 21–23
    19th century xiv, 25–31, 36–38
    20th century 82, 242, 245–252
Theatre of the Absurd 167, 177
theatre clubs 10 28–29, 30, 95, 97, 103–104, 112, 122, 125, 156, 165, 167, 207, 214
Theatre of Cruelty 177–178
theatre managers x, xi
Theatre Regulation Act, (1843) 1, 25, 159, 161, 167, 200, 214, 217, 227–229, 233, 235, 245

'Theatre Revolution' xiv, 123
Theatre Royal
    Stratford East 8, 10, 11, 17, 118, 225
    Theatre Workshop 6, 17, 195
theatre society 10
theatre-going x–xi, 19
Theatres Act, (1968) 122, 136, 137–138, 234, 236, 238, 240, 245, 246, 250, 251–252
Theatres National Committee 115
This Was a Man 62
Thorndike, Dame Sybil 68, 90, 191
Three Hundred Club 97
Thursby, Charles 52
Times, The 14, 35, 43, 46, 47, 52, 53, 58, 97, 117, 140, 222, 224, 235, 238, 240, 241
Times Educational Supplement 223
Tinker, Jack 250
Titus Andronicus 221, 237
Toller, Ernst 242
Tolstoy, Leo xv, 31, 38, 242
Tomorrow with Picures 173
Torquay Pavilion 176
Tourneur, Cyril 237
Travers, Ben 17, 76–78
Tree, Sir Herbert Beerbohm 30, 46, 60
Trevelyan, John 198
Trevor, Austin 110
Trewin, J.C. 107
Troubridge, St Vincent 82, 113, 182, 185, 192
Tudor theatre 18–20
Tynan, Kathleen 155
Tynan, Kenneth 113, 119, 155–156, 157, 159–161, 168, 169, 176, 188, 190, 193, 196, 209–210, 224
Tyrer, Howard 65

Index

Ullswater, Viscount 66
Ulster Unionists 39
University College, London 229
US and *Soldiers* 146, 148–155
US 146, 148–155, 151

Vadja, Ernest 72
Vale of Laughter 78
Variation on a Theme 117
vaudeville 53
venereal disease 29, 37, 48, 50,
      53–54, 86, 165, 166, 230, 248,
      249
vice squad 234
Victim 207
Victor 200
Victoria
      Queen 3, 4, 27, 69, 130, 177,
            231–233, 234, 235
      Queen Victoria 232
Victorian theatre x, xiv, 26–31,
      36–38
Vietnam war 13, 148–155, 238
View from the Bridge, A 112–114, 119,
      173
Virgil 96
Vitrac, Roger 200
Vizetelly, Henry 38
Vortex, The 59–62, 93
Votes for Women 42

Wagner, Richard 31
Wain, John 170, 198
Waiting for Godot 123, 167, 178–180
Walpole, Sir Robert 4–5, 17, 23–24,
      158, 226, 236
war
      Boer war 39
      II World War 87–88, 95, 105, 155,
            156
      appeasement 138–145
      I World War 39, 50, 69–70, 87,

88, 95
Ward, Dame Genevieve 71
Wardle, Irving 205, 222–223, 224,
      235–236, 238
Waste xv, 43, 48–49, 168
'We All Wore Green Carnations' 100
Weavers, The 242
Webb, Beatrice 50–51, 52
Webb, Sir William 20
Webster, John 171
Wedekind, Frank 156, 177, 197–198,
      206–211
Weiss, Peter 200
Wells, H.G. 40, 46, 50
Wells, John 6, 17
We're No Ladies 109
Wesker, Arnold 191–192, 198
West, D.J. 91
'West End Apathy' 168, 169
Westminster Theatre 117
Westwood, Gordon 85, 91–92
What Made the Iron Grow? 138
When Parents Sleep 230
Whigs 25
White, Michael 156–158, 162, 172,
      174, 199–200
Whitehouse, Mary 129, 131–132,
      246
Whitman, Walt 96
Whitworth, Phyllis 97–98
Wickham, Glynne 23
Widgery, Lord 251
Wife Without a Smile, The 35
Wigg, Colonel 5
Wilde, Oscar 57, 84–85, 88, 89, 100,
      101, 172
Wildeblood, Peter 89
Willatt, Hugh 210
William III 23
Williams, Tennessee xii, 82,
      105–108, 110, 167
Willis, Ted 185

271

Wilson, Harold, Cabinet 1–3
Wilson, Cecil 178
Wilson, Harold 1–17, 127, 149, 158,
    195, 226, 234, 238
Wilson, Mary 6, 9, 10
Wimbledon Theatre 203
Wolfenden Report 91, 129
women
    sexuality 37, *see also* lesbianism
    on stage 18, 22
    women's rights 36–37, 48, 57
Wood, Charles 171, 216, 226
Wood, Peter xi, 115, 137, 204

Woolf, Virginia 47
World of Paul Slickey, The 173,
    186–190
Worth, Irene 124, 129
Wyndham, Sir Charles 50

Yeats, W.B. 43
You Weren't Always on Top 6
Young Idea, The 185
Young Woodley 74–75, 101

Zola, Emile 38